Teaching medical sociology

Proceedings from the International Seminar on Training Programs in Medical Sociology, Leuven, Belgium, August 1976.

Teaching medical sociology: retrospection and prospection

Edited by

Yvo Nuyens

Janin Vansteenkiste

The Catholic University of Leuven, Belgium

Martinus Nijhoff Social Sciences Division
Leiden/Boston 1978

ISBN 90 207 0719.1

Distributors for North America
Kluwer Boston Inc.
160 Old Derby Street
Hingham, MA 02043 USA

Contents

List of contributors IX

PART ONE: Introduction 1

Teaching medical sociology: retrospection and prospection . 3
Y. Nuyens

Introductory remarks 13
J. Vansteenkiste
A.P. Woudenberg

PART TWO: Future developments 21

1. Health care in the future 23
   A.J.H. Thiadens

1.1. Introduction 23
1.2. Passive health care 25
1.3. Transitional phase 31
1.4. Active health care 32
1.5. Summary and conclusion 35

2. The profession of medical sociologist in the future: implications for training programs 37
   S. Bloom

2.1. Introduction 37
2.2. Background data for understanding the occupational role of medical
     sociology 37
2.3. The role of sociology in medicine 40
2.4. The manpower of medical sociology: sources and training 46
2.5. The substance of medical sociology training: its relevance to outcome . 54
2.6. Summary and conclusions 56

3. The medical profession in the future: implications for train-
    ing programs   61
    P.J. Thung

3.1. The 19th century origin of the medical profession   61
3.2. The medical profession as a thing of the past   63
3.3. Relevant developments in medical education   66
3.4. Conclusion   69

PART THREE: The current status of medical sociology training   71

4. The current status of medical sociology training in the U.S.A.   73
    Hans O. Mauksch and Robert A. Day

4.1. Introduction   73
4.2. Health studies as incidental studies   73
4.3. The role of key individuals, departments, schools and foundations . .   74
4.4. Emergence of medical sociology as a special field   76
4.5. The emergence of specific training programs   77

5. Reflections on training in medical sociology for undergradu-
    ate students of sociology at the University of Warsaw . .   87
    M. Sokolowska

6. Basic assumptions in medical sociology teaching in medical
    schools   95
    E.G. Pattishall

6.1. Background   95
6.2. Basic assumptions   99
6.3. Conclusion   104

7. Basic assumptions in teaching medical sociology in medical
    schools: the case of West Germany   107
    M. Pflanz and J. Siegrist

7.1. Historical background   107
7.2. The institutionalization of medical sociology   109
7.3. Teaching medical sociology: basic assumptions and problems of realiza-
      tion   111
7.4. Research policy and the identity of medical sociology   114

PART FOUR: Educational objectives 119

8. Medical sociology training for sociologists 121
   M. Stacey

8.1. Introduction 121
8.2. Objectives in teaching and learning 125
8.3. Approaches to teaching 126
8.4. A main objective: to show interrelations between society and health care
     systems 127
8.5. General approach 130
8.6. Sociology and its application: detachement and environment 134
8.7. Sociologists and workers 137

9. Medical sociology training for medical doctors 141
   C.W. Aakster

9.1. Introductory remarks 141
9.2. Goals as dominant options 141
9.3. The newly (re-)formulmated objectives of medical schools in the Nether-
     lands 142
9.4. The relevant environments of medical schools 144
9.5. The transformation system of medical schools 146
9.6. The realization of social disciplines-based objectives in medical educa-
     tional systems 149
9.7. Suggestions for a new education of doctors 151

PART FIVE: Description of didactical situations 153

10. Teaching methods and practical training in sociology de-
    partments 155
    Margot Fefferys

11. Teaching methods and practical training in medical
    schools: the case of Maastricht 161
    H. Philipsen

11.1. The new faculty 161
11.2. The characteristics of the educational program 163
11.3. Bottlenecks in the education system 166
11.4. Implications for the teaching of medical sociology 169

PART SIX: Evaluation methods of eduational processes   . . .   171

12. Evaluation methods as instruments for improvement of
    courses and programs   173
    J. Daniëls

12.1. Evaluation and the instrucitonal process   173
12.2. The full context of evaluation (formative and summative evaluation)   . .   175
12.3. Formative course evaluation   178
12.4. Recommendations for course evaluation   187

13. Evaluation methods as part of training programs   191
    E. Nihoul

14. Curriculum construction: reflections on a workshop   . . .   209
    J. Vansteenkiste

14.1. Introduction   209
14.2. Indications for curriculum construction featuring the formulation of objec-
      tives and the selection of content   211
14.3. Situating the didactical method for curriculum construction   218
14.4. Analysis of the didactical method for hidden assumptions   224
14.5. Beyond the evident explanation of a workshop's   230

PART SEVEN: Evaluation of the seminar   233

15. Critical evaluation of the seminar   235
    Derek Gill

15.1. New developments in medical eduation   237
15.2. Teaching medical sociology in medical schools   240
15.3. The development of educational objectives   243
15.4. The teaching and development of medical sociology   245
15.5. The future of medical sociology   252

PART EIGHT: Bibliography   257

16. A selected bibliography of recent articles   259
    J. Vansteenkiste

Acknowledgements

The editors wish to express their gratitude and appreciation to:

The Ministry of Health;
The Ministry of Education;
Nationaal Fonds voor Wetenschappelijk Onderzoek;
Katholieke Universiteit Leuven;
Janssen Research Foundation, and Sabena.
for their financial support

The Research Committee on the Sociology of Medicine, International Sociological Association; and World Health Organization, Regional Office for Europe.
for their sponsorship

Multi-taalbureau (L. Verdegem); and Department of Sociology of the Katholieke Universiteit Leuven (Mrs. Van Meerbeeck)
for their technical help.

List of contributors

Aakster C.W., Senior Lecturer in Medical Sociology, Institute of Social Medicine, Rijksuniversiteit Leiden, the Netherlands.

Bloom S.W., Professor of Sociology and Community Medicine, Department of Community Medicine. Mount Sinai School of Medicine, New York, U.S.A.

Daniels J.W., Director, Onderwijskundig Studiebureau, Limburgs Universitair Centrum, Belgium.

Day R.A., Assistant Professor in Behavioral Science, Department of Behavioral Science, College of Medicine, University of Kentucky, Lexington, U.S.A.

Gill D.G., Chief Section of Behavioral Sciences, Department of Community Health and Medical Practice, University of Missouri, Columbia, U.S.A.

Jefferys M., Professor of Medical Sociology, Department of Sociology, Bedford College, London, England.

Mauksch H.O., Professor of Medical Sociology, Executive Officer, The American Sociological Association, U.S.A.

Nihoul E., Professor of Medical Microbiology, Laboratorium voor Bacteriologie en Virologie, Rijksuniversiteit Gent, Belgium.

Nuyens Y., Professor of Medical Sociology, Department of Sociology, Division for Medical Sociology, Katholieke Universiteit Leuven, Belgium.

Pattishall E.G., Professor of Behavioral Science, Department of Behavioral Science, College of Medicine, The Pennsylvania State University, Hershey, U.S.A.

Pflanz M., Professor and Head, Institut für Epidemiologie und Sozialmedizin, Medizinische Hochschule Hannover, Hannover, Germany.

Philipsen H., Professor in Medical Sociology, Medische Sociologie, Medische Faculteit Maastricht, Maastricht, the Netherlands.

Siegrist J., Professor of Medical Sociology, Abteilung Medizinische Soziologie, Universität Marburg, Marburg, Germany.

Sokolowska M., Professor of Sociology, Department of Medical Sociology, Institute of Philosophy and Sociology, Polish Academy of Sciences, Warsaw, Poland.

Stacey M., Professor of Sociology, Department of Sociology, University of Warwick, Coventry, England.

Thiadens A.J., Project Manager, Werkgroep 2000, Amersfoort, the Netherlands.

Thung P. J., Professor Relations Between Natural Science and Medicine, Medische Faculteit, Rijksuniversiteit Leiden, the Netherlands.

Vansteenkiste J., Research assistant, Department of Sociology, Division for Medical Sociology, Katholieke Universiteit Leuven, Belgium.

Woudenberg A. P., Regional Officer, Office for Health Education and Social Sciences, World Health Organization, Copenhagen, Denmark.

PART ONE

INTRODUCTION

Teaching medical sociology: retrospection and prospection

Y. Nuyens

This volume contains a selection of papers presented at the International Seminar on Training Programs in Medical Sociology, held from August 23rd to 26th, 1976, in Leuven, Belgium.

The seminar was organized by the Department of Sociology, Division of Medical Sociology, University of Leuven, in collaboration with the Research Committee on the Sociology of Medicine of the International Sociological Association and the Interfaculty Group for Medical Education. The organization of the seminar was financially supported by the World Health Organization, the Belgian Ministries of Health an Education, the Belgian National Fund for Scientific Research, the Catholic University of Leuven, and the Janssen Research Foundation.

The occasion for the organization of this seminar lays with the Research Committee on the Sociology of Medicine, which, among other things, tries to act as a catalyst for the genesis of international meetings, focusing on matters that are relevant for the professsion. Training in medical sociology only recently became a matter of international concern. At the International Conference on the Sociology of Medicine in Jablona, Poland, in 1973, attention was focused on the role of medical sociology in medical training and, in a rather exemplary fashion, also on the strategies, methods and curriculums of the sociology of medicine for undergraduate and graduate students in sociology. The trend report on the training of medical sociologists that was presented at the World Congress of Sociology in Toronto, Canada, in 1974, illustrated the lack of systematic knowledge in this field and pointed out the need for critical reflection on this issue.

This need for critical reflection on training can be explained, for the greater part, by the accelerated development that has taken place in medical sociology in the last two decades. Between Chapter Four of Parsons' *The Social System* and today, a great widening of medical sociology's action radius can be observed, and, in addition, medical sociology (parallel with general sociology) has become characterized by processes of specialization, professionalization and institutionalization.

This development raised some questions as to the influence of training in this process of social change, as well as to the impact of these developments on training itself.

H. Mauksch, in his analysis in Chapter 4 of the development of medical sociology in the United States, distinguishes four sequential steps, viz.:

- Health studies as incidental studies. They usually represented the work of one or two scholars who were either interested in knowledge for knowledge's sake or in arousing public sentiment for health reforms. Within this period, every notion of specialized training remained absent.
- The role of key individuals, departments, schools and foundations. After World War II, a lot of well-established sociologists began to do research on various topics in health, thus bringing this kind of research to the attention of most sociologists. Parsons, Merton, Hughes and Hollingshead are names frequently mentioned in this context. Large-scale and conceptually and methodologically well-organized research projects such as *The Student Physician* and *Boys in White* aroused the interest and expectations of public authorities and private foundations, which hoped to find in social research unexplored opportunities for solving policy problems developing rapidly in a health care system that was then still in its organizing phase. For training, this had the implication that support by government and private foundations was largely associated with support of research and scholarship.
- Emergence of medical sociology as a special field. Separate sections and committees on medical sociology were established, first within the national professional association, later on a more international level. They started to recruit their own members, organize meetings, symposiums and conferences, publish professional journals etc. – in other words, the discipline had entered its institutionalization phase. Obviously, the training problem was soon to be (re)discovered.

- The emergence of specific training programs. Since the late 1960's an increasing number of university-based, medical sociology-oriented doctoral programs have been organized. However, when a financing institution furnished funds for programs (e.g., the Center for Health Services Research and Development backed twenty such training programs in 1972), it was not because of its primary interest in sociology as a discipline, but also because of the presumed contribution which specially-trained sociologists could make to various needs in health care. The result, with respect to training, is a tension between, and an incipient problem formulation about, on the one hand, an explicit and primary commitment to the discipline and, on the other, a clearly-stated priority to develop technically-competent specialists who can serve the needs of the health field.

From this historical outline we may conclude that medical sociological training has always aligned itself with, and has always adapted itself to, certain expectations and demands of society (public authorities, policy agencies, medical faculties, professional groups). Yet, on the other hand, it has been hardly (or not at all) successful in grafting its own demands onto that same society, let alone in providing form and content to these expectations.

When, for example, health care in a first-definition phase was viewed as a policy problem (booming costs, uneven distribution of services, differential usage of health care) and policy agencies called on the contributions of social research in order to broaden their knowledge of these problems, the dominant theme in training became: 'a good medical sociologist must be, first and foremost, a well-trained research sociologist'.

The special aspects of work *as* a medical sociologist are, in this context, assumed to be part of a professional super-structure, to be built upon the scholarly substructure of general sociology. What the term 'a well-trained research sociologist' actually implies for training programs can only be derived from an analysis of such programs. As an hypothesis, we may assume that a congruency has been realized between academic sociology and the policy expectations that have been formulated − at least on the level of an overdevelopment of quantitative, survey-oreinted research methods.

Another example may be taken from medical training. The changed morbidity profile, in which chronic and degenerative diseases are the major focus of concern and where care rather than cure becomes the major orientation of medical activity, reveals the limited span of a medical training that draws its body of knowledge and skills exclusively from the contribution of the physical sciences. Medical training, therefore, will refer expectations and demands to the behavioral sciences, in order to bridge, with the latter's help, the gap between training and practice and alleviate the situation's problematic nature, thus bringing it once again under control. In more academic terms: the behavioral sciences are expected to realize a problem-oriented approach within medical training. In practice, this means that medical sociology must be able to translate its body of knowledge, research findings and theoretical insights (in other words, the substantive achievements of the discipline), and adapt them and make them useful into a setting which is beyond the discipline's control.

In other words, medical sociology is facing a dilemma which Philipsen has formulated in this volume as: 'when a student tries to solve problems such as headaches and tiredness in general practice, it is not so simple to give the student a clear insight into the power relations in the national health care system...'

In relation to the training of medical sociologists, this dilemma gives rise to a behavioral science movement within the training. The four types of this movement, as described in Chapter 2 by Bloom, (basic science of behavior, clinical science of behavior, social behavioral science and science of community behavior) all have a common behaviorist signature – they represent a translation and adaptation of medical sociology to the needs of a medical training predominantly formulated in clinical, individualizing and behaviorist terms. This sort of medical sociology, which is tuned to the demands of medical training manifests itself in the series of handbooks and readers that rarely present themselves as aides for the training of future medical sociologists, but usually aim instead at a public of medical (and sometimes also health) practitioners. In the introductions to these books one finds statements such as: 'We anticipate that many of our readers may be new to the discipline of sociology and therefore our introduction has two specific aims: firstly, to provide a general framework... secondly, to introduce the reader to some of the basic sociological approaches and concepts' (Cox and Mead). Or: 'I want to consider some of the features of present-day medical practice that have led to the inclusion of sociology as a useful preparatory discipline and then go on to introduce some of the sociological concepts I consider salient to medical practitioners' (Tuckett).

Referring to Straus' classic dichotomy, we may say that we are dealing here with sociologists in medicine or 'practitioners who use some of the tools of sociological analysis to illuminate problems and issues thrown up by medical policy-making personnel'. The fact that such a providing function exists is not problematic in itself but its dominant development may be questioned, or, as Johnson puts it: 'What is interesting is that those who pioneered and left were concerned primarily with knowledge and understanding while those who followed rapidly became problem- and client-centered'.

It is clear that the case of medical training and the noted policy expectation about research both act as indicators for a wider societal process involving the structural features of the medical sociology scene, where 'the sources of research funds and attitudes of those who have the power to allow or refuse researchers access to medical situations and personnel' play a major role.

In his analysis of recent American developments in this field, Bloom states:

'Large-scale government support at first accepted the view of academic sociology. It no longer does. In the meantime, graduate training as a whole has become dependent upon federal support... The government agencies which continue to offer such support now are adding the condition that a more direct effort should be made to prepare future sociologists for the specific applications of sociological knowledge. In health, this refers to health services roles... The curriculum of graduate training will be changed to include more experience in the setting of work and the more systematic teaching of applied and policy-making skills...'

In practice, this evolution suggests an outline of the structural framework in which the discipline may realize its optimum efficiency or in which the transition from 'learned profession to policy science' may be achieved. At this point, we can correct the above-mentioned observation that (training in) medical sociology has always aligned itself with certain expectations and demands made by society. Indeed,

Bloom observes that, in recent years, medical sociology itself has been directing its energies increasingly toward issues which are visibly relevant to application.

These trends of research are represented as follows:

FROM	TO
a social psychological frame of reference	institutional analysis
small-scale social relations as subjects of research	large social systems
role analysis in specifically limited settings	complex organizational analysis
basic theoretical concerns with classic social analysis of behavior	policy science directed toward systematic translation of basis knowledge into decision-making
a perspective of human relations and communication	power structure analysis

This development illustrates the basis which has been laid within medical sociological research, and the points of application which have been suitably created, to meet society's demand for an applied, useful, policy-relevant health service role. To attribute this development solely to external factors would betray a one-sided approach. As with any social fact *qua* social fact, medical sociology is shaped through a dialectic of internal definition and external formation, an internal definition that Bloom illustrates as follows:

'As it has established its position, both as a legitimate sub-field of sociology and as a collaborator with the medical professions, there is evidence of increasing attention by medical sociology to the application of its knowledge... We seem now to have reached security in the legitimacy of this contribution, and to be turning to the effort to establish an organized dimension of applied social science'.

Particularly will established medical sociology speak of the conclusion of a first phase in the development of the medical sociological profession. This first phase is held to be primarily a period in which a body of knowledge is developed in which the capabilities of the discipline as a field of inquiry are tested and in which medical sociology attempts to have its scientific contribution to the problems of health care recognized. In this period, emphasis was clearly and exclusively on research and, moreover, higly centered within university/academic settings. In this context, there was no need for specific training in medical sociology, since any specific requirements of knowledge, skills and attitudes were thought to be part of what one acquires after having mastered the fundamentals of sociological knowledge and skill.

Society's demand for medical sociology now seems to be changing. We may refer not only to the pre-structuring by various policy-making agencies of specific applications of sociological knowledge, but also to the observation that an increasing number of medical sociologists practice their profession outside the framework of the academic research- and teaching-centers. In various settings, such as health insurance companies, health education organizations, welfare agencies, and even in medical associations, sociologists are given advisory and policy-making tasks. Thus, they are defined in new health services roles. It is clear that the current types of training, producing basic research sociologists for the most part, are not optimal for meeting these new role demands.

Against this background, how to teach medical sociology, as well as what to teach, become vital questions for the future of the discipline.

Uncritical fulfillment of this social demand by training through emphasizing applied and policy-making skills will enhance the risk against which authors like Freidson and Pflanz have warned. 'Medical sociology has focused on the areas that the medical practitioner himself has considered problematic, adopting the conception of what is problematic from the profession itself without raising questions about the perspective from which the problem is defined', says Freidson, while Pflanz states: ' Few medical sociologists have succeeded in breaking away from the confines of a medical value system, and most have taken these values for granted and as justified... The expectation that a sociologic analysis of the large and comprehensive systems of public medicine might make essential contributions to a better understanding of the functioning of institutions and organizations, of professions, communities and the family has seldom been met...'

With this unilateral institutionalization of the problem- and client-centered approaches within training, the dilemma of 'separation or symbiosis' (always applied by sociologists to the relationship between medicine and sociology) threatens to be grafted onto the relationship between general and medical sociology, with clearly more chances for separation than for symbiosis.

Johnson also points out this danger in the present development when he advocates the rediscovery of sociology for medical sociology, indicating as possible paths: widening the sociological perspective in health and illness; becoming aware of, and increasingly avoiding, constraints on research; seeking firmer roots in mainstream sociology and reexcavating the theoretical tradition. Such an option not only constitutes a warning but provides a valuable counterweight against a far too lopsided development of medical sociology in the direction of a policy science.

The above discussion reveals why the training problem of medical sociology can hardly be separated from the question of medical sociology's charter in society: what role is medical sociology able and willing to play against the back-ground of greatly increased societal expectations? Pflanz anwers this question with:

'Some are even convinced that the whole building is ripe for demolition and should be replaced by a new and better one. If today's medical sociology and its achievements are measured by its own pretensions and by public expectations, we are confronted with rather discouraging results. Whether patients, physicians or nurses, the general population, institutions, health officials, or the press, no one has derived substancial benefit from the ideas, the words, or the activity of medical sociology. Although medical sociology conceives itself as a critical science that aims to contribute an improvement of the conditions of life, it has nearly everywhere gambled away its assets by its uncritical adoption of existing values, whether they are those of the establishment, of public opinion, of a party or parties, of various ideologies, or the values of an action-oriented and bureaucratic medicine. Far too seldom have these value systems been seriously questioned in a search for alternatives of importance for the present or the future...'

The contributions to the International Seminar on Training Programs in Medical Sociology that follow should be read, interpreted and implemented against the background of the themes discussed above. Although the seminar's central focus was on the training of medical sociologists as a guide for the orientation and development of the discipline, the link with physicians as well as with educational scientists was structurally built into the program. The special attention given to the sociologist's role in medical training is justified by the fact that the introduction of behavioral sciences and the structural presence of sociologists within medical training settings has recently penetrated the Continent as well.

This development raises questions about the role fulfillment of sociologists within their new work setting, the contribution of their own training to this role fulfillment, and the impact of these new tasks on the social status and orientation of medical sociology as a discipline.

From the viewpoint of scientific reflections on training programs, educational scientists have recently been providing teaching methods as instruments for discussing and solving teaching problems within a certain framework. The focus of this framework is the formulation of teaching objectives to be set in the line of a task definition which may or may not be situated within a wider social context: in addition, these teaching objectives constitute the fundamentals of teaching contents, curriculum construction and evaluation procedures. The experimental application of this method during the seminar clearly revealed the span and limits of this approach, which will be dicussed in more detail in this volume.

In the light of the above remarks, the contributions to this volume can be grouped around five topics:

1. Developments within health care, the medical profession and the medical-sociological discipline (Thiadens, Thung, Bloom).
2. Accounts of current training programs and attempts at evaluation thereof (Day, Sokolowska, Pattishall, Pflanz, Siegrist).
3. Formulation of teaching objectives (Stacey, Aakster).
4. Case studies of didactic situations (Jefferys, Philipsen).
5. Evaluation methods of educational processes (Daniëls, Nihoul).

A critical comment on the seminar (Gill) and a selected bibliography on training programs (Vansteenkiste) conclude this work.

Sincere thanks are due to all who have contributed to the seminar.

References

Bloom, S., 1976, 'From learned profession to policy science', in Sokolowska, M., *Health, Medicine, Society,* Warsaw, Polish Scientific Publishers, 432-447.

Freidson, E., 1970, *Professional Dominance,* New York, Acherton Press.

Johnson, M., 1975, 'Medical sociology and sociological theory'. *Social Science and Medicine* (9), 227-232.

Nuyens, Y. and L. Claus, 1976, *'La ensenanza de la sociologia de la medicina en Europa y USA',* Papers Revista Sociologia, 5, 11-29.

Pflanz, M., 1974, 'A critique of Anglo-American medical sociology', *International Journal of Health Services* (4), 3, 565-574.

Introductory remarks

J. Vansteenkiste

In the seminar's opening sessions, the importance and relevance of an international reflection on training programs in medical sociology was indicated from various angles.

Professor M. Field, the President of the Research Committee for the Sociology of Medicine of the International Sociological Association, sketched the objectives of this Committee which, among other things, tries to act as a catalyst for the genesis of international meetings in which medical sociologists from all over the world can meet their colleagues from other countries. The rapid growth and institutionalization of the discipline, in addition to the changing societal expectations, give rise to questions about the content and orientation of training in medical sociology. In Field's opinion, such a seminar may contribute to a focusing of the problem-definition and provide elements for solutions relative to training in medical sociology.

Professor H. Janssens, the Chairman of the Belgian Inter-University Consultation Board for General Practitioner Training, discussed mainly the modern practitioner's changed training needs. He defined the broadening of the training perspective as acquiring 'knowledge and skills in those aspects of human existence which are of fundamental importance to enable one to provide assistance and to approach the patient as both an unassailable individual and as a social being'. For the realization of these objectives, medical trainers call in the help of the social sciences, notably medical sociology.

Dr. A. Woudenberg, Regional Officer for Health Education and Social Sciences of the W.H.O., stressed the interest of the W.H.O. in medical sociology and discussed the application of behavioral sciences in medicine and public health. He examined health education as an example of the application of sociology and psychology to medicine – mentioning only one example, however, of the multidimensional tasks sociologists should perform in health care, tasks varying from theoretical and applied research to policy-advising and policy-making functions.

A. P. Woudenberg

The Seminar on the Social Sciences in Medical Education, which was held in Hannover in October, 1969, and of which this volume is a product, recognized a number of trends which have been developing for several years within the health professions, the social sciences, and society at large. In medicine there has been a gradual re-kindling of interest in the social, cultural and environmental aspects of health and medical care. In the social sciences there has been a delineation of health and medicine as the focus of a major system of human behaviour. In society there has been a growing awareness of the potential which medicine possesses for enhancing the well-being of mankind, a growing sophistication in medical knowledge, and a tendency to define good health and adequate medical care as basic human needs and rights.

The kind of philosophical background against which the Seminar was held has been appropriately described by the late medical historian Henry E. Sigerist. Sigerist stressed that the nature of medicine in different societies and at different periods of time is related to the prevailing social and economic characteristics and to the technical means available to medical science.

'...The position of the physician in society, the tasks assigned to him and the rules of conduct imposed upon him by society changed in every period. The physician was a priest in Babylonia, a craftsman in ancient Greece, a cleric in the early and a scholar in the later Middle Ages. He became a scientist with the rise of the natural sciences, and it is perfectly obvious that the requirements upon the physician and the tasks of medical education were different in all these periods.'

In this context, discussion quickly brought out the rather exclusive devotion to the natural sciences – characteristic of medicine for the past 100 years – as a logical response to the scientific developments of the period. Prior to about 1870, the physician's orientation and the tasks he performed with respect to organic disease were necessarily limited by the absence of knowledge about etiology and methods of preventing and treating disease.

A hundred years ago the great health concerns of society were the infectious diseases. Massive unpredictable and uncontrollable epidemics, diseases of mothers and infants, and infected wounds were the great killers of mankind. Limited means for controlling both pain and infection had prevented the development of safe and effective surgical intervention. Against this background, the breakthroughs in the natural sciences which began in the 1870s and led to asepsis, safe anaesthesia, advances in surgery, immunology and chemotherapy, so quickly and dramatically altered medicine's potential for responding to disease that it was quite logical for it to focus on those particular functions in which it had suddenly proved to be effective. In keeping with developments in scientific knowledge, on which its newly-found capacity for intervention was based, medicine became almost exclusively concerned with the structure, the function, the chemistry and the genetics of the human organism.

In the summary and conclusions of the Seminar's Report, the feasibility of change was discussed; i.e., some participants expressed doubts about the possibility of effecting the changes they wished to make. It was generally agreed, however, that the discussions at the Seminar could be seen as a step toward the accomplishment of those changes – a step in a social movement to improve and broaden medical education. The process cannot be completed in one step. Every social movement must expect to encounter resistance. But this is not insuperable and should not be exaggerated; obstacles that cannot be eradicated can sometimes be circumvented. Indeed, one of the functions of medical social scientists is to study the processes of change and how change may be induced in medical education.

Above all, those advocating reforms should avoid a defensive attitude. Those who believe that little can be done will do little. The problem is not a trivial or peripheral one. The whole discussion on the teaching of social sciences in medicine is centrally related to the recognition of social change, to creative adaptation to change, and to the task of learning how to direct it better and prepare for the changes of the future.

Another event I would like to refer to is the WHO Regional Office's *Workshop on Teaching Social and Preventive Medicine (Educational Methods)*, which took place in Edinburgh from the 5th to the 13th of september, 1972.

The consultant, an education specialist, stressed in his introductory statement that the Workshop should be viewed as a dialogue between those who were essentially pedagogues but not necessarily expert in social and preventive medicine, and those who were experts in social and preventive medicine but not necessarily trained in pedagogy. Participants should not be considered the 'pupils' of the educational specialists, for the latter had just as much to learn as the other participants – in particular about methods of coming to terms with real educational problems rather than with purely theoretical ones. Certain consequences were expected to result from the Workshop activities. The first of these would be an increased awareness of the large variety of ways in which the teaching of social and preventive medicine could contribute to the overall undergraduate medical curriculum. The Workshop would certainly not be concerned with an attempt to determine what the scope and content of social medicine should be, but it would include work on a job analysis which might direct attention to the wide variety of tasks for which the teaching of social and preventive medicine must prepare the undergraduate.

Another consequence might be the formulation, in terms both relevant and useful, of definitions of the specific and general educational objectives which should guide attempts to teach social and preventive medicine. It would also be important to survey some of the main educational strategies, methods and resources which could help those who had to achieve the specified educational objectives. Some consideration should also to be given to the overall strategy of course planning and curriculum design, while some time would have to be spent in considering problems which arise when an attempt is made to find out if stated educational objectives are, in fact, being achieved.

Finally, I would like to call your attention to a *Report on a Symposium on the Preparation of Health Personnel in Health Education, with special reference to Postgraduate Education Programmes*, organized by the WHO Office, and held in Cologne from the 10th to the 14th of November, 1974.

I draw from this report because I think that training and teaching in health education is relevant to training programmes in medical sociology, and vice versa.

In many European countries, the integration of health education into other professional activities will require that health education be accepted as a separate subject within the existing curricula of the educational institutions for the different professions involved. The first step will have to be an administrative decision about the desirability of such an innovation. Once this decision has been made, the next step will be the acceptance of the subject-matter by the relevant training institutions and the provision of teachers and educational material. This may prove to be more difficult than it sounds, and a number of problems may be envisaged.

The main problem will be the acceptance of health education as a separate subject. Before any attempt is made to persuade the governing body of a medical faculty or school of public health to allocate a substantial amount of time to health education in the existing curriculum, there must be certainty that the proposed subject-matter is of an academic standard. This involves not only a set of principles and methods, but also a theoretical basis and empirical evidence of effectiveness.

The instructor or the subject must be of a high enough academic status and level of professional prestige to be listened to: for example, a member of a faculty board or of the governing body of a school of public health.

The problem of where health education should be taught must be resolved: if health education is to become an integral part of the medical and paramedical, as well as the educational professions, it must be taught in the undergraduate courses of all the professions concerned.

Even if we find an academically respectable instructor and are successful in raising the subject-matter to an academic level, we shall still have the problem of competing for time with other more 'relevant' subjects. This is because the curricula of students are already over-crowded, and we shall have to convince a curriculun committee that it would be useful to reduce the number of hours devoted to, say, anatomy, and give a corresponding number of hours to health education.

When we have overcome all these hurdles, the problems will not end, because we shall be faced with the greatest of them all: the acceptance of the subject-matter by the students. We must remember that students are intent on becoming professionally-qualified as soon and as painlessly as possible and the introduction of a new subject will meet with a certain scepticism, if not with outright opposition. To be accepted by the students, the subject must be a part of the qualifying examination and have obvious future advantages.

In many instances the problems listed above will not be easily overcome, and an alternative solution should be considered. In many academic institutions the students have for some time now been taught a number of social sciences as part of their degree course. In many instances the subjects, such as psychology and sociology, form an integral part of their curricula. It seems, therefore, more practical and more promising to build on what already exists instead of trying to achieve the recognition of health education as an academically acceptable subject, and at the same time to fight for the integration of this subject into an already overcrowded curriculum. There are perhaps certain advantages in treating health education as an applied aspect of behavioural sciences (sociology, psychology) in medicine, instead of as a special subject in its own right.

In general terms, the contribution of the behavioural sciences (psychology, sociology, anthropology) to medicine is in two main areas: firstly, in the study of the institution of medicine, the organizations and the professions involved in dealing with the client-population; and secondly in the study of medical problems and their solution. This last is concerned mainly with the study of the distribution of the problem in a population (epidemiology); with the study of the causes (etiology) and the solutions of the problem – part of which the study of the causes (etiology) and the solutions of the problem – part of which lies within the sphere of health education. In the case of behavioural sciences, the problems under study will be related to the social environment or to human behaviour.

In many medical schools the teaching of behavioural sciences has a long tradition and they are already included in the curriculum. Yet health education, although a part of this subject-matter, has not been widely accepted. This, then, is the problem we are facing and should be considering in great detail, because the whole future of health education teaching on this higher level depends on its solution.

If we accept that health education is an aspect of the applied behavioural sciences in medicine, then its future will depend on the future of behavioural sciences in medical schools.

In mentioning and quoting from the three reports, finally, I hope that I am more or less in line with what was said in the introduction to the programme of this Seminar: namely, that the tasks set out for sociologists in health care are not few and one-dimensional but cover a large variety ranging from theoretical and applied scientific research to policy advice and policy-making. I also hope, that this International Seminar will focus on the professional requirements of training programmes in medical sociology for behavioural scientists and medical doctors, critically evaluate existing initiatives, and formulate an efficent strategy for the future.

I hope that the present work of the WHO Regional Office for Europe in health manpower development can contribute to these objectives.

PART TWO

FUTURE DEVELOPMENTS

Training is always situated within a certain social context. Therefore, any scientific reflection on training programs should take into account the social framework in which the training takes place and for the realization of which a contribution is expected from training. When training is indeed expected to make such a contribution, this implies that either acknowledged or expected social developments be incorporated in this framework. In relation to the theme of this seminar, this means that general outlines should be made of the developments that will determine the structure and content of future health care, and this within a changing social, political and economic context. While training programs in medical sociology presently have relevance mainly for the training of (medical) sociologists and medical doctors, the expected and/or desired developments in task definitions and professional practices of both professions can subsequently be dealt with.

Dr. A. Thiadens extrapolates on the main lines of the development of health care in the future. These transitional trends picture the possible evolution of the present, mainly passive, health care into more active health care. He examines the most important implications of these trends for the behavior of those seeking help as well as for those providing it.

In his analysis of the profession of medical sociologist, Prof. S. Bloom observes considerable structural changes. During the time that sociologists were developing the domain of medical sociology and acting primarily as sociologists-in-medicine, it was generally accepted that prerequisites should not be acquired in any specialized training, but rather in a basic program of research sociology. Dominant in professional practice, therefore, was the academic research function. Recently, however, a shift could be observed with respect to an increased financial support of a type of specialized training that was expected to prepare future sociologists for the application of their knowledge in the domain of health and the performance of health services roles.

Prof. P. Thung, in this volume, explains why he expects 'not much of a future' for the medical profession in its present form. This form, developed in the nineteenth century, has fulfilled and outlived all its original objectives. On the one hand, modern health care has outgrown its original scope and, on the other hand, looking at the present developments in medical training, one must conclude that it is no longer feasible to train people for one comprehensive medical profession. Programs should be differentiated and tuned to the varieties of qualifications required by modern health care. 'Only deprofessionalization can save professionalism,' Thung asserts. Electives are the only innovating force, since they break with the uniform curriculum. It is in this perspective that medical sociology should define itself. Medical sociology should not join the battle for more lecture time within the framework of the archaic comprehensive medical curriculum.

1. Health care in the future

A.J.H. Thiadens

1.1. Introduction

The way in which patients in China are treated in hospitals and medical centres differs essentially from the Western manner.

The central factor is the team approach. The relations between the patient, the medical attendant and the nurse are based on equality and mutual respect. It is the duty of the medical staff to serve the patient. The patient is stimulated to ask questions about his case which are dealt with extensively by the medical staff.

In consequence the patient is closely involved in the process of his recovery. Conversely, the patient is expected to take a positive attitude towards the treatment and to help his fellow patients when he is already convalescent and able to perform simple actions. The ambulent patients take an active part in the care of those who are bedridden. They read the paper to them, perform simple domestic chores, keep them company and thus become familiar with the social and medical problems of the bedridden patients. In this way they are often able to counsel the medical team in attendance. When the patient has to undergo an operation, the surgeon and the nursing staff tell him exactly what he can expect. The patient is consulted about the method of operation that would be best for him and he can choose for himself between anaesthesia by means of narcosis or by means of acupuncture. The relation of confidence that is thus created has a positive effect on the process of recovery and may be looked upon as an integral part of the Chinese mode of treatment.

In the wards an informal atmosphere of solidarity prevails.

The patients choose representatives from among their midst who are to submit their views and suggestions to those in charge of the wards. Every morning there is a discussion with the medical leaders or the medical teams for the purpose of deciding upon the working program of that day with the patients and the nurses.

In this description of a situation in a hospital in China in 1973 the patient is seen to be an ally of the doctor and the nurse.

In Western Europe all those concerned seem to be drawn along passively on the current of the medico-technical developments. When the current narrows down into the channel of the hospital, it becomes all too evident how haphazardly they drift past each other. The distance between patient and medical staff becomes greater and greater. The doctor and the nurse are traditionally the persons who give advice, the patient is the person who seeks advice.

The extreme specialization in medical science and nursing constantly widens the gap between those giving and those seeking advice. More and more medical and non-medical specialists are involved in the examination and elimination of the disorder.

The treatment of disease and the guidance of the patient are increasingly being affected by teams of workers, but personal contact with the patient is becoming less and less. As the person seeking advice, the patient becomes the non-expert *par excellence*. Those seeking and those giving advice are going through a serious crisis. This critical situation is symptomatic of the whole phenomenon of health care.

Is it still possible for the two parties to get out of this critical situation? Is it still possible for them to become allies? Is there a remedy for health care in our Western countries?

In my opinion an answer to these questions is possible only if we have the courage to analyse the present situation in an historical perspective. Does not the present crisis indicate a turning of the tide? Are we not passing through a transitional phase?

The health care being criticised might be defined as a passive health care. We, as people seeking and giving advice, are half-heartedly heading for an active health care.

Now what are the characteristic features of this passive and active health care? And what consequences does this have for the confrontation of those seeking and those giving advice?

1.2. Passive health care

In passive health care the patient is primarily regarded as a person requiring, demanding and seeking advice. In the hospital the reparative care deminates. A physiological disorder is repaired. The disease is treated. The patient as an individual is dissociated from human relations.

1.2.1. The patient in passive health care

Medicine, as it is still functioning at present in many places, isolates the physiological aspect from the totality of man. It aims at repairing defectively functioning parts of the organism. In this way the patient is degraded from a human being to a thing, namely the object of the treatment. In medical practice it is forgotten that man is not only subject to a number of physiological processes but also to physic and social factors, and that he reacts to his illness in his own way. Although it is known that many disorders are psycho- or sociosomatic, this fact is hardly taken into account in the treatment. In actual fact it is merely the symptoms that are combated. In those cases where the psycho-social factors *are* recognized as a reality they are frequently labelled hysteria, affectation or lability. For the patient this means that he is often treated impersonally. It is irrelevant who or what he is. Something is evidently wrong with his organism. That has to be dealt with. He is degraded from a person to an individual. This individual is not ill, but has a disease. He loses his identity and becomes a medical record: a case history; two curves on squared paper, a red one and a blue one.

He is regarded in a different light and changes from a person who is ill to a disease. Because of the monopoly of medical science and because illness is the only lawful and socially tolerated way of evading one's obligations, one is also obliged to somatize one's feelings of uneasiness and to express them in the form of physiological complaints. The patient, who enters the hospital more or less out of necessity, passes from his familiar world into completely unfamiliar surroundings. The hospital is found difficult to live in. The patient can appropriate only a very small territory; if the worst comes to the

worst, nothing but a bed and a bedside table. He is indeed cast out of
the existing and familiar sphere, and thus the concept existential (from
exist) at once becomes relevant. The space of the world he lives in is
narrowed, but also socially isolated. The part of the hospital outside
the room he lies in, remains as unfamiliar and mysterious to him as it is
to an outsider. The outer world is banished altogether and is only
represented now and then by visitors, who are admitted in carefully
restricted numbers. As an aid-requiring object of treatment, freed
from social obligations, he is therefore also dissociated from relations
with those humans with whom and through whom he normally also
tries to become human. As a pre-eminently dependent and non-expert
person he is a patient: the person undergoing everything. There is a
marked distinction between the two categories, the greater the risk of
polarization of views to prejudices. Undoubtedly a marked distinction
between the sick and the healthy will also result in a fixation of roles
on either side. On the part of the patient this feeling of isolation, apart
from certain characteristics of the patient's role (the right to be
exempted from a number of social obligations, the duty to accept
advice, the disease as an unpleasant matter), will probably have to do
with feelings of anxiety and uncertainty of the patient. The hospital
tends to infantilize the patient, it forces him to follow the stereotyped
pattern of the hospital, it curtails his freedom, it does not offer him any
alternatives, deprives him of all responsibility, and does not give him
any possibility to participate in decisions about his own body. In
passive health care the present-day patient seems to be a person who
asks for an authority that is to solve his problems for him. Perfectly
accustomed as he is to a dependent role, he does not demand the right
to make his own decisions. He does not even seem to be aware that
the position he occupies as a patient is sometimes in glaring contrast
with his other positions in society, in which he does bear responsibility. It is as if this forms part of his being a patient.

Recapitulating: in passive health care the patient is primarily a
person seeking and demanding advice, an object of treatment; he has
a disease, is dependent, undergoes reparative care, and is approached
as an individual in a special category. In passive health care the
patient experiences the hospital as a workshop for repairing organs. It
is a business rather than a home of and for the sick. It is a

working-community rather than a living-community. It is isolated in our society. It has the character of a boarding-school rather than of a hotel, and inside this boarding-school everyone wears his own uniform. The patient views his pyjamas as the clothes of a convict. The hospital is as it were a white reservation. When he leaves it, he loses his bearings, he has to get accustomed to life again. He no longer has any orientation. It is as if he were driving on a dark road, where the traffic marks have suddenly disappeared. It is as if the body he has does not belong to him.

Passive health care is out-of-date. We are in a transitional phase. How do hospitals now present themselves to their clients?

We have just finished a study about the normal circulars published by the hospitals themselves. We were interested in the way hospitals supplied information to their clients. The investigation was restricted to the general hospitals, 35% of the total, including the university hospitals. The following points emerged:
- The patients are hemmed in by rules and orders.
- Thinking is done by the nurses; they take over the patient's capacity of self-determination.
- Doctor decides about everything; he is the one who knows best.

The aim of the circular is to help the patient adapt to the whole system. However, the picture it presents is misleading. It is stated in many of the circulars that the hospital will try to make life as pleasant as possible.

This is, of course, pure nonsense. It is not the aim of the hospital to be a hotel, and the patient is certainly aware of this. Moreover the text does not elaborate on this in any way. It merely mentions that great care is given to the preparation and serving of the food.

The patient is expected to obey a number of rules. Sometimes cynical references are made to promotion of independence and a sense of responsibility. This means that the patient, I quote, 'will spontaneously obey the rules so that he has not to be reminded every now and then. It is in your own interest to accept the system. Surely you will not grieve all these nice doctors and dear nurses who are labouring night and day on your behalf.'

The circulars do not mention the possibility of any difficulties. No mention is made of dying, death, pain, stress, etc. What is presented is a mockery. The reality is quite different. The patient is bound by rules. He is not permitted to smoke, drink, eat, or do anything else, without permission.

Like a child he has to ask permission for almost all kinds of normal activities. He eventually loses every wish to speak his mind.

It is unlikely that this is a true picture of how Dutch hospitals function at present. Health care is no longer merely passive. Some of the texts in the circulars appear to be very out of date and conservative indeed and hospitals often harm their image by publishing them.

1.2.2. Doctor and nurse in passive health care

The doctor usually exhibits an authoritarian behaviour pattern. However, this does not justify considering the nurse as a 'trained incapacity'.

Doctors give insufficient explanation, if any, to the nurse on the nature of the disease, the diagnosis and the therapeutics, if any. It is still unusual for the doctor to make allowances for the nursing organization inside the hospital. He comes at the time that suits him; not at the time that is most suitable in connection with the nursing organization of a ward.

In this passive health care there is still a great difference in status between doctors and nurses, and consequently a great hierarchical difference as well.

Doctors and nurses work simultaneously, but the work of the nurse is, more often than not, work *for* the doctor instead of *with* the doctor. Each party thinks in claims. This is the province of the doctor and that is the province of the nurse, the latter being subordinate to the former in the caste-like structure of the hospital. The extreme specialization threatens to empty the profession of the nurse of its meaning even further. However, I think it is preferable that a nurse should herself, from the point of view of her own profession, indicate what are the bottlenecks in passive and active health care, in order that she may cooperate in a friendly way with the doctor and the patient.

As for the doctor, it is precisely in the hospital that his approach to the patient is concerned with a particular aspect of the case. His attention is chiefly directed at the treatment of the disorder of an organ. As a doctor he is the one who knows what the matter is and who decides to do something about it. In other words, as a specialist he has grown to be an organ specialist. The organ specialists will have to recognize that they can hardly function horizontally any more. They are confronted with a permanent shortage of time, amongst other things, owing to the rapid development of technical medicine, the necessity of keeping abreast of the professional literature, and the team discussions with other organ specialists. This forces them in a direction where less and less justice is done to the patient as a human being. These considerations tend to stress the need to adapt horizontal specialisms such as social work and almoner services in such a way that this deficiency may be eliminated. Unfortunately many specialists in passive health care are completely tied to the hospital both in their training and in their specialist work. This might be one of the reasons why problems such as resocialization, for instance, are insufficiently recognized by them.

It is symptomatic of the authority of doctors and the development of more and more medical specialisms that Dr. William Poe, professor of social medicine at Duke University, advocates a new discipline in the medical faculty, viz., marantology (from the Greek word *marantos*, meaning withered, spent). Marantologists would have to care for those who are no longer wanted by anyone, the aged, the incontinent and the incurable people, those guilty of the sin of remaining alive, but not responding to our manipulations.

As a professional group doctors still form a closed unit with the character of a privileged class. Certain codes, marked mutual solidarity and secrecy, and the handling of particular status symbols (addressing one another as colleague) contribute to this exclusivity.

The doctor is in a position of authority towards the patient because it is exclusively he who is assumed to have knowledge of disease and its cure.

Recapitulating: in passive health care the doctor and the nurse present themselves as experts in giving advice. In treating disease doctors act as menders of organs. The emphasis is on the physiological dysfunctioning which is taken in hand, the patient serving as the object of treatment. The doctors know everything about disease and health.

We mentioned above that hospitals do themselves an injustice by publishing circulars. It is also interesting to observe how the hospitals themselves present their own nurses and doctors. We have made the following list of their activities:

Activities of the head-nurse:
- Post-cards and stamps are available at the desk of the head-nurse.
- If your bed-light is out of order, contact the head-nurse.
- Permission can be given by the head-nurse to have a look around the ward, or to visit another patient.
- Each patient has to be accessible at all times to the doctor and the head-nurse.
- Do not leave your room without the permission of the nurse on duty.
- Doctor and nurse decide which patients are allowed to watch T.V.; the T.V. set is switched on and off by the head-nurse.
- Lights go out at 10 o'clock. Exceptions can only be made by the nurse.
- Any wishes, any complaints, which we trust you will not have, are to be discussed with the head-nurse.

This is the picture that hospitals present of their nurses. In another list we mentioned:

Activities of the doctor:
- Nothing is said about his real physician's work.
- Patients may only take a shower if the doctor gives permission.
- The doctor decides whether you may smoke.
- There is a phone plug in your room; you may have a phone if the doctor allows. Social aid can only be given by request of the doctor. Only he knows what kind of aid might be required in your case.
- No food may be taken into the hospital by the visitors; doctor knows what is best for you.

This is how hospitals are still presenting themselves. It gives no real idea of how they function in practice.

It is clear that we are coming into a transitional phase. Within this transitional phase we can observe many trends. In any case, it is clear that the passive health care is out-of-date, and that we are progressing towards active health care.

1.3. Transitional phase

There is a growing feeling that it is no longer economically justified to
be concerned *ad infinitum* about everybody. There is a desire to check
the wild growth of super-specialisms. Growing uneasiness can also be
found about the fact that people are becoming more and more liable to
disease in our society, in spite of all the facilities and the progress of
medical science. Now that the morbidity pattern is shifting, more
attention should be given to the psycho-social disaeses, and in
particular to those people who are chronically sick.

As the citizen becomes emancipated he no longer accepts being
labelled a patient, a human being that has to suffer everything, in
particular being degraded to an errand-boy delivering notes from the
general practitioner to the specialist.

But it is also among the persons traditionally giving advice, the
doctors, that doubts are beginning to arise. More and more doctors are
beginning to realize that the way they act has become fundamentally
ambiguous: that disease means health at a different level, that the
prevention of death may sometimes be cruel and stupid, that the
elimination of suffering, though not of pain, may be wrong, that
combating symptoms may be shortsighted. During their consulting
hours general practitioners are being flooded with complaints of a
psychosomatic character. These doctors come to the conclusion that
as individual doctors they cannot do much to improve the micro-
climate of the individual patient, and even much less to improve his
macro-climate. They feel that medical authority often means impo-
tence.

Among the nurses too passive health care tends to be criticized. The
professional reality does not come up to the professional expectations.
The flight of the profession into specialization is noted with concern,
partly for the same reasons as in the case of the doctors. There is a
considerable drop out among nurses.

The patients as the persons traditionally seeking advice are growing
more and more conscious of being critical consumers as well.

They are beginning to realize that it is their own body which is
concerned, with which they identify themselves.

They also find that many of the persons traditionally giving advice

are compromising in this critical situation by suppressing the symptoms and having recourse to valium. They are therefore rightly uniting
in patients' councils and consumers' associations of patients, at least
in the Netherlands.

Are there, is this transitional phase, any indications of the character
of the active health care we are hesitatingly heading for? What do we
mean by active health care and what does this mean for the identity
crisis of those seeking advice, the patients and those giving it, the
doctors and the nurses?

1.4. Active health care

In active health care the patient no longer seeks, demands and needs
advice, but he is a co-operator, a co-helper, a working ally and a
co-administrator of the health care. The emphasis is no longer on a
physiological disorder, but attention is focused on the integration of
the physiological, the social and the physic level at which dysfunctioning may occur. No longer does the treatment of a disease dominate the
guidance of a patient. In active health care the treatment of the disease
and the guidance of the patient are integrated. The patient is no longer
degraded to an individual dissociated from his human relations, but he
is continuously associated existentially with the network of human
relations within which he is trying to become a human being. What
consequences does this have for those seeking advice and those giving
it?

1.4.1. The patient in active health care

It is not only from a therapeutic point of view that the patient of the
future will be emancipated. A fundamental choice must also be made
in favour of the right of everyone to arrange his life freely in his own
way.

In active health care everyone is entitled to have the chance of
becoming healthier. He must therefore be able to break through the
isolation, to communicate, to participate and to enter into relations.

He must have the opportunity to be creative and must be enabled to choose from a number of real alternatives. In active health care people are aware that everyone has a future; even the elderly person, the invalid, the sick person can develop within a limited or a narrowing scope.

In self-care, people need to co-operate with their own relatives, friends and family in order to realize everyone's optimum development. The profile of the patient in active health care could then be characterized especially by the fact that he is a co-operator, co-helper and a working ally. As the object of a treatment he is at the same time its subject. It is no longer the fact that one has a disease which dominates the situation, but the experience of being ill. The emancipated patient now only accepts integral care. This integral care respects him as a human being interwoven with his sociosphere. The patient in active health care will therefore experience the hospital primarily as a house of and for the sick, where patients and fellow-workers are equal. In this house everyone's need of privacy is respected. Treatment and guidance are integrated. Patients take part actively in their own and each other's cure. They can continue their life-pattern as much as possible. Visitors are also responsible for the patient's welfare. All fellow-workers are allies. The living and working functions of all rooms are integrated. The hospital is on a human scale. It is integrated with the built-up area. It is founded in joint consultation with the region. From the genuine guidance he receives during the dying process and in the coping with crises, the patient in active health care will be able to infer to what extent the treatment of the disease is integrated with the guidance.

1.4.2. The doctor and the nurse in active health care

In active health care the doctor and the nurse speak the same language as the patient and they are aware that they know only a part of the process of his growing less and more healthy. Emotional reactions and psychic stresses will no longer be labelled hysteria and affection. The nurse is no longer the extension of the doctor or the representative of the dependent patient. The nurse, as a guiding expert, will co-ordinate the total guidance of the patient. According to the nature, the intensity and the duration of the care which the patient needs, the nurse will on her own authority be allowed to consult other means of guidance.

The nurse and the doctor are allies and will try to integrate the treatment of the disease and the guidance of the patient. In this team work the patient will be accepted as a working ally, who also bears responsibility.

In other words, in active-health-care hospitals a therapeutic climate is created in which the roles of seeking advice and giving it will alternate more and more. In other words: a therapeutic triangle is formed: patient - doctor - nurse.

The rigid hierarchy disappears and gives way to equality on a basis of everybody's own contribution. There is also scope for giving vent to one's emotions.

Recapitulating: the doctor and the nurse as persons giving advice in active health care are no professional solvers of problems, but they help the patient to solve his problems for himself. They are aware of bearing a partial responsibility in the process of recovery. In a therapeutic climate the treatment of a disease is integrated with the guidance of the patient. Equal care is devoted to physiological and social and psychic dysfunctioning.

The doctor and the nurse no longer treat the patient as an individual individually, but as a team of allies.

1.5. Summary and conclusion

The crisis in which the persons seeking and the persons giving advice are involved is symptomatic of the whole health care.

This crisis is part of the transitional phase from a passive to an active health care.

In many places passive health care with the concomitant concepts of health is still present in the confrontation of patient, doctor and nurse.

At the same time, however, there are indications that we are heading for active health care.

– The question is to what extent we are willing to recognize the trends in this transitional phase in order to stimulate development towards an active health care.

Are we prepared to accept the consequences of this active health care as patients and as persons giving advice? How are we training our students? Can and will we protect them from becoming professional solvers of problems?

I hope that this analysis of the present situation may make us more aware of our responsibility for the future and may motivate us to co-operate in a health care to which we are all entitled as human beings.

2. The profession of medical sociologist in the future: implications for training programs

S. Bloom

2.1. Introduction

After some background data about the general occupational role of medical sociology, I will describe the role patterns of sociology within the institutions of medicine, especially medical schools. I will then discuss the manpower of medical sociology, its sources and types of training. Finally, I will analyze the work of medical sociology in terms of the actual role demands, asking whether our current types of training are appropriate for their intended outcomes. It should be noted that throughout, I refer to the situation in the United States. [1]

2.2. Background data for understanding the occupational role of medical sociology

Throughout its history sociology has been, and continues to be, primarily a teaching occupation, and the sociologist a college or university teacher. The best estimates are that over 85 percent of sociologists are employed in institutions of higher learning. (Lutterman, 1975). This places the sociologist in a large general occupational category, but within this group, sociologists are relatively small in numbers. In medicine also, sociologists are proportionately a small group.

More specifically, there were 2.7 million full-time teachers of all

---

1. The groundwork for the ideas presented here appear in two previous papers: 'From Learned Profession to Policy Science', presented at the Conference on Medical Sociology in Warsaw, August 20-26, 1973, and to be published in the Proceedings, edited by Magda Sokolowska; and with Robin Badgley, 'Behavioral Sciences and Medical Education: the Case of Sociology', *Social Science and Medicine*, 7: 927-941, 1973.

types in the United States in 1972-73. Of these, 620,000 worked in colleges and university, in 2600 institutions; one-third teaching in universities, one-half in 4-year colleges, and about one-seventh in 2-year colleges. [2]

The number of students is extremely large, and at least until recently, increasing. About 60 percent of all persons in the United States between 18 and 21 attended college in 1972, compared with 40 percent ten years earlier. [3]

In general, sociology is one of the smallest academic disciplines. In universities and colleges in the year 1971, for example, 11,323 sociologists were employed. By comparison, there were almost 17,000 psychologists and more than 60,000 medical scientists in colleges and universities in the same year. [4]

These are total figures for each discipline and tell us nothing, of course, about the relative importance of their activities in medicine. What we do know is that the history of the five major medical 'basic sciences', (anatomy, physiology, biochemistry, pathology, and pharmacology) contains close and integral involvement in medical education in Western European countries for at least a century. In the United States, the movement toward making these disciplines equal in importance to clinical medicine in the training of doctors began around 1875, and consolidated as a clear institutional pattern by 1920.

---

2. Of the total 2.7 million, about 1.7 million were women. Only about one-fourth of college and university teachers, however, are women: 155,000. Women are more likely to work in the 2-year colleges and to teach certain subjects, such as nursing, home economics, and library science.

3. All figures presented so far in this section are from the U.S. Department of Labor, Bureau of Labor Statistics, *Occupational Outlook Handbook,* Washington, D.C., U.S. Government Printing Office, Bulletin 1785, 1974. Denominators include total population ages 18-19, 3,059,000 in 1969; from ages 20-24, 6, 594, 400. Cf. Statistical Abstract of U.S. Printing Office, 1969. It should be noted that the percentages reported from the *Occupational Outlook Handbook* are different from a more recent report: *Special Labor Force Report 155,* 'The High School Class of 1972'. According to the latter, the highest proportion of high school graduates who entered college reached 51 percent in 1968, and then began to fall. By 1972, it had dropped to 49 percent. See Nelson N. Foote, 1975.

4. In 1975, there were 7,271 members of the American Sociological Association (ASA) 2,101 associate members, and 1,039 student members. The Section on Medical Sociology of the ASA averages about 10 percent of the total, or more than 800. Cf. Statistical Abstracts, 1973; *ASA Footnotes,* August, 1975.

Medical sociology, on the other hand, is only beginning to be perceived as an established partner in medical education. What was still described in 1963 as its 'promise' (Reader, 1963) became a decade later the unequivocal assertion:

'Sociology has already contributed much to medicine... has (in its work related to medicine) developed a distinct body of knowledge, and in fact, reached the position where it can contribute substantially to decision making in medicine'. (Kendall and Reader, 1972)

As it has established its position, both as a legitimate sub-field of sociology as a collaborator with the medical professions, there is evidence of increasing attention by medical sociology to the applications of its knowledge.

The literature reveals a remarkable degree of concern about its development. (Caudill, 1953; Clausen, 1956; Reader and Goss, 1959; Reader, 1963; Suchman, 1964; Graham, 1964; Bloom, 1965; McKinlay, 1972). Most of its continuing self-scrutiny, however, was – at least until recently – focused on the evaluation of its contribution to knowledge. We seem now to have found security in the legitimacy of this contribution, and to be turning to the effort to establish an organized dimension of applied social science – of which an example is seen in table 2.1.

Williams, first in 1963 and again in 1972, sought to show how the knowledge of medical sociology was actually being applied. Hyman (1967) reviewed 'the uses of sociology for the problems of medicine'. In my own review of the field in 1972 I concluded that, in the trends of research, there were indications that medical sociology was directing its energies increasingly toward issues which were visibly relevant to application. I described the trends of research (Bloom, 1973) as follows:

FROM	TO
a social psychological frame of reference	institutional analysis
small-scale social relations as subjects of research	large social systems

role analysis in specifically limited settings	complex organizational analysis
basic theoretical concerns with classic social analysis of behavior	policy science directed toward systematic translation of basic knowledge into decision-making
a perspective of human relations and communication	power structure analysis

Care must be exerted, however, to avoid the assumption that the organization of the applications of science follows directly from knowledge. Historical evaluations of the relationships between knowledge and its applications tend to falter and get lost in what might be called the fallacy of rationality.

This is a recognized problem in the history of medicine. Both the medical historian Sigerist and the sociologist Freidson have documented the practice of writing medical history as though it were an orderly progression from important discovery to important discovery, ignoring the critical influence of various social and political factors. Actually, as Freidson shows so clearly, there are two histories of medicine, one a history of ideas and the other of the organization of its practices. The influence of one upon the other is profound but by no means direct, rational, and inevitable (Freidson, 1970).

Sociology appears no less prone to the same fallacy. It is not enough, therefore, to document the trends of medical sociology's knowledge development, if we seek to understand its role *in* medicine. We must look directly at the position, status, role requirements of those sociologists who are employed as medical sociologists. Once this is done, the implications for training future medical sociologists may seem obvious, but here again, I think we must not take anything for granted.

2.3. The role of sociology in medicine

Although sociologists have conducted research on various aspects of medicine for at least three-quarters of a century, the organized field of inquiry which we now know as 'medical sociology' is only about thirty

Table 2.1 Sociomedical knowledge: its applications

STUDIES OF	FOCUSED ON	
	Behavioral or psychological function as such ('basic') and viability of the action system of individual actors ('applied')	Social, social-psychological, and sociocultural factors in other aspects of health and disease 'basic' and their management' ('applied')
Biology and ecology of disease and health	1. Ecology of mental disorders; production and reproduction of successful or unsuccessful coping behavior in families; basic studies of motivation, learning perception, etc.	2. Social factors in the epidemiology of cancer, rheumatoid arthritis, etc.
Response to health and disease	3. Communication of mental health concepts; social-psychological careers of mental patients during and after hospitalization; emotional factors and coping behavior in relation to leukemia, death and other stressful situations	4. Factors affecting acceptance of fluoridation or other public health programs; the impact of influenza on a community
Organization of medical facilities and other groups affecting health	5. Social structures and functioning of a mental hospital; mental health in schools and industry (i.e., impact of schools or industries as sociocultural systems on the viability of the action systems of their members)	6. Social structure and functioning of the general hospital, health departments, group practice of medicine, etc.
Education, career development, and professionalization as a social process	7. Career development in all the 'mental health' professions (i.e., all those whose primary concern is with helping other achieve a more viable action system); development of new roles in the field of mental health (e.g., the mental health worker)	8. The development of student physicians; choice of public health as a career; social factors in revising education

Source: Richard H. Williams, 'The Strategy of Sociomedical Research,' in Freeman, et al., 1972: 463.

years old. During the decade after World War II, sociologists were engaged in research roles, studying problems of health, illness, and the social relationships and institutional processes associated with those problems (Badgley and Bloom, 1973). Their participation in the education of physicians came later. However, even in the early research stage, their work involved them with medical education. Medical education itself, or 'socialization for the professional role', was one of the first research problems that was intensively studied by important teams of sociologists (Merton, 1957; Becker, 1961). Also it was in the medical schools mainly that the research was conducted, and where the first positions for sociologists were created.

Thus even though the first ten years were characteristically years of intellectual trial in which the capabilities of the discipline as a field of inquiry were being tested, medical sociology found itself at the same time within what was called the behavioral science movement, participating in several different types of educational activities. Four main types of behavioral science emerged that can be described as follows:

A. *The basic science of behavior*. An attempt to create a new natural science, synthesized from the knowledge and methods of a variety of single disciplines and focused on a group of problems explaining the behavior of the whole organism as opposed to the reductionism of the separate disciplines. The approach is that of the basic sciences of preclinical medical education. Because of the emphasis on laboratory study and the experimental method, psychology was most often chosen to integrate with the biological sciences in this effort.

B. *The clinical science of behavior*. An attempt to expand the knowledge base of clinical medicine to include psychosocial as well as biological factors which might contribute to the explanation of pathology in the human individual.

C. *Social behavioral science*. A view of behavior in the study of health and illness which selectively incorporates three of the major social sciences – sociology, anthropology, and social psychology – in the development of a preclinical basic science of human behavior.

D. *The science of community behavior.* The application of social
   science to problems of health and illness in populations, especially
   as defined by the field how known as community medicine. This
   involves the expansion of the methodologies of public health, such
   as epidemiology and biostatistics, to include modern social science.

If we dichotomize the two basic variables,[1] the orientation or approach to knowledge, and[2] the substantive content which is emphasized, the four types of behavioral science described above fit the
pattern shown in fig. 2.1.

Orientation

		Basic science	Applied science
Bio- psychological		(A) Basic science of behavior	(B) Clinical science of behavior
Socio- cultural		(C) Social behavioral science	(D) The science of com- munity behavior

Contant
emphasis

Fig 2.1. Types of behavioral science in medical education in the United States.

Each of these types of educational approach is associated with its own
type of work setting. In a sense, this may be interpreted as an
expression of the pluralism which is identified with the United States
when its institutions are functioning at their fullest freedom. Stated in
another way, this is a decentralized system, with varying types of
ownership, size, and authority structure, operating with little if any
constraint on educational ideology; and the result is a varied pattern.
   The model for Type A was the Mental Health Research Institute at
the University of Michigan. There, a collection of behavioral scientists came together as a group which originally, in 1949, had been

formed at the University of Chicago by James E. Miller (Miller, 1955). Seeking 'an empirically testable general theory of behavior', biological scientists joined with psychologists and a wide spectrum of other disciplines, adding sociologists only later in its history. The Institute was part of the department of psychiatry of the medical school, but functioned essentially as a separate research unit. Teaching was mainly at the post-doctoral level for both physicians and other scientists. Although a new journal was started, *Behavioral Science*, and other similar efforts can be traced to its influence, the Michigan Institute type of model does not appear to be a significant force at the present time in the academic life of this country.

Type B describes one of the earliest and most widespread approaches in the institutionalization of the behavioral sciences in medical education. Typically, it was represented by a small subsection of social and psychological scientists on the faculty of a department of psychiatry. The responsibility of such groups was to teach a preclinical course as a general preparation for the clinical study of medicine. As part of psychiatry, it tended to be weighted toward the problems of mental health. In 1951, Norman Cameron, as commissioned by the American Psychiatric Association, presented a curriculum plan for such teaching (Cameron, 1952). Cameron's plan was widely adopted and dominated this type of teaching for more than a decade.

The content of the type B approach was strongly influenced by developmental psychology, and, as time passed, it became more like a standard psychiatry curriculum. This was in spite of efforts by the National Institute of Mental Health (NIMH) to encourage the creative development of what Cameron began. NIMH created the Human Behavior Training Grant Program specifically to finance the salaries of new faculty members to teach behavioral science. This support was substantial, beginning in 1960-61 with five grants for a total of US$ 139,256 and grew to US$ 1,245,381 for grants to forty medical schools in 1968-69 (Webster, 1971: 306). These grants tended to be used more for psychiatrists than for adding new types of personnel. At best, only one out of four of the grantee institutions hired social scientists (Thurnblad and McCurdy, 1967).

The conclusion is inescapable (in my judgment) that psychiatry, the first and most promising host for medical sociology, changed its mind. It is not appropriate to analyze this case in greater depth here, except to summarize very briefly the facts. In effect, psychiatry never went beyond a token acceptance of social science, and sociology in particular, as a collaborating partner in medical education. Very quickly, it returned to the position that the basics of psychiatric knowledge itself, especially psycho-dynamics and psychopathology, were the best preparation for physicians in the understanding of human behavior. This was the premise used to hire psychiatrists to teach behavioral science rather than to use new programs to build strong social science divisions for research and teaching in the medical school. My own evaluation of the history of Type B is that power factors overwhelmed the original objectives. It became a means to increase the strength of psychiatry competitively in the medical school rather than a means of introducing behavioral science as a meaningful part of the knowledge basic to medicine.

Type C, 'social behavioral science', is perhaps the closest to the standard definitions of social science. Anderson and Seacat (1957), in their early review of the field, made the distinction very clear between two operating definitions of behavioral science:[1] the general comprehensive multidisciplinary approach, which I have called the 'basic science of behavior', (Type A) and (2) the social behavioral science, defined to include only sociology, anthropoly, and social psychology. The earliest significant institutionalization of this approach occurred, at Syracuse University under the direction of Robert Straus. This unit moved to the University of Kentucky Medical School when the latter was still only a conception, and it has survived and thrived as a Department of Behavioral Science ever since the medical school became operational.

In general, it is this type which, historically, appears to have the most strength as a social structure in medical education where medical sociology can be the effective partner of medical educators. This was the conclusion of the most recent study of the field (Badgley and Bloom, 1973). Kentucky is now only one of an increasing number of examples, including the University of Toronto (Badgley, 1971) and others.

Type D., 'the science of community behavior', is a combination of the oldest and the newest frames of references for social science in medicine. It was in public health, or 'social medicine', that sociology first found a home for research and teaching concerned with health and illness. In nineteenth century Germany and England, this was expressed explicitly by movements which asserted, 'medical science is intrinsically and essentially a social science' (Rosen, 1949; Badgley and Bloom, 1973:930-931). In the United States, however, there was a long period of hiatus, in which there was, at best, a casual relationship between the two. With the growth of community medicine, the situation has changed. Social scientists, now including economists and political scientists, are important participants, as members of divisions within departments of community medicine. Mount Sinai School of Medicine offers one example. Alternatively, in a school of Public Health like that of Columbia University, a similarly strong role for medical sociology has appeared.

There are other work settings which can be described for medical sociologists. For example, it is now quite standard for medical sociology to be among the courses in the undergraduate college curriculum of sociology departments. Therefore, in the colleges and universities quite separate from medical schools, medical sociology is an accepted sub-specialty and manpower needs are defined to include qualified people in this field. The same is true in graduate programs. For the latter, however, the training programs characteristically include some form of collaboration with professional schools such as medicine, nursing, dentistry, etc... Thus, on a joint appointment basis, medical sociologists work in their parent department and in one of the types of setting described in fig. 2.1.

For the purposes of this discussion, the important point is that it is in the settings of the university, particularly as they are connected to education in the health professions, that the role of sociology in medicine must be placed.

2.4. The manpower of medical sociology: sources and training

The early contributors to medical sociology included some of the most prominent academic sociologists of modern times: Parsons, Merton,

Hughes, Hollingshead, Faris. However, neither then, nor later did these scholars identify themselves as specialists in medical sociology; nor did the profession at large. Rather, each was known mainly as a theorist, and the fact that some of their major research was about medicine was regarded as incidental to the importance of their scholarly contributions to the general development of sociology as a field.

Indeed, the belief was strong among many of the early medical sociologists that the prerequisites for such work were *not* in special training, but rather in the best possible basic program of research sociology. Substantive knowledge about the world of medicine, familiarity with its institutions, and first-hand experience in its settings were thought to be part of what one acquires *after* having mastered the fundamentals of sociological knowledge and skill. Moreover, there were in the next generation of medical sociologists many whose background fit this description. Freidson (1962, 1970), Becker (1961), King (1962) and Robert Straus (1957, 1969) are but a few examples of scholars who, in their graduate training, had no special preparation for medical sociology, whose doctoral dissertations were in other fields, but who are now well known as 'medical sociologists'. The view that no specialty training is the best training is, of course, characteristic of academic sociology. It represents, no more and no less than the prevailing ideology of the university where the social controls of sociology are based. Moreover, as I will try to show this point of view was to persist, even to the point of dominating the large-scale federal support program for training medical sociologists which began formally in 1960 in the National Institute for Mental Health (NIMH).

Against this background of strong ties to the mainstream of its parent field, and the resulting conservative (speaking only in educational terms) attitude about how to train future medical sociologists, there were some different opinions which found expression very early. Several organizations, the private foundations more than the government, marked the sociology of health as a field for their special interest and exerted their influence to move sociology toward a new type of professional role. The Russell Sage Foundation was among the first. Although closely tied to the leadership of general sociology, Russell Sage was always committed to social service and the application of social sciences for community problems (Glenn, Brandt, and Andrews, 1947). They forecast accurately the needs of professions like medicine and social work for closer collaboration with sociology. In 1944, they created a Department of Studies in the Professions. Similar foresight was shown in the policies of the Common Health Fund and the Milbank Memorial Foundation.

Government support, unlike the private foundations, in the early stages was almost entirely limited to research (Williams, 1972). NIMH, as one of nine institutes comprising the National Institutes of Health, began in 1946 with the passage of the National Mental Health Act (Lutterman, 1975). Its first operating budget in 1948 was US\$ 4,000,000, growing to more than US\$ 61 million by 1967, and always included both research and training. In its first years, however, its training support was entirely for the clinical fields of psychiatry, clinical psychology, psychiatric social work, and psychiatric nursing. Not until 1957 was the training program broadened to include research training. In 1958, the first research training grants were awarded to sociology by NIMH on an experimental basis, followed in 1960 by formal activation of the Social Sciences Subcommittee of the Training Branch to administer what began as seven programs and grew to a peak of seventy-seven in 1973.

Once the federal government had committed itself to the support of science, the scale expanded rapidly. The effect was to reinforce the academic perspective because these funds went to the universities exclusively. This situation continued for two decades, described as 'the idyll... when science was generously supported and left alone' (Culliton, 1976). The search for knowledge for its own sake was dominant; the uses of knowledge, at least for the scientist, were secondary.

Although the major beneficiary of these policies was biomedical science, the sociomedical sciences, as they came to be called, were not neglected. They received about nine percent of the total research support of NIMH. More specifically, in 1948, NIMH awarded thirty-eight research grants for a total of US\$ 373,226; by 1961, there were 1,286 active grants for a total of US\$ 30,492,087 (Williams, 1972:476). In 1961, there were 113 principal investigators from the social sciences with NIMH grants, 50 in anthropology, sixty-three in sociology. In addition there were 574 principal investigators from psychology (45 percent) and Williams notes that there were a significant number of social psychologists among them (Williams, 1963:442).

This was the situation in research when the federal government began to commit support to the training of social scientists. It was clearly a growth situation. In 1957, NIMH doubled its previous year's research funding from US$ 3.8 million to US$ 7.3 million. By 1967, the amount had grown to more than US$ 18 million, and in 1970 to US$ 20 million. Here, in effect, was the main market for the training programs, a large and growing research enterprise in behavioral science of which sociology alone accounted for more than US$ 5 million in 1967, or one-fourth of behavioral science research (20 million) and six percent of the NIMH research total (62 million).

The character of the training programs directly reflected this situation. What at the start had been specifically health relevant became general and 'basic'. For example, the pilot NIMH training programs at Yale and the University of North Carolina which started in 1958 were not at all the models for those that came later. Once the NIMH social science training program was formalized, the strategy of the program broadened. The view which prevailed has been described by some of those who made policy at the time:

'...It was impossible to know what aspects of social science (sociology) would prove valuable to the general mental health effort. *Quality training* was what was needed, and the by-products of the process would feed into manpower and research of the mental health effort. Programs that looked at deviant behavior, social disorganization, the family, ageing, and so forth, were all regarded as reasonalbe content areas for support, and the scope of relevance became virutally all inclusive'. (Freeman, Borgatta, and Siegel, 1975)

This was the perspective until 1973. In the interim, the two pilot programs of 1957 grew to seventy-seven, and level of support went from 85,000 to over 5 million dollars, as shown in Table 2.2. Only six programs were specifically in the field of medical sociology, and the range of subfields and interdisciplinary types of programs was very wide (See Table 2.3..).

Table 2.2. NIMH Social sciences research training program*

Fiscal year	No. of grants	No. of stipends	Total funds available*
1957	2	14	$ 84,916
1958	2	14	84,941
1959	3	27	146,865
1960	7	35	314,128
1961	13	70	420,665
1962	22	130	801,448
1963	39	226	1,332,704
1964	54	333	2,084,763
1965	62	403	2,796,515
1966	67	488	3,329,412
1967	72	575	3,891,063
1968	69	605	4,048,071
1969	77	626	4,818,518
1970	76	595	4,664,400
1971	79	586	4,892,941
1972	77	570	5,211,684
1973	77	567	5,129,208

* includes unexpended balances from prior budget periods.
Source: Kenneth. G. Lutterman, 'Research Training from the Perspective of Government Funding,' in N.J. Demerath, et al., 1975, p. 310.

Table 2.3. Problem of disciplinary area of social sciences research training in 1972-1973.

		Number of grants
Economics of Human Resources		2
Anthropology of Cultural Change		12
Political Science -		
Alienation, Urban Conflict		3
Sociology		43
(Subfields)		
Socialization	2	
Ethnic and Minority Problems	2	

	Number of grants	
Urban Problems	1	
Family Problems	4	
Complex Organization	4	
Social Change	4	
Education Problems	1	
Comparative Social Change	4	
Deviant Behavior	5	
Methods of Research	4	
Evaluation Research	2	
Demographic Research	2	
Demographic Research	2	
Medical Sociology	6	
Social Psychology	2	
Interdisciplinary		17
Evaluation and Policy Research	2	
Economics - Political Science - Psychology		
Public Affairs - Sociology - Political Science -		
Economics - Psychology - Public Health		
Organizational Behavior	1	
Sociology - Education - Business Administration -		
Psychology		
Urban Problems	3	
Sociology - Political Science - Economics		
Political Science - Urban and Regional Planning		
Psychology - Sociology - Economics		
Social Psychology	4	
Psychology - Sociology		
Anthropology - Psychology - Sociology		
Ethnology - Sociology - Psychology - Anthropology		
Sociology - Psychology - Political Science		
Law and Social Science	2	
Sociology - Law		
Anthropology - Sociology - Political Science -		
Criminology - Law		
Social Psychiatry	3	
Psychiatry - Sociology ʼ		
Psychology and Political Science	1	
History and Social Science	1	

Source: Kenneth G. Lutterman, 'Research Training from the Perspective of Government Funding,' in N.J. Demerath, III, Otto Larsen, and Karl. F. Schuessler, editors, *Social Policy and Sociology,* New York, Academic Press, Inc. 1975, p. 311.

Eventually, in 1973, the policies of the United States Government were to change sharply toward both training and research. In that year, the Nixon administration ordered all training support to be phased-out, scheduling zero support for 1977. Challenged by Congress, this order was stopped short of its final goal, but not until research training was severaly reduced. Not only were the size and amount of funding drastically curtailed, but also the former open academic perspective was replaced by objectives of manpower training specific to the applied needs of the health field.

What caused the change in government policy is a question that is not easily answered. There were indicators of a changing manpower demand as early as the mid-1960s. At that time, coincident with and quite probably related to the passage of medicare and medicaid in July 1965, health services delivery emerged as a central theme for support by the federal bureaucracy. A new agency was created, the National Center for Health Services Research and Development (in 1968) and, for a short time, it appeared that support for social science would only multiply, as the Center (NCHSRD) built a parallel program to that of NIMH. Within a few years, NCHSRD built a research training program of more than US$ 5 million. Abruptly, in 1973, this development aborted. Research training at NCHSRD was wiped out entirely by the Nixon administration's 1973 directive.

It is all too tempting to see the current negative climate toward biomedical and sociomedical training as the result of political ideological change. In the United States, the Republican Party is, after all, the conservative party, in favour of economies of government activities and, in its attitude toward the university, more suspicious and anti-intellectual than the Democrats. The facts are, however, that there are similarities between the parties as well as differences. In their attitudes toward research, some important conclusions are shared. For example, a recent issue of *Science* reported:

'Senator Edward M. Kennedy (Democrat, Massachusetts), as Chairman of the Senate Health Subcommittee, has just begun what he describes as a yearlong process of review and examination of public policy in the areas of biomedical and behavioral research. Out of this may come legislation that substantially reshapes the National Institutes of Health (NIH), by mandating a new emphasis on clinical research and the assessment of new biomedical technology.

'...Our committee does not come to these hearings with any deep distrust or disillusionment with biomedical and behavioral research'. Kennedy declared at the outset of the first day's session. But as the morning wore on, it became apparent that though 'disillusionment' may be too strong a term to express his feelings, 'dissatisfaction' certainly is not. For more than a year now, Kennedy has been challenging the research community to throw itself into activities that would show it is responsive to its social obligations *Science*, 20 June 1975) and he leaned on that theme as heavily as ever. His subcommittee collleague Richard S. Schweiker (R-Pa). was even more persistent, indeed, strident, in asking scientists to tell him why they have not done more for him (the public) lately. *It is going to be a rough, and extremely important, year* (my italics)' (Culliton, 1976).

My own interpretation is that it will be rough for the biomedical and behavioral sciences for more than just one year.

Medical sociology should be studied as a case example of the effects of the increased fiscal control by the federal government of the professions. In this case, we see a discipline, small but increasingly visible, among the university-based professions: these are most essentially *scholarly* professions, oriented toward the increased understanding of human behavior, and engaged mainly in roles of study and teaching. Because its subject and methods are defined as relevant to problems of health and illness, medical sociology found itself increasingly drawn into new roles first as research collaborator, then as educator, in medical education. In the process, it has been caught in the tides of medical manpower development, sharing the experience of institutional changes which were occuring in medicine. Only part of the path traversed by the biomedical sciences has been trodden by, medical sociology. It followed the same path to full-time teaching in medical schools, and to virtually total dependence upon federal subsidy. Unlike the other preclinical sciences, it has stopped short of a separate identity from its patent discipline; on the contrary, the university department of sociology has been retained as the main source of manpower training. The latter provides a strong structural resistance to the medicalization of sociology within the training programs for medical sociologists. Counter-efforts, such as the training program. of NCHSRD, have failed as part of the current funding crisis.

The question remains: what have these historical patterns signified in the actual character of training for medical sociologists and what do their trends portend for the future of such training?

2.5. The substance of medical sociology training: its relevance to outcome

What, precisely, do medical sociologists do? This is the question that must be asked when we assess how medical sociologists are trained. Is the educational preparation effectively related to the outcome? Are medical sociologists prepared for the role demands which they encounter in their work roles?

Those work roles, we said earlier, are diverse. So is the training. There is no necessary compatibility, however, in shared diversity.

Reviewing the work roles, in those situations where the basic science of behavior is emphasized, (fig. 2.1., type A) sociologists are required to collaborate in interdisciplinary teams and to be skilled in designing quantitative approaches to the study of complex problems of behavior. Where the cinical science of behavior is the focus, (Type B) the role demands emphasize social psychological skills: e.g., knowledge of human growth and development, research on small group relationships, and interviewing skills and concepts. Where sociologists work with a high degree of autonomy in a separate department of behavioral science, the roles are very varied and the full play of sociological knowledge and skill is called upon (Type C). In departments of community medicine, sociologists are expected to study large population groups and communities; the skills of survey analysis, community study, and organizational analysis are utilized in a quest to understand the provision of health service.

Perhaps the best preparation for such varied roles can be found in the most basic knowledge and skills of the field. Security in one's basic professional identity, it may be argued, is the necessary foundation for informed and effective versatility in the challenge to adapt to specific work tasks. In fact, this was the dominant pattern chosen by training programs. But here again, it is necessary to specify. What is the pattern of training for research sociology, at its most basic general level?

There appear to be two main points of agreement on how to teach research sociology. It is agreed that one cannot learn to do research only in formal abstract terms. 'One learns to do research – any kind of research – by doing it' (Hill, 1975:290). Thus, curriculum is less important than the availability of active research programs in which students can participate.

There is also agreement that some form of apprenticeship model is best for research training. Although this model transcends specific methodological and theoretical differences, it tends to favor the large department. Only with a socalled 'critical mass' of faculty is it likely that sufficient research will be on going to provide the necessities of effective apprenticeship. The exceptions are smaller departments which deliberately concentrate their resources in the study of particular research problems.

As the NIMH Social Science Training Program grew into the major source of research sociologists in the United States, the criteria by which it was evaluated rested upon these types of criteria. *Health relevance was secondary* to the general up-grading of social science training. The rational was that '...manpower for the health-related sciences could become available only when the existing general manpower shortage was relieved' (Freeman, Borgatta, Siegel, 1975:299). What were the results? When the program was just twelve years old, the following appraisal appeared:

'When a survey was conducted several years ago, one in three graduate students in full-time study was NIMH trained; a large number of recent Ph. D.'s either were supported directly by the program or had key professors and resources that came from it; medical sociology is a major specialty for sociologists now, and their research results are read by health professionals and published to a considerable extent in professional journals in the mental health field. Furthermore, social scientists hold not only research positions in state and federal health agencies but administrative and policy-making ones as well. It appears that something was purchased with the NIMH training grants.' (Freeman, Borgatta, Siegel, 1975:301).

Let us, for the moment, accept the judgment that the training programs of the past two decades have accomplished their major purposes, both for the general up-grading of social science training, and in relieving the basic manpower shortage of research social scientists. *What can we say about the future?*

Firstly, it is clear that the federal sources of support for social science training are changing their policies. The amount of such support is being drastically reduced. Also, qualification for those moneys that are still available is increasingly specialized.

Secondly as a result of the specialization of government support policies, major structural changes are likely to occur in the research training of sociology. The objective of specialized training support is to produce sociologists who can fill new types of work roles, especially in occupational settings other than traditional academic settings. The means of accomplishing this goal, as encouraged by present government policy, includes postdoctoral training, and interdisciplinary collaboration between sociology and the other social sciences. It can be expected, therefore, that sociology departments and also behavioral science groups in medical schools, will turn their attention to the task of post-doctoral training. For medical sociology, this represents a return to the pattern first developed by the Russel Sage Foundation post-doctoral fellowships. For general sociology, it means that pre-doctoral support will be reduced and that various collaborating relationships must be formed in order to achieve effective post-doctoral training.

For medical sociology, there may be a hidden benefit. The post-doctoral fellowship could satisfy the need for junior faculty teaching roles and could stimulate new research. At the same time, in the settings oriented toward social behavioral science and the science of community behavior, the situation is favorable for the specialized requirements of the new federal policies.

On the surface, the shift in government policy toward research training appears to be caused by disappointing results. This is definitely the tone of the citation above from the Kennedy subcommittee. However, not all portents for the future are discouraging.

2.6. Summary and conclusions

Medical education has always been central to the work roles of medical sociologists:

- First, in research, medical schools were the main settings in which sociologists were employed.
- Medical education itself was a focal subject of sociological research.
- Once the teaching of behavioral science was institutionalized, medical sociologists became part of the teaching team.
- As contributing collaborators with medical fields such as psychiatry, public health, and community medicine, sociologists were employed in academic positions, whether in graduate schools of public health or in undergraduate medical schools.

Because medical education in the United States is institutionally a part of graduate university education, there is a close continuity between the traditional and still most common occupational role of the sociologist and the position of its sub-specialist, the medical sociologist. This has been reinforced by the increasing acceptance of medical sociology as a legitimate part of basic sociology, with the result that undergraduate college training now includes medical sociology. As part of the same legitimization of medical sociology in its parent discipline, joint appointments between the medical school and departments of sociology are increasing.

In other words, the institutional controls for general sociology have been extended to include medical sociology, thereby strengthening the ties between the two. The influence upon training has been very strong: the medical sociologist is trained mainly as a basic research sociologist.

The dominant theme of such training has been, 'a good medical sociologist must be, first and foremost, a well-trained research sociologist'. The special aspects of work *as* a medical sociologist have been assumed to be part of a professional superstructure to be built upon the scholarly substructure of general sociology.

There are signs, however, that this pattern is being broken. Large-scale government support at first accepted the view of academic sociology. It no longer does. In the meantime, graduate training of sociology as a whole has become dependent upon federal support. The threat to withdraw such support, therefore, is profoundly disturbing not only to medical sociology. The government agencies which continue to offer such support are now adding the condition that a more direct effort should be made to prepare future sociologists for the specific applications of sociological knowledge. In health matters, this refers to health service roles.

Several effects of historical trends may be stated as forecasts of the future:

1. The training of medical sociology is being extended to include post-doctoral training.
2. The knowledge and skills required for effective work in health service roles by sociology is being reviewed with a new sense of urgency. The curriculum of graduate training will be changed to include more experience in the actual working environment and more systematic teaching of applied and policy making skills.
3. How to teach medical sociology as well as what to teach is also being investigated.
4. The role of the medical sociologist as a product of graduate education, is a required subject for intensive study if the total training process is to be effective. In other words, socialization of the professional role, a field of research that sociologists have developed with reference to the education of physicians, dentists, and nurses, should now be applied to medical sociology itself. The knowledge to be gained from such study has immediate policy relevance.
5. High priority has been assigned by policy makers in the government training programs to interdisciplinary research and training that brings together sociologists, economists, and political scientists. Future training programs can be expected to respond by joining these approaches into common effort in graduate research training.

References

Anderson, Odin W. and Milvoy Seacat, 1957, *The Behavioral Scientist and Research in the Health Field,* New York: Health Information Foundation.

Badgley, Robin (editor), 1971, Social Science and Health in Canada, Milbank Memorial Fund Quarterly, XLIX, Part 2.

Badgley, Robin F. and Samuel W. Bloom, 1973, 'Behavioral Sciences and Medical Education', Social Science and Medicine, 7:927-941.

Becker, Howard S., Blanche Geer, Everett C. Hughes, and Anselm L. Straus, 1961, *Boys in White: Student Culture in Medical School,* Chicago: University of Chicago Press.

Bloom Samuel W., 1965, 'The Sociology of Medical Education: some comments on the state of a field', The Milbank Memorial Fund Quarterly, 43 (April): 143-84.

Bloom, Samuel W., 1973, 'From Learned Profession to Policy Science: a Trend Analysis of Sociology in Medical Education', Presented at the Conference on Medical Sociology, The Polish Academy of Sciences and the International Sociological Association, Warsaw.

Cameron Norman, 1952, 'Human Ecology and Personality in the Training of Physicians', in American Psychiatric Association, Psychiatry and Medical Education, (Report of the 1951 Conference on Psychiatric Education), Washington, D.C.: American Psychiatric Association.

Caudill, William, 1953, 'Applied Anthropology in Medicine', in Kroeber, A.L., editor, *Anthropology Today.* Chicago: U. of Chicago Press.

Clausen, John A., 1956, *Sociology and the Field of Mental Health,* New York: Russell Sage Foundation.

Coombs, Robert H., and Clark E. Vincent, editors, 1971, *Psychosocial Aspects of Medical Training,* Springfield, Ill.: Charles C. Thomas, Publisher.

Culliton, Barbara J., 1976, 'Kennedy Hearings: Year-long Probe of Biomedical Research Begins', *Science,* 193:32-35 (2 July, 1976).

Demerath, N.J. III, Otto Larson, Karl F. Schuessler, editors, 1975, *Social Policy and Sociology,* New York: Academic Press; Inc.

Foote, Nelson N., 1975, 'Putting Sociologists to work', in Demerath, et at., 1975: 321-338.

Freeman, Howard E., E., Edgar F. Borgatta, and Nathaniel H. Siegel, 1975, 'Remarks on the Changing Relationship between Government Support and Graduate Training', in Demerath, et al., 1975: 297-306.

Freeman, Howard E., Sol Levine, and Leo G. Reeder, editors, 1963, *Handbook of Medical Sociology,* (First Edition) Englewood Cliffs, N.J.: Prentice-Hall, Inc.

Freeman, Howard E., Sol Levine, and Leo G. Reeder, editors, 1972, *Handbook of Medical Sociology,* (Second Edition) Englewood Cliffs, N.J.: Prentice-Hall, Inc.

Freidson, Eliot, 1961, *Patients Views of Medical Practice,* New York: Russel Sage Foundation.

Freidson, Eliot, 1970, *Profession of Medicine,* New York: Dodd, Mead.

Glenn, John M., Lilian Brandt, and F. Emerson Andrews, 1947, *Russell Sage Foundation, 1907-1946,* 2 volumes. New York: Russel Sage Foundation.

Graham Saxon, 1964, 'Sociological Aspects of Health and Illness', in Robert Faris, editor, *Handbook of Modern Sociology,* Chicago: Rand McNally.

Hyman, Martin D., 1967, 'Medicine', in Paul Lazarsfeld, et al., *The Uses of Sociology,* New York: Basic Books.

Kendall, Patricia L., and George G. Reader, 1972, 'Contributors of Sociology to Medicine', in Freeman, et al.,

King, Stanley, 1962, *Perceptions of Illness and Medical Practice,* New York: Russell Sage Foundation.

Lutterman, Kenneth G., 1975, 'Research Training from the Perspective of Government Funding', in Demerath, et al., 1975:307-320.

McKinlay, John E., 1972, 'Some Approaches and Problems in the Study of the Use of Services', *Journal of Health and Social Behavior,* 13:115-152.

Merton, Robert K., George G. Reader, and Patricia L. Kendall, editors, 1957, *The Student Physician,* Cambridge: Harvard U. Press.

Miller, James, 1955, 'Toward a General Theory for the Behavioral Sciences', *American Psychologist,* 10:513.

Reader, George G., 1963, 'Contributions of Sociology to Medicine', in Freeman, et al., (First edition) 1963:1-18.

Reader, George G. and Mary E.W. Goss, 1959, 'The Sociology of Medicine', in R.K. Merton, et al., *Sociology Today.* New York: Basic Books, Inc.

Rosen, George, 1949, 'Approaches to a Concept of Social Medicine, a historical survey', in *Background of Social Medicine.* New York: Milbank Memorial Fund.

Straus Robert, 1957, 'The Nature and Status of Medical Sociology', *American Sociological Review,* 22:200.

Straus Robert, 1969, 'A Department of Behavioral Science', *Journal of Medical Education, 34:662.*

Suchman, Edward A., 1963, Sociology and the Field of Public Health, New York: Russell Sage Foundation.

Thurnblad, R. and R.L. McCurdy, 1967, 'Human Behavior for the Student Physician', *Journal of Medical Education,* 42:158-162.

Vincent, Clark E., 1965, 'Support for Research Training in Anthropology under the National Institute of Mental Health Training Programs'. *American Anthropologist,* 67:754-761.

Webster, Thomas G., 1971, 'The Behavioral Sciences in Medical Education and Practice', in Coombs and Vincent, 1971:285-348.

Williams, Richard H., 1972, 'The Strategy of Sociomedical Research', in Freeman, et al., 1972: 459-482. 1963, 'The Strategy of Sociomedical Research', in Freeman, et al., (First edition) 1963:423-440.

3. The medical profession in the future: implications for training programs

P.J. Thung

To the main title of this presentation, 'the medical Profession in the Future', I have added a sub-title of my own which requires some clarification. In my opinion, the medical profession of the future is a subject of little interest since I do not expect there to be much future for the medical profession in its present form. In this talk I will first of all maintain that this profession originated in a not very distant past to serve purposes which were typical of that past. In the second place, I will argue that the realities of today's health care have outgrown the original scope of this same medical profession and that, having served its nineteenth century purposes, it now shows signs of becoming a thing of the past. In the third place, I will discuss the relations between these views and present developments in medical education, the main conclusion being that it is no longer possible to educate for one medical profession and that our programs should be differentiated to prepare for the variety of qualifications demanded by modern health care.

3.1. The 19th century origin of the medical profession

In most western countries, today's medical profession was established or consolidated during the mid-nineteenth century in close relation with administrative and legislative processes aimed at straightening out the chaotic conditions prevailing in the field of health and healing. Today, it is often forgotten that the legislation on which medical licensing and the medical profession were founded, had one clear purpose, viz. to eliminate confusion as to what was safe and accepta-ble medical practice and who were to be its accredited practitioners. The medical profession was thus institutionalized with the express purpose of being what is often cited today as its main shortcoming, viz., a closed group of initiates into a natural science-based craft of medicine, guarding a somatic definition of health and disease.

It should be remembered that at the time there were many approaches to health and disease, though often interrelated and not clearly defined. These ranged from traditional household remedies, pharmacists' prescriptions and barbers' procedures to more or less philosophical systems of explanation and advice. The emerging supremacy of the natural science-oriented brand of medicine had not yet been justified by superior successes in prevention or cure, but derived from its cultural position. It was affiliated with the two most prestigious movements of the day: natural science and technology. Although itself not yet demonstrably effective, academic medicine spoke the same language and tried to apply the same concepts and mechanisms as were so clearly successful in science and technology. Its main merit lay in the systematic description and analysis of symptoms and syndromes and in its efforts to relate these to causal mechanisms of disease.

Only rarely, before the twentieth century, did these efforts lead to unambiguously demonstrable explanations. And even more rarely were such explanations backed by effective means of prevention or cure. But the prevailing culturel atmosphere was sufficient backing for academic medicine, notwithstanding its practical ineffectiveness. Moreover, this very ineffectiveness helped to maintain the prevailing somatic and mechanistic definition of disease: it was the culturally acceptable description that mattered, not the effcicacy of the concomitant prescriptions.

And so, throughout the Western world, legislation and university education succeeded in establishing natural science-based medicine as *the* dominant and official approach to health care, while its initiates consolidated their social position as *the* medical profession. Next to the relative ineffectiveness of medicine, I draw attention to the limited range of action of this profession, which was rarely confronted with the vast reservoir of disease and malnutrition in the lower strata of society. This too was related to the prevailing cultural atmosphere: medicine was individually applied as part of the way of life of the upper social classes. Its unavailability to the majority of the population was usually accepted as were so many of the inequalities of the day.

3.2. The medical profession as a thing of the past

3.2.1. Contemporary demands

My thesis in this section is that the requirements of today's medical practice have outgrown the scope of the medical profession in two ways. In the first place because the concept of disease has broken through the nineteenth century's somatic definition, and in the seond place because equal availability of medical services is now claimed for all people. Both these developments are now overtaxing the medical profession, and require adaptations which are of a qualitative rather than an quantitative nature.

The more extended definition of disease arose through a number of factors. Medicine itself was one of these factors since during the last half century it grew increasingly effective in its analysis and treatment of somatic disease. Medicine became successful in identifying and manipulating causal mechanisms; it passed from the descriptive into the effective phase. But this also led to the recognition that a number of diseases resisted this type of analysis. It was then postulated that for the so-called functional disorders, and for the new category of psychomastic disease, other approaches were indicated. Also, success in fighting acute mortal conditions increased the frequency as well as the duration of chronic disease. And here, in the ups and downs of the chronic patient, the influence of other than somatic and mechanistic factors becomes unmistakable.

In other words, the generalized somatic definition of disease was no longer appropriate because of the very successes in dealing with specific somatic diseases and the lack of such success in other cases. But the recognition of psychosomatic and psychosocial mechanisms behind various disorders started a new trend. Soon, an increasing range of social and psychological determinants were discerned relating many aspects of our cultural surroundings to health and disease. The medical profession was obviously unprepared for these new developments.

The second aspect is the demand for health care to be made available to the entire population. This is also related to the success of contemporary medicine, although of course social and political factors were also important. General availability and accessibility is of course much more of an ethical imperative in the case of today's effective medicine than it was for its nineteenth century precursor. Again, however, new approaches become necessary since it soon becomes clear that the diffusion of upper class commodities into the entire population is not just a matter of increasing the supply. I am referring to the discrepancies between availability on the one hand and accessibility and acceptability on the other. These discrepancies are found at the national level, but even more markedly when we look at the international inequalities of health care effectiveness. And so it happens that new claims are put upon the medical profession. Preventive medicine, community health, rural health are among the new demands made upon this profession whose nineteenth century tradition has not prepared it for these new areas.

3.2.2. Indications that the profession is dissolving

This profession, in its traditional form, will not be able to survive the stresses described in the previous section. Of course the signs of erosion may differ from country to country, and in some places there may be considerable resistance, but the situation in the Netherlands does not differ in principle from that in other parts of the world. In the first place, there is a loss of coherence within the profession due to the diverging specializations and professional interests. Clinical specialists, general practitioners and physicians in administrative positions speak and think in different languages, move in different circles and are members of different professional organizations. We no longer believe in the fundamental interchangeability of all doctors, or in their basic comprehensive competence as members of one and the same guild. We also no longer allow them to register with more than one specialism, and find them gradually dropping such professional courtesies as not billing each other.

Other infringements on the position of the medical profession come from without. Non-medical appointments in administrative positions charged with matters of health policy have long been accepted.

However, the appointment of hospital directors who are not necessarily physicians is a more recent development in our country. And in university teaching, we have definitely been slower to supplement M.D.'s by Ph.D.'s than elsewhere.

More important of course, are the changing functions and relations in practical medicine. In some areas, changes have been slow and formal rather than effective. In Holland, as in other countries, nursing is now being recognized as a specific discipline which is supplementary rather than subservient to the physician. This recognition is reflected in the composition of boards, committees and other representative bodies. But at the same time, in many hospitals it has so far failed to influence effectively the intra-staff work relations. This is, however, definitely a matter of time, since in new hospitals, with young medical and non-medical staff, coöperation on an equal footing is increasingly usual.

The changes described so far may of course not affect the position of physicians as the only profession licensed to practice medicine. This position is, however, slowly being eroded in other ways. The so-called paramedical professions, such as physiotherapy and dietetics, though in many situations still formally subordinate to medical supervision, are in practice increasingly independent in their diagnostic as well as therapeutic activities. And finally, nonmedical psychotherapists are by now so strongly established that their legal recognition as independent agents of health care has recently been announced.

In the Netherlands, where all health care expenditure is subject to governmental regulations, the legal monopoly of the medical profession has always been and still is very strong. Officially, this monopoly shows minor cracks only, but these are indicative of pronounced changes in the cultural atmosphere and of longstanding movements towards more radical change. The joint medical faculties have advocated since 1967 the abolition of the present licensing system and the introduction of a variety of differentiated qualifications. A revision of our 1865 law on medical practice is now being prepared. The first draft of this revision is a typical compromise after several years of discussions and has already attracted criticism for not being a radical breakthrough. Finally, and perhaps most important, it is becoming increasingly clear that the comprehensive medical licence impedes adaptation of educational programs to the demands of modern medical science and practice. As a consequence it now becomes likely that university education, in which the medical profession had its historical roots, will also be instrumental in its future dissolution. This is elaborated in the next section.

3.3. Relevant developments in medical education

3.3.1. Comprehensive versus elective curricula

Up to the 1940's or 1950's, the primary product of medical education in most parts of the world was intended to be a general physician with a comprehensive orientation in the medical sciences and with an at least basic competence in the various fields of medical practice. It has long been recognized that this objective is incompatible with the rapid growth and diversification for several decades, of both science and practice. Pressure for the inclusion of new developments and specialties led to increasing congestion of the curriculum. This is not only a quantitative problem concerning the amount of material to be covered, but it also qualitatively impairs the educational process. Inevitably, more and more material is presented and absorbed in an encyclopaedic and superficial manner and this negatively conditions the students to independent thinking and the personal pursuit of knowledge. Leaving no time or energy and certainly giving no incentives for developing personal interests and abilities, the comprehensive general medical curriculum induces shallow and even prejudiced ways of thinking.

This problem has long been recognized and medical faculties have tried to remedy these deficiences in many ways. Integrated courses and problem oriented teaching are among the teaching methodologies which may be successful. One approach, however, is more radical and therefore has met more resistance than others, viz., doing away with the uniform one-stream curriculum. Elective courses are very exceptional in medical education on the continent and at most occupy a small fraction of the curriculum. In my own faculty at Leiden at present 5 percent of total curriculum time is used for electives and the national average is of the same magnitude. However, in other countries, especially in the U.S.A. and Canada, the principle of differentiated programs is firmly established. Of course there are many ways to effectuate this differentiation. There may be a limited number of alternative programs or there may be one general program with time allotted for free electives, or again programs may be extremely flexible with opportunity for adaptation to individual taste and abilities. However, the main thing about electives is that they offer opportunities for trading in quantity for quality. In well-designed elective programs, the choice of area or subject is subordinate to the process of independent study or problem solving. Elective programs should not primarily be a way of early specialization in specific branches of medicine. They should provide the student not with specific knowledge but rather with experiences and skills which are applicable in many fields. They should also enable him to choose his future speciality realistically by testing his own talents and inclinations.

3.3.2. Curriculum structure and the profession

It is of interest that resistance to the idea of elective curricula is based on the educational fallacy of a direct relationship between teaching and learning. The comprehensive medical curriculum is patronized by the defenders of the traditional comprehensive licence for the practice of medicine, because it supposedly guarantees the overall basic competence of the physician. It was actually once designed and maybe even functioned as such in the nineteenth century. Today, however, this argument is just as fictitious as is the nineteenth century medical licence itself.

The situation on most of the West-European continent, and also in those third world countries with which I am familiar, is that medical faculties today are required or feel obliged to have one *uniform* general medical curriculum as *a basic preparation* for all medical specialisms. This general medical curriculum culminates in a uniform basic medical licence, to which all specializations are additional extras. The uniform medical licence, in turn, guarantees the continued existence and socially favoured position of a unified medical profession.

3.3.3. Medical sociology and the future of medical education

The previous section leads to the conclusion that many medical faculties are providing an outdated type of program, which is educationally detrimental, for the sake of an antiquated professional identity which is medically nonfunctional. All this, however, is an inheritance from the past and bound to wear away. But when we look towards the future what trends and promises do we find?

As indicated above, one of the most promising innovations in my opinion is the elective element in the medical curriculum. Together with problem-oriented teaching, it opens the way to continued educational growth and is truly future-directed. This view has specific implications for our educational strategy and also for sociology.

I expect that medical personnel in the future, even within the lifetime of today's students, will be spread over a wide spectrum of qualifications and competences. These will range from engineers, medical sociologists and bacteriologists working at macro-level as for instance in preventive medicine and hygiëne, to clinical technologists working with and for individual patients perhaps without ever seeing one face to face. It will also include clinical specialists and family physicians in the present sense, to psychotherapists, social case workers, physiotherapists and many others. In this range, the professional identity of the medical doctor will dissolve, and the new categories will outgrow the boundaries of what today is called medical and non-medical. At the same time, the university will have to expand and differentiate its teaching programs which will similarly outgrow today's faculty boundaries. This differentiation may then build on today's elective programs and it is at this area that medical sociology, like other future-directed disciplines, should concentrate its efforts.

It is evident in the past decades, the scientific and clinical biases of academic medicine have not been helpful in developing such areas as community medicine, medical sociology and medical psychology. On the other hand, the cultural climate in many countries is now becoming increasingly favourable for these disciplines and students are generally very much aware of the shortcomings of the classical program. In this situation, however, I want to warn against a tendecy to swing the balance the other way. In view of the future differentiation of health workers, I expect that while many of them will require a lot of sociological insight, many others will not. More important, however, is that it would be wrong for medical sociology to join the battle for teaching time in the archaic comprehensive medical curriculum. This is exactly what a dozen other new specialities have recently done. In our country, during the last ten years, I have seen gerontology and sexuology, industrial medicine and radiation hygiëne, medical psychology and dietetics all put in similar and well documented claims for hours in the general medical curriculum. They have all thus wasted the opportunity for being truly innovative forces. What they should have done and what I hope that medical sociology will do, is join forces with those who are trying to break up the antiquated comprehensive curriculum. The reasons for this will be repeated by way of conclusion.

3.4. Conclusion

Medical sociology is warned against investing too heavily in today's comprehensive basic medical curricula. The only argument invoked in favor of this type of curriculum is that it supposedly guarantees the basic general competence of all physicians as members of the licence-holding medical profession. This general medical licence, however, is a thing of the past and the general medical curriculum leads at most to a shallow encyclopaedic amateurishness. Today's physicians function professionally on the strength not of their university education but of their post-doctoral training. Moreover, they are ill-prepared to follow the rapid growth and diversification of medical science and practice.

In the future, health care personnel will be variegated not only in their fields of interest and experience, but also in their task descriptions and eventual licences. Medical professionalism, in the sense of job-competence, will then be pluriform by right as well as in fact. To prepare for this future pluriform professional competence, medical faculties should do away with the fiction of preparing for one unified medical profession. The first breakthrough will be the establishment of elective programs as a major component of the curriculum. At this breakthrough and at these programs, medical sociology should direct its efforts, in order to make a real investment in the future.

PART THREE

THE CURRENT STATUS OF MEDICAL SOCIOLOGY TRAINING

Training programs in medical sociology, both for sociologists and for physicians, can rely somewhat on experience and tradition, however limited these may be. This enables a preliminary evaluation to be made in which the main lines of development are indicated and tested for the changed role expectations and task performances. Such an evaluation may furthermore provide insights and orientations for the optimizing of future training programs developed from the evolutions described in the preceding section. The highly situational and culture-bound nature of these training programs, however, risks their being ignored in the analysis of such overall trends. The concrete elaboration and testing of such rather general and abstract evaluations by means of a few national case studies may reduce this risk.

In his lecture for the seminar, R. Day discussed the major trends and perspectives for medical sociology training in sociology departments. Medical sociology is presently imprisoned in the confines of symbolic interactionism and structural functionalism. Developments within general sociology like meta-theory, phenomenology, ehtnomethodology, critical sociology and neo-marxism have not found much of a home in the medical sociological sphere. This explains why medical sociology in its present situation is not equipped to deal with today's health care problems. The paper that is included in this volume, co-authored with H. Mauksch, deals mainly with the morphology and development of the American training situation raising questions concerning theory versus application on the one hand and disciplinary integrity versus interdisciplinary development on the other.

M. Sokolowska, in her paper, discusses the characteristics of the training program in medical sociology for undergraduate students of sociology at Warsaw University. Although the general knowledge of sociology remains prerequisite, specific knowledge relevant to the health field has to be developed. Sociology of medicine, elements of clinical and epidemiological knowledge and biology may be the bases for such a program. Training programs should structure medical sociologists, not only for the important role of teaching in medical schools, but also for such tasks as planning and administration in the health care system.

Prof. G. Pattishall reflects on the function of medical sociology in the training of futur physicians. From his evaluation of the experiences of medical schools in the U.S.A. in incorporating behavioral sciences, he infers some guidelines for promoting the role of medical sociology in medical training. These guidelines can be summed up by stating that the success of medical sociology will depend on how well it can succeed in performing a bridge function for all clinical disciplines.

The present state of institutionalization of medical sociology in German medical schools is examined by Prof. J. Siegrist and Prof. M. Pflanz. The main problems in Germany arise from the way medical sociology is organizationally and hierarchically dependent on the medical institutions. This explains why medical sociology in the country came under the umbrella of the 'medical model' which exerts increasing pressure for practical problem-solving attitudes. Ways of coping with this strain may be found in a stronger alliance with psychology and psychosomatic medicine on the one hand, and with social medicine, public health and preventive medicine on the other.

4. The current status of medical sociology training in the U.S.A.

Hans O. Mauksch and Robert A. Day

4.1. Introduction

One of the indices of the status of an area of specialization in a discipline can be gleaned from the characteristics of the educational preparation for this special field. Within sociology, medical sociology offers a significant object lesson for the sociology of sociology (Day, in preparation) if one observes how the mode of training in this field has developed and what its current outlook is.

This paper will combine a brief report on a survey of medical sociology training in sociology departments in the United States with some consideration of the antecedents of the current status of education and medical sociology and its outlook. The fact that the area of medical sociology has taken the shape of formalized training programs in universities in the United States has to be viewed not only from the point of view of academic development but has to be appreciated within a broader social, political, and economic context.

What follows here, then, is a very brief attempt to pinpoint different stages and/or emphases in the emergence of medical sociology training programs in the United States and to show a few of their more prominent relationships to the broader social contexts and settings in which they have evolved. Four such stages in the development of medical sociology can be suggested: 1) health studies as incidental studies; 2) the role of key individuals, departments, schools and foundations; 3) the organization of medical sociology as a special field; 4) the emergence of specific training programs.

4.2. Health studies as incidental studies

Here we are referring to those sociologists and other social scientists who have had an individual scholarly interest in health, sickness, and health services and also to the more reform-oriented people in the fields of public health and medical social work and welfare. This would include a vast array of studies that go back at least as far as Elizabeth Blackwell's *Essays in Medical Sociology* (1902). McCartney's research also provides evidence of a small, but fairly steady stream of medical sociology articles in the major sociology journals during the period of 1895-1954 (McCartney, 1965). The major portion of studies of this type occured between 1920 and 1950. As mentioned above, they usually represented the work of one or two scholars who were either interested in knowledge for knowledge's sake or in arousing public sentiment for health reforms. According to Straus' distinction between the 'sociology *of* medicine' and 'sociology *in* medicine,' (Straus, 1957) they tended to be sociologists of medicine for the most part. It is interesting that these early studies rarely involved research support either from governmental funding agencies or from private foundations which subsequently were to have such an extremely important impact on the course of research and training within medical sociology and the health fields generally.

The notion of specialized training was practically absent during this period and the development of a coterie of followers of the authors and their products is not very noticeable in this period. The studies identified with this area were either within the framework of existing areas of sociological inquiry or were directly applied to the health field. Just to cite two examples of the former one can fit the work of Oswald Hall (1948) into the field occupations and the study by Faris and Dunham (1939) into the array of ecological studies of the urban scene. Sigerist (1943) and Davis (1938) are just two of the many examples of the latter type of literature.

4.3. The role of key individuals, departments, schools and foundations

Following the end of the Depression and World War II, medical sociology began to emerge as an identifiable field. One of the most important factors was the interest and research efforts put forth by key individuals in prestigious sociology departments. Many well-established sociologists began to do research on various topics in health, thus bringing this kind of research to the attention of most sociologists. Parsons devoted a section of his classic work, *The Social System*, to the topic of medicine and the medical profession. His work with L.J. Henderson on this topic is equally well-known. One of his students, Robert K. Merton, who was then already a major figure in the profession, also became interested in the area in the early 1950's.

Arising largely from the meetings of the University Seminar on the Professions at Columbia University during the 1951-52 year, Merton, George Reader of Cornell Medical School, and Patricia Kendall received a grant from The Commonwealth Fund to conduct a study of medical schools. This grant resulted in *The Student Physician* (1957) and numerous other publications. It also pulled together many researchers (Samuel Bloom, Natalie Rogoff, Renee Fox, David Caplovitz, Rose Laub Coser, *et al.*), who later were to continue working in this new area. In 1958, The Commonwealth Fund again warded a grant to the Bureau of Applied Social Research to study internship and residency programs of medical students. This was the beginning of a prolonged informal training program in medical sociology at Columbia.

At the University of Chicago the development of medical sociology was largely linked to the sociology of occupations and work. While others such as Burgess and Warner were also involved in research linked to health, Everett C. Hughes served as the central figure in the emergence of an identifiable area of training in the sociology of health. The number of dissertations at Chicago in this area of specialization testifies to this influence as does the continuing careers of Chicago graduates (H. Smith, E. Freidson, A. Strauss, H. Mauksch, H. Becker, F. Davis, J. Roth, and R. Habenstein, *et al.*).

During the post World War II period there were, of course, other institutions at which individual scholars emerged with an interest in the health field. Columbia and Chicago are cited as major examples of places where training and socialization had their roots in the leadership of selected faculty members and the stimulus of the subject matter itself. Yale University needs to be mentioned since it represents, in a way, the transition from a pattern of informal training to the formalization of training programs. Yale can be identified with the development of formal pre-doctoral training programs in medical sociology. Under the leadership of August B. Hollingshead and Jerome K. Myers, Yale initiated a pre-doctoral training program, first supported by The Commonwealth Fund and subsequently by The National Institute of Mental Health. It was the first program funded by N.I.M.H. and can claim among its graduates a large number of currently prominent medical sociologists (Robert Straus, George Psathas, Robin Badgley, Ray Elling, Leonard Syme, Albert Wessen, et al.).

The development of training for medical sociology in the United States cannot be evaluated without an awareness of the roles played by the federal government, and, particularly, several private foundations. Of central importance is the development of the programs of the Russell Sage Foundation, the pioneering work of Odin Anderson at the Health Information Foundation, the support of the Milbank Memorial Fund, and the involvement of the Commonwealth Fund. All of these played an important part in supporting scholars and in financing various training aspects of medical sociology. N.I.M.H. support was the largest in monetary terms and its influence weighs heavily over the development of medical sociology training programs during the 1960's. During this period training support was largely associated with the support of research and scholarship. In some instances, particularly the Russell Sage program, this involved post-doctoral support to foster the development of experience and specialization. This era saw the emergence of the formal, pre-doctoral, grant supported, training programs in medical sociology.

4.4. The emergence of medical sociology as a special field

During the late 1950's a movement towards formalizing an organization of medical sociologists gave rise to the emergence of the Section on Medical Sociology of the American Sociological Association. Its first organizational meeting was held during the A.S.A. convention, 1959. From the point of view of the sociology of medical sociology, the formation of this Section and its history deserves considerable attention, particularly as a problem of boundary formation and as a case study of competing perceptions and interests in how medical sociology ought to exist. From the point of view of the patterns of training medical sociologists, the salient issues during the early years involved several crucial questions which influenced curricula and careers and the place of medical sociology in the discipline. One of these issues was the very question of disciplinary identity of medical sociology. An early move towards the conceptualization of a 'medical behavioral science' lost out to those who insisted on a strong foundation in sociology for this specialized field.

Another issue which was raised in the early years of the Section addressed itself to the role of the medical sociologist and whether it should be seen as that of scholar, or as a link to the practitioner. This dialogue included suggestions that those trained in medical sociology should be certified by a group which whould include physicians. Here, too, the commitment to the discipline of sociology won out. The medical sociology section provided a structure and a definition of membership. Although the majority of its members continued to be sociologists whose education did not involve a specialized training program, the Section provided legitimacy and stimulation to the formalization of the education of medical sociologists.

4.5. The emergence of specific training programs

During the 1960's training programs in medical sociology became the prevalent pattern for preparing future specialists in the field of medical sociology. A variety of funding agencies, primarily federal ones, joined N.I.M.H. in supporting some university-based, medical sociology-oriented, doctoral programs. The newly formed Center for Health Services Research and Development appeared as a major source of support in 1968; it supported close to twenty training programs by 1972. As programs became formalized, reliance on them gave rise to new issues. Partly the need for formal proposals and contracts, and partly the institutionalization of the programs themselves, articulated some of the issues which had previously been implicit in the development of medical sociology. One of these is the very place of career-specific and applied educational programs in sociology. The various granting agencies were mandated to offer support not because of their primary interest in sociology as a discipline, but because of the presumed contribution which sociologists with special training could make to various needs in health care. Academic sociology departments, understadably, started to look with some concern on the establisment of programs which combined money, external legitimacy, with the capability of seducing the 'pure' scientist. This legitimate concern and the inevitable marginality of medical sociology faculty on this issue continues. The training programs in medical sociology vary from an explicit and primary commitment to the discipline to a clearly stated priority to develop technically competent specialists who can serve the needs of the health field. A number of programs are not located in sociology departments but are in schools of Public Health or in other designated locations of universities.

Questions have been raised about the current status of the training of medical sociologists in the United States. Within the discipline, the role, the size, and the consequence of these programs are subject to critical evaluation. This is important, partly because it has yet to be demonstrated that the training of sociological specialists in the health field associates their applied contribution with a reciprocal accretion of sociological substance and theory. In contrast, the funding agencies are asking about the consequence of the dollars which they have invested and they seek evidence of impact and influence.

As a member of several committees concerned with these questions, the senior author initiated a survey of sociology departments in U.S. universities to obtain baseline data needed to formulate further questions. What is offered here is merely a synopsis of these data which were obtained by circulating a mail questionnaire to all graduate sociology departments (174) listed in the 1972 American Sociological Association's *Guide to Graduate Departments of Sociology*.

141 schools responded to the questionnaire. Of these, *sixty* indicated that they offered no courses and no programs in medical sociology, *fifty-six* schools reported that they offered courses in medical sociology but did not consider this to constitute a formal medical sociology program. The claim to have a formal program was made by *twenty-five* schools. It should be remembered that several of

the schools who did not respond are known to the authors as having training programs in medical sociology. Thus, it may not be inappropriate to consider the actual number of programs proportionate to the ratio between schools responding and schools receiving the questionnaire.

Programs vary in size according to number of faculty members involved, courses offered, and students enrolled. Six of twenty-five programs responding had five or more faculty members primarily committed to medical sociology. Table 4.1. shows the distribution of faculty members in schools having medical sociology programs and in those who offer courses but no formal programs. As expected, the

Table 4.1. Number of medical sociology faculty members

Number of faculty	Types of schools			
	Programs		Courses only	
	N	%	N	%
0	—	—	1	2
1	3	12	23	41
2	4	16	23	41
3	5	20	5	9
4	7	28	2	4
5 or more	6	24	2	4
TOTAL	25	100	56	101

majority of the latter group have only one or two faculty members identified with this field of specialization. Conversely, it is worth noting that one-fourth of schools offering formal training programs do so with either one or two faculty members. These programs generally have fewer students.

A total of eighty-nine faculty members were reported to be involved in these twenty-five training programs. Of these, approximately one-half are shown in table 4.2. to be jointly appointed with a professional school. The predictable marginality of medical sociology

Table 4.2. Faculty members' appointments and type of school

Type of appointment	Types of schools			
	Programs		Courses only	
	N	%	N	%
Full appointment in sociology	29	33	68	75
Joint appointment with professional school	43	48	11	12
Full appointment with professional school	2	2	5	5
Other	15	17	7	8
Total	89	100	91	100

faculty members, at least in some schools, is suggested by the fact that only one-third are fully appointed in their sociology department. The ratio of extra-departmental commitments is predictably lower in those schools which only offers courses. While this involvement in joint appointments is prevalent among schools with medical sociology programs, only 50 percent of the eighty-nine faculty members re-

Table 4.3. Number of medical sociology graduate majors

Number of majors	Types of schools.			
	Programs		Courses only	
	N	%	N	%
0	5	20	42	75
1-4	3	12	9	16
5-9	8	32	4	7
10-14	7	28	0	0
15 or more	2	8	1	2
TOTAL	25	100	56	100

ported have any of their salary funded by grants. Grant support for salary in excess of 40 percent is reported by 37 percent of these faculty members. In schools offering only courses, 80 percent of the faculty members report no grant support at all. However, approximately 10 percent of faculty members in both types of schools, report that 100 percent of their salary is supported by grants.

Does a graduate training program in medical sociology require special courses in this field of specialization? Two programs report that they do not offer any special courses and that their specialization occurs through experience and research guidance. More than half of the programs offer between three and seven courses as their repertory of this area of specialization. In many instances the reports indicated that the specialized courses are oriented to the field of health and its problem categories rather than to theoretical divisions within the discipline of sociology. As expected, those schools offering four courses or more are more likely to fit some of them into the traditional sociological categories such as Social Psychology or Formal Organization. In order to integrate the issue-oriented focus of the training programs, all schools offering a training program have some type of institutional relationship with a health care agency or professional school. The largest number of affiliations are with schools of medicine; hospitals and schools of nursing appear as second and third in frequency. Notwithstanding the effort by funding agencies to emphasize the need for sociological involvement in community health agencies, formal association with such organizations is relatively scarce.

Approximately 180 graduate students are considered majoring in medical sociology in those schools which identify themselves as having a program. Table 4.3. shows the distribution of these schools by the number of majors in the program. This table also shows that majors have been reported from those schools who did not consider themselves as having formal graduate programs in medical sociology. One non-program school even reported that it had in excess of fifteen such majors, a response which will be checked in a follow-up study. The questionnaire included questions about financial support. Nine of the twenty-five program schools replied that they had no traineeships to offer their graduate majors. In all other instances the number of traineeships offered involved usually between two and three students less than those reported to majors in medical sociology. Among those programs which reported that they were supported by a training grant, 35 percent used one-third or less of the grant funds for student support. 25 percent reported that they had allocated in excess of two-thirds of their grant funds to the support of students.

It would testify to the very process of institutionalization and formalization if the preparation of medical sociologists would be identified only with formal training programs. The survey indicates that one needs to take a look at least at the number of students who take courses in medical sociology, but who are not declared majors in this field. The twenty-five program schools reported that, during one academic year, nearly four hundred students took a medical sociology course. This means that, in these schools, over two hundred graduate students take at least one course in medical sociology which may influence their choice of dissertation and direction of interest. The fifty-six schools reporting that they offer courses but no programs, indicate that about three hundred and fifty students a year take a graduate course in medical sociology.

A careful look at the proces by which graduate students choose the field of medical sociology as their career is particularly important these days when the lure of federal support is waning, if not disappearing. Although economic deprivation and poverty is never a desirable condition, it may be that the impending crisis of program support may force a serious re-examination for some of the assumptions which have emerged in the field. One of the questions which needs to be raised refers to the objectives of formal training programs.

In the preparation of sociologists who can function effectively in the health field, one can distinguish at least four types of goals which may explicitly or implictly be the agendas of trainig programs. For one, there is the development of specialized technical competence applicable to the health field and expertise in the literature of this substantive area. This preparation for competence in task performance is normally the main thrust of any graduate training in the arts and sciences. The peculair characteristics of the health field, its sub-cultural characteristics, language, rituals, and cognitive style have, secondly, led the training programs in medical sociology to include – covertly or deliberately – training in role performance. Some of the objectives of these training programs are quite explicit in seeking to enable the medical sociologist to relate and to communicate effectively with physicians and other health professionals.

Although it has already been mentioned, the emphasis on application and evaluation must be identified as the third theme of training programs. On this issue training programs vary widely. However, all of them are involved in a quasi-confrontation with the traditional aims of graduate training which places basic research even ahead of preparation for teaching. There are additional subtleties to this issue. This orientation can be interpreted as ranging all the way from preparing the technical expert who will assist the implementation of established goals to the training of change agents, if not re-volutionaries. The fourth and, generally, least overt agenda of training programs is the development of a career commitment to the health field. This agenda is explicit with many of the granting agencies and, occasionally, even specified in their enabling policies. Among the teaching faculty, the students, and the supporting agencies, there is probably some difference in the mix of these three objectives.

Whatever the validity of these factors, which have influenced the flavor of training programs, these developments are associated with the appearance of a sectarian flavor in the recruitment, training, and careers of medical sociologists. This phenomenon is not only philosophically dangerous and harmful to sociology; it is also contrary to the realities of the situation. On one hand, entry into the health field continues to be available to sociologists without this specialized preparation. On the other hand, even more importantly, the application of various segments of sociological knowledge to the health field ranges across the entire span of the discipline and cannot be conveniently synthesized in one package called medical sociology. This is not stated here to question the justification and need for the training of specialists in this applied field. The issue is raised to caution against the disruption of the place of medical sociology as an integral part of the discipline. There is harm to sharp boundaries.

All of these issues will affect the future of training programs. This is particularly so in the light of what appears to be the national trend in funding agencies. They want policy-oriented social research and they want commitments by trainees to remain in health-related fields. Hence, any continuation of funding will probably shift even more toward the development of technical skills with less emphasis on expertise in basic disciplines. Parallel to this trend is a movement towards an interdisciplinary 'behavioral science' approach. The stresses of the current situation can be identified with the two dimensions of theory versus application on one hand, and disciplinary integrity versus interdisciplinary development of the other hand. These two dimensions can be thought of as a two-by-two table with four cells. Each cell implies a different role and a different type of education. However, as these sometimes hidden, and sometimes heated debates surrounding training proceed, it might be well to question the basic assumptions of this four-fold table. Are these dichotomies real and do they indeed involve mutually exclusive consequences? Should there not be reciprocity between applied, policy-oriented research and the accretion of theory? Can increased awareness and training in interdisciplinary issues not simultaniously foster the growth of sociology?

Because of the nature of this field, its social visibility, prestige, and public support, medical sociology is particularly exposed to some of the questions raised above. With the years of prosperity and fashionable support of sociology on the way out, those who will continue to be committed to the teaching of future medical sociologists must face some of the various questions suggested here. One of these questions is whether the issues confronting the training of medical sociologists are not actually merely more exposed aspects of fundamental questions affecting the entire discipline and the graduate training of all future sociologists.

References

Blackwell, Elizabeth, 1902, *Essays in Medical Sociology,* London: Ernest Benn.

Davis, Michael M., 1938, 'Social Medicine as a Field for Social Research', *American Journal of Sociology*, 44 (September, 1938), 274-79.

Day, Robert A., (in preparation), 'Towards the Development of a Sociology of Sociology: The Case of Medical Sociology', Unpublished doctoral dissertation, Department of Sociology, University of Missouri-Columbia, Mo.

Faris, Robert E. L., and H. Warren Dunham, 1939, *Mental Disorders in Urban Areas*, Chicago: University of Chicago Press.

Hall, Oswald, 1948, 'The stages of a Medical Career', *The American Journal of Sociology*, 53 (March, 1948), 327-36.

McCartney, James L., 1965, 'Medical Sociology: A Case Study of a Special Area Receiving Much Support', in *The Support of Sociological Research: Trends and Consequences*, unpublished Ph. D. dissertation, University of Minnesota.

Sigerist, Henry E., 1943, *Civilization and Disease*, New York: Cornell University Press.

Straus, Robert, 1957, 'The Nature and Status of Medical Sociology', *American Sociological Review*, 22 (April, 1957), 200-04.

5. Reflections on training in medical sociology for undergraduate students of sociology at the University of Warsaw

M. Sokolowska

I am going to talk about a course in medical sociology given at the University of Warsaw for undergraduate students of sociology. This program was started in 1971 and is still the only teaching program in Eastern Europe.

I believe that there are two basic conditions indispensable to teaching health and medicine to undergraduate students of sociology. Firstly, it must be the sociology of a given country. Secondly, there must be a sufficient number of sociologists able to teach health and medicine to the students. If either of those conditions is not fulfilled, there can hardly be any teaching in this area. The majority of the people present here are perhaps not fully aware of the fact that many countries hardly have sociology in the sense which is applicable and relevant to including the teaching of health and medicine in its program.

Our experience began with the medical school of Warsaw. Medical schools in Poland are not part of the university. They are separate, even the administration. In the early sixties the Dean of the Medical School contacted the Department of Sociology of the University of Warsaw and asked for someone who could provide a fifteen hours' course in sociology. He did not specify what was actually wanted. One colleague, a well-known marxist sociologist, agreed to give this course, and she gave a very well organized course in the theory of social development. But after having given this course she refused to repeat it, saying that the students were not interested at all, that they either slept during the course, did not appear, or did something else during lectures. Present at this talk was a well-known non-marxist sociologist who observed ironically that the future medical doctors could not possibly be interested in class struggle and that he could do the job better. For the next year, the medical students of Warsaw were provided with a well-prepared program in symbolic interaction and were also informed about life in a Navajo tribe in the USA. But after a year he too refused to carry on. The Medical school was probably disappointed because for years nobody asked us to do anything.

Curiously, the Medical School did not seem to be interested in the reason for this failure. No consideration was given to how sociologists are being educated or how they are being prepared to teach in medical schools. This is a broader problem, not specific to Warsaw and Poland. Usually, the only observation made by a medical school is that sociologists, as teachers, are too abstract. But nobody asks the question, why?

Our investigation of this situation started from quite a different angle, namely from the university Department of Sociology. This is the primary place where students of sociology get their training, where they are being prepared for their future careers. Some of them may eventually become teachers in the medical faculty. Our scrutiny led us to the immediate conclusion that, apart from the medical school, we ourselves, the so-called medical sociologists, are also astonishingly little occupied with the basic curriculum of the sociological students.

On the contrary, we are preoccupied with the medical curricula. A great variety of publications, discussions and conferences etc. concentrate on the question of how to teach in medical schools, when to introduce sociology, social science, the social sciences behavioural sciences, medical behavioural science etc. into the medical curriculum; how teaching should be organized within particular medical departments, independent units, part-time appointments etc. But a striking silence surrounds, or rather surrounded up to a few years ago, the place where those prospective teachers are created.

Let us devote some words to the present conference. It represents a few centres, which are rather atypical both for the world situation and for their own countries. Of course, the participants of this conference, present an equally biased sample.

Most sociological centres in the world do not, however, bear any resemblance to such an international conference. There is a general lack of interest in health and medicine among those sociologists, who design and execute sociological curricula. It means that the future planners, administrators, politicians, etc. who are often trained sociologists, in any case here in Poland, have no idea what health and medicine and health system are. Those activities of medical sociologists which are primarily centred on medical curriculum are therefore short-sighted, especially in societies which are not so de-centralized, post-industrial, pluralistic, etc., but which represent a majority of the countries all over the world.

For instance, Polish sociologists are trained with the main aim to study society at large, to be social planners and administrators for all societal fields and areas; except health and medicine, which has been assigned solely to medical doctors. Somehow it goes without saying that the domain of health belongs totally to them, while the sociologists may either rely uncritically on material supplied by doctors or must altogether renounce the study of medical facts and phenomena, which often happens.

To some extent this situation has been created by the situation in the United States: by the relation between American sociology and American medicine; by the tremendously high status of professions in the USA in general and of the medical profession in particular, as compared with the relatively low status of sociologists. However, this is not the case in Poland; rather the reverse would be true in some cases. Nevertheless, we are influenced by the American situation, and although our local scene is quite different, health and medicine have up till now, or rather, until a short time ago, been determined and conceptualized exclusively in clinical terms. Therefore, this is an 'alien body' in the theoretical and empirical study of society. It simply does not fit into it. Medicine is considered generally to be a very interesting area (for instance the technical developments of medicine) but it is not conceived as a definite sphere of social life, expressable in concepts and methods familiar to sociologists.

I believe that even the best medical curriculum will not help to achieve our ultimate goal: to socialize prospective doctors. The effects of this situation are two-fold. I have in mind the Polish medical doctors, our epidemiologists, for instance, who are willing to come to the social planners and administrators with their socio-medical problems but who find rather rigid fellows, not understanding anything about health and medicine as a definite sphere of social life and societal concern and action.

Therefore, in the very interests of medicine, the situation should be reversed: the medical doctor should officially enter the scene to ask how the prospective social planners are trained and to demand that their training include health and medicine.

What are a few main characteristics of the training in medical sociology for the undergraduate students of sociology at the Warsaw University.

In the first place, we are not faced with the situation which Sam Bloom talked about. We have no behavioural movement. Our sociology can hardly be called that. It is much more oriented towards traditional social sciences, and also much more towards social policy.

In the second place, the medical sociology taught at our university is not actually medical sociology. We attempt to be an integral part of the basic sociological training, congruent, where possible, with what the students get in several other courses and seminars. It seems to us, that it would be of rather dubious value to start with quite different approaches and concepts, different from what is generally taught. In Poland, as in many other countries, there is basically one binding program of sociology and not only for sociology, for the whole country and we intend to keep knowledge of health and medicine within these lines. Of course, we do bring some specific aspects but still keep within the general program.

I agree considerably with the first goal of teaching in medical sociology which was discussed earlier and which Robert Day talked about: the medical sociologist must be first and foremost, a good sociologist. We can discuss for hours what this means, but this is another question and I am not going into it here. Anyway, if a sociologist has to get prestige within the medical world, his or her knowledge must be distinct, tied up and based on the parent discipline. This statement sounds like a truism and probably the majority of you have heard it many times before but as I have already said, this audience is by no means representative. In fact, this truism is still far from being realized. Of course, in addition to general sociological knowledge, skills and imagination a specific knowledge relevant to the health area must be developed. However, it is the general knowledge of sociology which is the first condition, sine qua non, for future teachers of sociology in medical schools.

Now we come to that specific knowledge which is embraced by the title of the course 'medical sociology'. It should not be a course in epidemiology or clinical sciences. The students should of course become familiar with epidemiology, clinical sciences and other areas of health but this should be done in the tradition of the sociology of knowledge rather than from the viewpoint of medical sciences. In addition, the students should possess intuition and sensitivity to orient them in the medical world, in which they are supposed to work. We claim to be specialists in human behaviour and yet we do not equip our students with a basic knowledge of behaviour enabling them to understand the rules governing medical culture and to act correspondingly. This is one of the main reasons for several frustrations, so well-known to young sociologists 'lost' in the medical world, of various disappointments and conflicts described plentifully in the sociological-medical literature.

What is more, this literature and our own behaviour seem to contribute to these failures, since we tend to point out the 'ridiculous' traits of our prospective partners, to stress all possible differences between us and 'the practitioners'. This label, originating from the USA and often used by sociologists with reference to doctors, is generally disliked by them, at least in the country where I live. It is understood as the expression of nonchalance of young people who enter the medical world and who are à priori convinced of their own 'superiority'. It does not contribute to the feelings of sympathy.

It is not always necessary to raise antagonism, because it will work against us. One can achieve a lot without it, just knowing what is to be expected, how medical people react, what their sensitive points are, how the processes of socialization can be included in the professional role of a doctor or a nurse, both in norm and in reality. It is my opinion, that even some of the best, almost classical sociological texts devoted to the medical school, as for instance Merton's *The Student Physician* or Becker et al's *Boys in White* do not supply our students with the information necessary to perceive, to feel, to understand the very 'substance' of the medical environment.

On the other hand, we have to face the fact that any course dealing with 'diseases' and their clinical symptoms, is usually received by our students with tremendous interest, often exceeding the interest they show for the professed goals of their training. The students do not seem to care too much whether it is 'sociological' at all. They especially like to hear about mental diseases. It is something to which they can easily become attached, they love deviate behaviour in all forms. Presentations dealing with various aspects of the technical developments of medicine, with the transplantation of kidney or heart for instance, are also found to be extremely interesting. We have to find some balance between this kind of interest and our aim to provide systematic knowledge of medicine and health system. It is not an easy task. Keeping the enthusiasm of our students alive as much as possible, I would be inclined to pay special attention to our main goal. Especially in the early years of the experience in training in medical sociology, when we have just taken our first steps into the departments of sociology, it is necessary to present our subject as a sociological area and not as a quite distinct sphere, however exciting it may be. I would not be afraid of being *plus catholique que le pape'*, in other words to be more 'sociological' than is, in fact, necessary in the future, when our 'establishment' will be strong enough. Otherwise we may be easily swamped in the scraps of clinical information which are interesting not only for sociologists but also for the general public, but which do not contribute to the development of the sociological study of medicine as the system of knowledge and action.

Recently a new program was under consideration in Warsaw and it is quite possible that it will soon be put into operation. It is aimed at bringing together medical students and sociological students and at developing joint sessions for them. We intend to take medical students from a different part of Warsaw and to make them enter a university to which they are strangers, both psychologically and geographically. Perhaps the word 'integration' would be an exaggeration. We would simply like to enable both groups to meet, at the undergraduate level, before they get socialized to their working roles, which are so distinct and so far apart from each other.

The so-called 'problem orientation' is another question which I would like to discuss. The course in medical sociology provides a convenient place to present this approach to the sociological students. As we know, any 'problem' is of an interdisciplinary nature, and the phenomena under study within this framework require more than just the sociological viewpoint. I am not familiar with the situation in other countries but I suspect that there too, and not only in Warsaw, the general sociological training does not provide enough opportunity to develop problem orientation in the students and to prepare them for work in interdisciplinary settings. Certainly this is the contribution which the area of health can make to general sociological education. Actually, our faculty in Warsaw has already observed this special value of 'medical' sociology.

I would also like to discuss a question which has not been touched upon so far, namely the biological approach. Medical sociologists, at least in Poland, are somehow considered by the sociological community to be the best 'specialists' in biology. This is probably because of our affiliation with medicine, which is still perceived as a 'biological science'. This, of course, a naive assumption. Even if we were the best medical doctors, we would still not be biologists. We would be trained in the specific applied biological knowledge, more pathological than physiological. Nevertheless, this is the approach which is somehow tied up with us and I think that we should take it seriously into consideration. If we decide to proceed in this direction this will be undoubtedly a quite different area of study of the genetic-biological endowment of man, of the important context and set of variables for the study of social structure. The 'general' sociologists definitely push us in this direction. It is true that this could be a real contribution to sociological theory, perhaps the only one we can make. I cannot see any other possibility, at least at the moment.

In conclusion, I would like to say that the teaching role of a sociologist, a teacher in medical schools, belongs to one of the most important aspects of his or her working role. The sociologist must be properly trained in order to fulfil this very important task. Medical schools could ask the departments of sociology how their prospective teachers are being trained. This may not be the practice with biologists, chemists or physicists involved in teaching in the Medical Faculty, but the social and behavioural sciences are quite a different matter. The interest shown by medical schools could be a strong encouragement to sociologists, for sociologists all over the world like to 'feel' their contact with and the reaction from 'real life', to see the practical application of their 'abstract' knowledge. It could help to solve several deep complexes of many sociologists, located precisely in this sphere. Many sociologists envy doctors, because they are able to see the direct effects of their work, and are thus convinced of their own utility. I can imagine how proud our department of sociology would be to get a letter from, say, the chancellor of the medical school of Warsaw informing them that the number of jobs for sociologists in medicine is still increasing and asking how the students are being trained for them. Since departments of sociology and sociologists are basically the same everywhere, I think that this idea is pertinent not only to Warsaw. Needless to say, medicine and medical doctors enjoy a very high prestige among sociologists. I hope I have succeeded in convincing you that this is the most important area of action at present, especially for the participants of this conference.

6. Basic assumptions in medical sociology teaching in medical schools

E.G. Pattishall

Medical sociology, as one of the behavioral sciences, is playing an increasingly important role in medical education today. While the major behavioral sciences of psychology, sociology, and anthropology do not share quite the same academic stature and curricula as the other basic medical sciences, there is much reason to believe that the curriculum time and attention paid to the behavioral sciences will continue to increase (Webster, 1971).

6.1. Background

Perhaps a few words should be given to the background of the behavioral sciences and how they have developed in medical schools. Most physicians in the practice of medicine will readily admit that most of the patients who seek their help (somewhere between fifty and eighty percent) are suffering from an illness that has a major behavioral or social component. They will also admit that most of their *education and training has taught them to deal only with the physiological, biochemical, and pathological aspects of diagnosis and treatment; the behavioral, the social and the psychological components have either been ignored or dealt with in a very superficial manner*, without an opportunity to acquire the specific knowledge and skills needed to work with the psychological, social, and behavioral components. Nor has the practising physician been required to demonstrate this important knowledge and skill in order to enter the practice of medicine.

The incongruency becomes *amplified if one considers the impact that the miracle of modern medicine has had on the patterns of diseases* which affect mankind. The tremendous success of medical advances has: almost eliminated the threat of the traditional infectious diseases of childhood and adulthood; alleviated the threat of pain, and reduced the certainty of death from trauma and emergencies. By preserving life, we have increased the number of people who survive to older ages, the number of disabilities, and the population with degenerative diseases. Thus, the 'fruits' or consequences of modern medicine have created a different pattern of disease: acute diseases have been replaced by chronic diseases, pain has been replaced by misery, miracle drugs have led to addiction, disability has led to handicaps, old age to senility and dependence, etc (Jefferys, 1975). The problem for us in medical education is that we have designed our educational program so that the medical students will learn the knowledge and skills necessary to deal with the acute diseases, which require less psychological and sociological understanding, while we give almost no attention to the chronic diseases, which require a significant amount of knowledge and skills to deal with the tremendous psychological and sociological problems involved. In other words, when the major pattern of diseases was of an acute nature, it required much more knowledge and understanding of the physiological biochemical, anatomical, etc. dimensions, but now that the pattern has changed more to chronic diseases, the greater needs are for more knowledge and understanding of the psychological, the sociological, the cultural, the family and the community aspects of human coping and adaptation. An understanding of and an ability to work with 'the human condition' is of equal or greater importance to modern medicine than the traditional basic sciences or the clinical training for specialization.

The *technology of modern medicine* has developed rapidly over the past 25 years, primarily because of the tremendous financial support that has been given to biomedical research. Knowledge has proliferated and medical specialties have become *fragmented into subspecialties, to the extent that medical education has put more and more emphasis on science and reductionism, technology, and specialization rather than holistic factors, humanism, and primary care*. The focus of medical education and human biology has been so distorted that concern for the person with a disease has been replaced by a narrow focus on the disease and the disease process, as though they existed completely independent of the patient, the family, and the community.

Fortunately, the public, medical educators, and medical students are beginning to rebel so that at least some of the priorities of medical education are being reordered. There have been rather *slow, but constant changes in medical curricula over the past 20 years* so that the social, the behavioral, and the humanistic components have been revitalized. A most important part of this trend is the support given by the funding agencies who, while not necessarily enamoured of the behavioral sciences, are insisting that their financial support go to the training of primary care physicians, toward medical care for those who do not have access to medical care, and toward a more humanistic and caring health-care system. The effect is that medical educators have to take a closer look at the training environment in medical schools, the faculty and teaching role-models provided, and the values and expectations of the patient (the consumer of medical care). This trend can best be summarized in terms of relevance, rehumanization, and renewed social commitment (Pattishall, 1973).

In the early 1950's, psychiatry had begun to articulate and demonstrate the relevance of the psychological and social factors in all areas of medicine. In an effort to teach the psycho-social factors and to develop the broad base of scientific support and credibility enjoyed by the other medical specialties, psychiatry began to look toward its colleagues in the social science departments in the university. These new social science colleagues were able to assist psychiatry with its own professional identity and with the new emphasis on medical research in clinical departments. The clinical psychologist, who had been building a considerable fund of knowledge and skill in the measurement of human attributes, was soon followed by the social psychologist, the physiological psychologist, the medical sociologist, and the cultural anthropologist; each bringing to psychiatry and medical education experience in research on human behavior, especially in research design, measurement, and statistics.

This was a fortuitous development for the social scientist, since he needed a real-live-patient situation in which to develop and extend the theoretical and practical study of human behavior. These research skills and body of basic knowledge about human behavior also added a much-needed dimension to the understanding of biological function and dysfunction in medicine.

The basic content of this early teaching of the social sciences in schools of medicine was most related to considerations of the doctor-patient relationship, interviewing, and psychosocial factors involved in being sick. As the cooperative teaching exercises between psychiatry, psychology, sociology, and other clinical specialties became more formalized, the non-physician faculty members were encouraged to offer special teaching sessions dealing with special elements within their own disciplines. One of our major problems has been that we have been particularly hard pressed to support our concepts and knowledge with adequate 'hard data'. *With the goal of gaining acceptance in the medical curriculum, we have steadily but surely been re-examining our content in terms of generalizations and knowledge based on empirical data and relevance to medical problems* .

An important milestone in the newly-established identity of the behavioral sciences in the *U.S.A.* was the *incorporation of behavioral science in The National Board of Medical Examiners Part I Examination.* Back in 1967 The National Board began studying the behavioral science teaching programs at the national level and found that behavioral science teaching had been increasing in most medical schools, and yet it was not being tested as a necessary component of the basic sciences. On the basis of the recommendations of an ad hoc committee on behavioral science testing, the number of behavior-related items in the Part I Exam was increased so that by June 1972, the Part I Exam included a full quota of behavioral science items. In 1973, the behavioral sciences were given equal weight along with the other basic science disciplines of anatomy, biochemistry, microbiology, pathology, pharmacology, and physiology.

Having had a vested interest in this development as a member of the ad hoc committee, and as the first chairman of the Behavioral Science Test Committee, I may not be completely objective in my comments about it, but I do feel strongly that this acceptance of the behavioral sciences represented a highly significant event in terms of visibility, equality, and relevance of behavioral science as a required basic science. The impact of this event on the teaching of behavioral science is still being felt. In fact, the most recent rumblings include a concern by some psychiatrists that the behavioral sciences may have indeed become a little too autonomous, too related to other fields of medicine, and less relevant to basic psychiatry. I consider this an extremely short-sighted view.

6.2. Basic assumptions

If we are going to promote and develop the contributions of medical sociology in medical education, then we must be guided by certain basic assumptions which will determine the content, format, and impact of medical sociology teaching in schools of medicine. I should like to list several basic assumptions which have been derived from experience with the teaching of the behavioral sciences to medical students.

6.2.1. Sociology in medicine versus sociology of medicine

I realize that this is a sensitive point for sociologists, but it is very important from the medical perspective that the medical sociologist think of himself or herself as applying sociological concepts, knowledge, and techniques in an attempt to analyze, integrate, and teach sociological generatizations and knowledge involved in medical problems (Straus, 1957). This interest will show medical students and physicians that the medical sociologist does have a body of knowledge which is directly relevant to disease, treatment, and health. Medical sociologists attempting to practise the sociology of medicine will be perceived as attempting to use the medical setting primarily to clarify what are essentially sociological questions. I recognize the importance of expanding the body of knowledge of sociology, through the sociology of medicine, but here we are dealing with the priorities of the medical institution and they must be adhered to if medical sociology is going to be regarded as more than a peripheral discipline.

6.2.2. Medical sociology as a behavioral science

Medical sociology must be defined as one of the behavioral sciences and be part of a multidisciplinary effort. *This means that medical sociology should not attempt to stand alone in the medical cur-*

riculum, but should be integrated as an important part of the other behavioral sciences: psychology, anthropology, and behavioral biology. Without this attempted correlation and integration, it will be seen as a fragmented and highly-specialized discipline, but without much central relevance to the multivariable and interacting components of medical problems.

6.2.3. Medical sociology in the basic sciences

Medical sociology and the behavioral sciences must be recognized as a basic science and as a discipline that is basic to *all* fields of medicine (Straus, 1959). While it has much to contribute to psychiatry, or community medicine, or family medicine, or preventive medicine, it can contribute as well to other medical specialties. This may not always be understood if the sponsoring department is psychiatry, or community medicine, etc., but it is important for the maximum development and application of medical sociology as a basic discipline in its own right, and not as a stepchild to only one department.

6.2.4. Bridging the gap between medical sociology and clinical disciplines

The general trend in medical education is toward more links between the basic sciences and the clinical sciences (NICHD, 1972). It is especially important that medical sociology use this as an opportunity to integrate and to demonstrate the relevance of medical sociology in the solution of medical problems. Often this can be demonstrated best through the teaching and learning experiences of the medical student attempting to understand, diagnose, and treat an ill patient. It can also serve to illustrate the interaction between the biological, the social, and the psychological factors in illness and health.

6.2.5. Use of the inductive process and empirical data

In teaching medical sociology, we must recognize the importance of the inductive process in the learning and the practice of medicine. The student-physician gets inductive data from the patient, considers it in comparison with other data, gets more date, and then develops an hypothesis or hunch as to the disease process, the diagnosis, or the conclusion. This is a learning-practising format which may be quite different from that of the sociologist, who may approach a problem with a theory or model. This is one of the fatal errors of traditional psychoanalysis which has attempted to offer a theory or speculation into which behavior and symptoms are fitted, rather than relying on empirical data for its conclusions. The medical student understands and respects the teacher who remains close to the empirical data, paying full homage to the world of symptoms or behavior as it presents itself, rather than attempting to construct or indoctrinate the world to fit or test their own theories or models of the world as they think it should be.

6.2.6. The language of medical sociology

One of the major criticisms that medical students often make about the behavioral sciences in general, but about sociology in particular is that the terms and language often sound 'fuzzy' or vague. We are more apt to get into this difficulty when we try to teach or explain a phenomenon without sufficient empirical data to support our explanation. We recognize that a science must have its technical vocabulary or language, but it must evolve out of the data and concepts, not precede it. One of the accusations is that we sometimes try to present common sense ideas with invented and sometimes irrelevant words. While I think this criticism may be too hasty, it is important to constantly examine our teaching for highly specialized jargon.

6.2.7. Medical sociology and social ills

It is important that teachers of medical sociology do not cultivate the image of responsibility for the abolition of the ills and inequities of society. Obviously, the medical sociologist possesses more knowledge and perhaps even the skills to teach and implement various social change issues, however, we must keep in mind that this is a responsibility and a commitment of all faculty members in a medical school and we will be more effective teaching agents, as well as change agents, if we keep it in that perspective. Similarly, we must not take sole responsibility for the rehumanization of medicine, but should insist that all programs and learning experiences in the student's training share this responsibility.

6.2.8. Identification and synthesis of relevant content

The most important but difficult task of the medical sociologist, as well as the behavioral scientist, is the identification and synthesis of a disciplinary content which recognizes the interaction of the bio-psycho-social components of the development of disease and the maintenance of health. This involves much more depth than the usual teaching session on the doctor-patient relationship, the influence of social class, or the ills of the present health care provision system. We are increasingly able to provide supporting empirical data for our knowledge and generalizations; knowledge and generalizations that often run contrary to conventional wisdom; which we are often accused of promoting.

6.2.9. A viable format for teaching

The early format of interviewing a patient and of attempting to demonstrate the importance of psychosocial factors in illness was well received, but most often lacked an academic substance and an awareness on the part of the student that he or she was really learning something that could be tested or evaluated. One mythical assumption in the medical student culture that has often worked against us is that if it can't be tested then it must not be very important. While medical students are just as intelligent, inquiring, and competent as graduate students, they do have a learning perspective that screens all learning experiences in terms of: (1) do I have to learn this in order to survive in medical schools?, and (2) how is it going to make me a better doctor?

While the lecture format is still the most prevalent in medical school, there is some recognition of its inefficiency and ineffictiveness. The fantasy of the faculty members that they may give a great lecture or become a great lecturer dies hard. My estimate would be that in reality more than 90% of all lectures in medical school (not just in behavioral science) are not the best use of a medical student's or faculty's time.

One format which we found effective consists of putting all of the lecture content (narrative, data, tables, etc.) in the form of a printed handout which is provided to students so that it can be read before each class session. The class session consists of raising special points for emphasis, answering questions about the content, presenting a videotape or live patient to illustrate specific content or behaviors, and the presenting of a medically-related problem which can only be solved if one has read the handout. This frees the professor to do what professors should do, and that is interpret, translate, integrate, inspire, and serve as a role model directed toward the relevance of the content.

One of our major stumbling blocks has been that we have attempted to teach medical sociology or behavioral science as a pure discipline, or have attempted to concentrate only on the experiential or field experience, or have attempted to fit the major content into a research experience model, or have attempted to follow the model of the clinician by teaching everything around patient care. We must show more creativity by attempting to find new combinations of teaching formats for different levels of abstraction, generalization, knowledge, and skills.

6.2.10 Medical sociologists need training in a medical setting

After surveying some of the major graduate education programs in medical sociology, I was amazed to find that many of them do not provide training in a medical center. Perhaps this is why the perspective of sociology in medicine comes as such a shock to a new faculty member who has been trained primarily in the perspective of the sociology of medicine. As we mentioned above, the teaching and learning environment of a medical setting is quite different from that found in a university department on campus. This is frequently demonstrated when a member of the sociology department (or psychology) is asked to come over and teach the medical students about the behavioral sciences; such topics as social class, role theory, deviance, social mobility, etc. The social scientists were most often quite willing to try to be of help, partly because they were interested in exploring the possibbility of some affiliation with a medical center for research, but also because they recognize the psychosocial factors as being important and that doctors should know more about them. While the visiting faculty member from oncampus would often deliver an excellent lecture, attempting to pull together all that is known and being investigated, in, for example, role theory, the medical student would be duly impressed and appreciative, but the content would be rejected and regarded as worth-less, since they could not see how this theoretical material provided by some outsider would make them a better doctor. *In other words, the lecturer lacked the awareness or perspective of the learning environment of this unique subculture called medical education.* The lecturer often left feeling hurt and misunderstood, sometimes concluding that medical students are not educable. Every attempt should be made to provide the graduate student in medical sociology with sufficient training and experience in a medical setting, doing both teaching and research, until he or she develops this awareness and perspective.

6.3. Conclusion

In summary, the success of medical sociology teaching in schools of medicine will depend in large measure upon the extent to which we emphasize sociology in medicine; the inclusion of medical sociology as one of the behavioral sciences; medical sociology as a basic science; bridging the gap between medical sociology and all clinical disciplines; use of the inductive process in teaching and learning; critical examination of the language of medical sociology; the sharing of responsibility for social change; identification and synthesis of relevant content; investigation of viable teaching formats, and provision of medical setting training and experience for graduate students in medical sociology.

References

Jefferys, Margot, 1975, Foreword in Cox, Caroline and Adrianne Mead (Eds.), *A Sociology of Medical Practice,* London: Collier-MacMillan, p. 318.

NICHD, 1972, *Behavioral Sciences and Medical Education,* Washington, D.C., D. H. E. W. Pub (NIH) 72:i41, p. 183.

Pattishall, Evan G., Ir., 1973, 'Basic Assumptions for the Teaching of Behavioral Science in Medical Schools'. *Soc. Sci. and Med.*, 7: 12: P. 923-926.

Straus, Robert, 1959, 'A Department of Behavioral Science', *J. Med. Educ.,* 34,: p. 662-666.

Straus, Robert, 1957, 'The Nature and Status of Medical Sociology'. *American Sociological Review,* 22, p. 200-204.

Webster, Thomas, 1971, 'The Behavioral Sciences in Medical Education and Practice', in Coombs Robert H. and Vincent, Clark E., *Psychosocial Aspects of Medical Training,* Springfield, Illinois, Charles C. Thomas, Pub.

7. Basic assumptions in teaching medical sociology in medical schools: the case of West Germany

M. Pflanz and J. Siegrist

7.1. Historical background

It is true and not true as well to say that medical sociology in Germany is a very new branch of sociological and of medical sub-disciplines. Although the term 'medical sociology' was not used in Germany before 1955, the idea itself has a long tradition in German medical thinking. We shall not attempt to delineate the whole development of thinking in an area which today we would call medical sociology, but we must mention two classics of medical sociology: the writings of Virchow and Salomon Neumann (around 1848) and the book by Müller-Lyer *'Sociology of Suffering'* (*Soziologie der Leiden* 1914). About the same time a more pragmatic approach was chosen by Alfred Grotjahn, the great man of German social hygiene, who emphasized the necessity of a union between social hygiene, and sociology and economics. The Swiss medical historian H. E. Sigerist was already using a sociological approach to the history of medicine when he was teaching at Leipzig, just as he did later in the United States. The most influential figure for an entire generation was probably Viktor von Weizsäcker, one of the most important promoters of medical sociology and psychosomatics in Germany from the early thirties until the years after World War II.

However, the birth of 'modern' medical sociology in the Federal Republic of Germany can be dated exactly: it is the 30th of June, 1958. On this day René Köning invited some sociologists and physicians to attend a guest lecture by A. B. Hollingshead at Cologne (Pflanz, 1973). In the following months a remarkable activity in this field could be observed. There appeared a supplement to *'Kölner Zeitschrift für Soziologie und Sozialpsychologie'* fully devoted to medical sociology. Another important attempt to establish a new sub-discipline of medical sociology was a paper given bij Schelsky at the annual meeting of the German Hospital Association in 1958, in which a systematic outline of 'sociology in medicine' and 'sociology of medicine' was presented. In 1961 almost at the same time two books on special topics appeared – one about the sociology of the hospital (Rohde, 1961), the other one about the relationships between social change and disease (Pflanz, 1961) – both attempting to introduce the reader to the field of medical sociology in general.

If we look at the list of publications in the vast field of medical sociology in the last fifteen years, including dissertations and other theses, we find a growing number of writings reflecting the increasing awareness of these problems. In spite of the rather large number of these publications we very often find expressed a feeling of isolation and even despair. For many years no author in medical sociology failed to point out the fact that in his eyes medical sociology in Germany is totally underdeveloped. This changed only recently. But one still wonders whether the lamentation about the poor status of medical sociology in Germany might have worked as a self-fulfilling prophecy. This problem is not restricted to publications but can still be found with respect to the institutionalization of medical sociology in Germany. It was some years before the first association of medical sociologists was established. Since 1969 a rather loose congregation of teachers in the fields of psychosomatics, psychotherapy, medical psychology and medical sociology has existed. The purpose is not only to discuss the first experiences with teaching in medical sociology but also to discuss and to assemble objectives for teaching in this field. Both functions were taken over by a new association, the German Society of Medical Sociology, in 1973. At about the same time the German Sociological Association established a Medical Sociology Section with the purpose of discussing problems of research at annual conventions. One can imagine that there would be great competition among all these groups in order to attract members and to gain status and power. However, this is not true. There is a large overlapping between all three groups, particularly on the level of the Boards. The situation is somewhat different for the German Society for Social Medicine. After a long period of competition between its members and medical sociologists (see below), a limited cooperation in the field of epidemiological research and policy has finally evolved.

7.2. The institutionalization of medical sociology

A new federal regulation of medical education began in 1970. On one hand the traditional oral examination was replaced by a centralized system of multiple choice examinations. On the other hand new sub-disciplines such as medical psychology and sociology, psychosomatics and social medicine were incorporated into the regular medical curriculum.

The pressure toward this special reform was augmented by the fact that several shortcomings of the actual health care delivery system had become widely recognized. The German student revolt in the late 1960's contributed to this change to a small extent only. The main impetus came from distinguished authorities within medical faculties, especially from the field of psychosomatics, internal medicine, anatomy, physiology and the history of medicine. The German society of sociology must bear the blame for not caring about these developments and failing to initiate training courses as a base for the recruitment of medical sociologists. Some teaching concepts of medical sociology have been developed and tested in three medical schools since 1965 (Giessen, Ulm, Hannover). However the official curriculum was not built upon these experiences but was rather the result of bargaining among different lobbies of the medical scene. In the meantime (by 1976) the contents of the official curriculum have been restated and rigorously adapted to the needs of a basic medical education.

The necessity of developing teaching programs under the pressure of new federal regulations for medical education rendered the medical faculties into a kind of 'shell shock' state involving apathy or meaningless behavior. It took some time before new institutions of medical sociology could be established, but after a first breakthrough they mushroomed. In less than four years thirteen out of twenty-seven medical faculties established chairs and institutions with the purpose of teaching medical sociology to undergraduate medical students. (Kaupen-Haas, 1976) The speed with which the establishment of these new institutions took place was very surprising and completely unmatched in any other academic discipline in Germany (see psychology as a comparison; Zloczower, 1973).

The kind of organizational and hierarchical ties of medical sociology to medical institutions varies tremendously. Some run independent departments – which is the exception – others are more dependent on medical institutions. The issue of dependency and autonomy is far from being solved in our country (Planz, 1975). Beside simple dependencies there are also a lot of subtle mechanisms meant to keep medical sociology in its place 'below clinical medicine and basic sciences', which is not unlike the situation in the United States and Canada (Badgley and Bloom, 1973).

At present, most medical sociological units in Germany are integrated in a 'psychosocial' center. Actually there are tendencies to incorporate them into centers of ecological medicine. This formal incorporation could have strong effects on the definition of scope and content of this new sub-discipline (see below).

In the situation as described it has not been possible to hire a homogeneous group of scientists for the newly created positions. Unlike in almost all other sub-disciplines of medicine the background of the new professors was rather diverse. Only seven out of thirteen are trained sociologists. The others came from the disciplines of medicine, psychology or psychoanalysis. It might be said that most of the professors are autodidacts in their field. Susser (1966) aptly described a similar situation in his report on the teaching of social medicine in the United States.

'Amateurism' comes into play and the status of the new field within the medical school is deteriorating. Perhaps it is not appropriate to see this development as only negative. It is possible that 'amateurism' has a larger potential content of innovation and creativity compared to the modes of self-recruitment in the old disciplines.

However, in a seminar in which the necessity and potential of postgraduate training in medical sociology is discussed, it seemed to us necessary to emphasize the mostly unreflected problems of recruitment, of incentives and of training *vs.* amateurism.

In summing up the present status of institutionalization it can be said that – in spite of a few local quarrels – medical sociology generally was not unwelcome to medical faculties. May be there was a feeling that the political activities of students would be channelled and relieved by medical sociologists. Since, recently, many potential activities of students were directed into other fields, it cannot reliably be said whether this expectation of some faculties was correct. The advent of medical sociologists in some places was exactly as described by H.O. Mauksch (1970) as the 'Decorator Syndrome', as the advent of a decorator who will redecorate one's home: 'He is sought after, he is wanted. This flavor of delight changes with the actual arrival of the decorator and his helper... his real presence is experienced as an inconvenience, an interruption, and an imposition'.

However, it would be unfair to place the blame only upon the others, the social structure or society, neglecting the disturbance likely to be made by medical sociologists themselves.

It's now up to the decorators to persuade their public of the utility and validity of their work. Let's consider this work in more detail.

7.3. Teaching medical sociology: basic assumptions and problems of realization

It might be said that medical sociology in the Federal Republic of Germany is trying hard to introduce nation-wide a highly standardized set of teaching objectives. As far as we know this accomplishment is rather unique in terms of numbers of hours devoted to teaching, in terms of agreement about the contents of teaching and in terms of coverage of medical students. However, it has to be admitted that there is no agreement in the world about the most relevant parts of medical sociology that should be passed on to the medical student that is comparable to the agreement in disciplines such as anatomy or physiology.

Even in Germany there is no test of relevance of the contents of teaching for the average medical student. This is not a unique situation in medical sociology since most professional associations of the medical sub-disciplines obviously arrange their lists of teaching objectives more according to an intra-disciplinary one-upmanship than in order to produce a comprehensive 'basic physician'.

Everybody would agree that standardization of teaching programs cannot be carried out so rigidly that creativity and imagination of the teacher are excessively impedimented. However, one must point out that the disagreements about content and format, about objectives and orientations, are greater in medical sociology than in any other pre-clinical or clinical sub-discipline. Even one quite fundamental contradiction is not resolved namely, whether the main orientation in the teaching of medical students should be a sociological one or a medical one. Just recently we got a beautiful example of this from the United Kingdom: in a conference a sociologist (F. M. Martin) preferred to teach only medically-relevant issues while a medically-qualified discussant (F. A. Boddy) wished to emphasize the need to communicate 'areas of study... which need to be more specifically rooted in, or developed from, the general discipline of sociology' (in R. M. Acheson and L. Aird 1976, p. 16-19 and 122-124).

However, among the majority of medical sociologists in the Federal Republic of Germany there is at least a minimal consensus concerning the following teaching objectives:

1. The medical student should get some basic information about demographic and socio-structural developments in contemporary societies, at least about those areas that are relevant to the understanding of existing forms and future modalities of medical practice and patient care.
2. The medical student should be able to evaluate societal influences on the notion of health and sickness. He should have some knowledge about the impact of social reality on the development and onset of illness as well as on the health and illness behavior of patients. This knowledge should create a better understanding of the psychosocial situation of people meeting the doctor.
3. Teaching medical sociology should lead to some sort of role distance in the process of professional socialization. The physician should understand the mechanisms of 'professional dominance'. He should be able to cooperate effectively with members of related professions in the health care system.

These basic assumptions make clear that teaching medical sociology does not only mean the transmission of cognitive information but also the training of the ability to communicate.

It is our opinion that only the teaching combination of knowledge, attitudes, and interactional skills will have some – if any – long-term impact on the physician's role performance.

What kind of practical results can we expect from teaching sociology in medical schools? Let us consider briefly some possible consequences.

- The medical student should be able to integrate specific sociological and psychological observations into history-taking as well as into the evaluation of the patient's state. He might learn to concentrate not only on the history of an illness (*Krankheitsgeschichte*) but also on the history of the sick person (*Krankengeschichte*).
- The medical student will learn to evaluate the functions of social control delegated from society to the physician.
- The medical student will be motivated to turn to fields of medical practice that were vastly neglected under the dominance of the 'clinical perspective' in medical education (for example, family medicine, occupational medicine, public health, preventive and social medicine).
- The medical student will be motivated to search for organizational innovations within his future working setting (for example group practice, patient-centered working conceptions, counseling activities).

There are many problems to be resolved before these objectives can be firmly established in medical education. First, in the Federal Republic of Germany there is still no obligation for medical students to participate in sociological courses. They can prepare themselves for the examinations by textbooks. Only recently have a few medical faculties incorporated medical sociology into a psychosocial course obligatory to all medical students.

A second problem arises from the fact that medical sociology and psychology are placed in the pre-clinical program. The complete lack of clinical experience narrows the range of topics. Some medical schools, however, have created interdisciplinary lectures with the new disciplines in the clinical stage as well as during the internship.

The present state of medical sociology is still week and contradictory. Many research results are not representative or cannot be transposed from one country or from one system of health care to another. A very important task of our discipline is to intensify research activities in those areas that are relevant to medical education and medical practice.

Recently the most important research organization in the Federal Republic of Germany – *Deutsche Forschungsgemeinshaft* – has decided that it will sponsor a coordinated research program covering a period of five to ten years, initiated by the Medical Sociology Section of the German Sociological Association. This decision could possibly be a milestone in the development of this discipline in West Germany.

But what about the present state of sociological research? How can the prevailing theoretical and practical orientations among medical sociologists be characterized? What dangers emerge from the incorporation of new disciplines into medical research? We think that illustrating the case of the Federal Republic of Germany would not be complete without a brief discussion of these topics.

7.4. Research policy and the identity of medical sociology

In the Federal Republic of Germany our discipline so far has not contributed significantly to any great breakthrough in either theoretical developments or empirical research. Most of the research done until now can be classified as an adaptation to Anglo-American scientific tradition (for an overview see Siegrist and Rohde, 1976). Perhaps the present state of theoretical and methodological discussions can best be documented by the comparison of three textbooks of medical sociology (Ferber, 1975; Geissler and Thoma, 1974; Siegrist, 1975).

There are probably only few medical sociologists in our country who adhere to the principle of value-free science. Most of them have a more or less distinct political orientation, the majority somewhere between the left-liberal and the left-radical. This has some consequences. One is that the public, including the medical public, cannot distinguish between the political orientation and the scientific approach; it is probably fair to assume that there must be some medical sociologists who are successfully hiding their scientific stance behind a strong political orientation. Besides that particular orientation there are many medical sociologists, who feel responsible for what they understand as 'health politics'. The vast majority of them belong to Alford's (1972) group of 'corporate rationalizers' trying to extend the function, power and resources of their organizations. It is not by chance that many medical sociologists do not set a high value on professional autonomy but are instead attempting to be useful to one of the larger groupings in our society, particularly the Unions or political parties.

A careful inspection would probably prove how right Alford was in stating that the relationship between the professional monopolists and the corporate rationalizers is a symbiotic one. Only occasionally does a medical sociologist in the Federal Republic of Germany belong to Alford's group of equal-health advocates, probably because the consumer-indigenous healthworker movement is very weak under the national health insurance system in our country.

The orientation of most medical sociologists in the Federal Republic of Germany towards medicine as an institution and/or as part of social reality is ambivalent. Many medical sociologists, on the one hand, are strongly critical of 'physicians' as a group. Wrapping their criticism in scientific terms does not obscure the fact that the basis of such criticism is often no more differentiated than public criticism. The authors wish to make clear that they feel much of the criticism is fully justified. On the other hand, most medical sociologists in our country identify themselves with the value frame of medicine as a social institution. Very few, if any, would subscribe to Illich's critique of medicine. The kind of antagonism towards medicine and the medical profession which prevails in some circles in the United States and the United Kingdom can scarcely be found in Germany. Here, there is very little discussion about the medicalization of society or medical power. Only very few sociologists in this field are committed anti-psychiatrists. Also, encouragement of self-treatment, consumerism or support for folk medicine does not exist at present.

The power and influence of the 'medical model' has been extended to the new sub-disciplines of medical faculties, and the pressure towards practical problem-solving attitudes is increasing. There seem to be two ways of coping with this new strain: the one is a stronger alliance between medical sociology and psychology or psychosomatic medicine. By taking this alternative practical ambitions of medical sociologists overlap with those of clinical psychologists (e.g., group or behavior therapy, counseling activities in clinical work and organizational matters).

The other way of coping is a stronger commitment to community orientation (Sokolowska, 1973). From this kind of orientation many theoretical and practical impulses could arise.

Social medicine, public health and preventive medicine could be powerful allies of medical sociology. It is a pity that compettition and struggle between social medicine and medical sociology have paralyzed this cooperation in our country. There are no clear distinctions in the context of work and no jurisdictional boundaries (Freidson, 1976) of both specialities in a division of labor. This particular situation created some conflicts beyond those due to emergence of a new para-medical profession.

The successes of medical sociology are deceptive. There are other goals to be accomplished than establishing professorships, departments or teaching programs. Medical sociology will flourish only if, beyond academic programs in medical schools, the professionals find fields of work in the non-academic field, distinct from social medicine, public health and epidemiology on the one hand and distinct from psychosomatics and clinical psychology on the other.

References

Acheson, R.M. and L. Aird, 1976, *Seminars in Community Medicine*, Vol. 1, *Sociology*, Oxford Univ. Press, London.

Alford, R.R., 1972, 'The political economy of health care: Dynamics without change', *Politics and Society*, 2, 127-164.

Badgley, R.F. and S.W. Bloom, 1973, 'Behavioral sciences and medical educations; the case of sociology', *Soc. Sci. & Med.*, 7, 927-941.

V. Ferber, C., 1975, *Soziologie für Mediziner*, Springer, Berlin.

Freidson, E., 1975, *Doctoring together: A study of professional social control*, Elsevier, New York, London, Amsterdam.

Geissler, Thoma (Hrsg.), 1974, *Medizinsoziologie*, Frankfurt, 1974.

Kaupen-Haas, H. and H. Döhner, 1976, Sozioäkonomische Bedingungen der Medizinischen Soziologie der BRD, 1. Teil, in *Medizinsoziologische Mitteilungen*, 2, 1976, 142-172.

Mauksch, H. O., 1970, 'Studying the Hospital', In: R. W. Habenstein (ed.), *Pathways to data*, p. 185-203, Aldine, Chicago.

Pflanz, M., 1962, *Sozialer Wandel und Krankheit*, Enke, Stuttgart.

Pflanz, M., 1973, 'Die Zunehmende Soziologisierung der Medizin', In: G. Albrecht u.a. *Soziologie, Sprache-Bezug zur Praxis-Verhältnis zu anderen Wissenschaften*, Westdeutscher Verlag, Köln, Opladen, 588-600.

Pflanz, M., 1975, 'Relations between social scientists, physicians and medical organizations in health research', *Soc. Sci. & Med.*, 9, 7-13.

Rohde, J. J., 1974, *Soziologie des Krankenhauses*, 1. Ed., 1962, 2. Ed., Enke, Stuttgart.

Siegrist, J., 1975, *Lehrbuch der Med. Soziologie*, Urban & Schwarzenberg, München, 2.A.

Siegrist, J. and J.J. Rohde, 1976, 'Zur Entwickelung der medizinsoziologischen Forschung in der BRD', In: *Soziologie*, 1, 24-38.

Sokolowska, M., 1973, 'Two basic types of medical orientation', *Soc. Sci. & Med.*, 7, 807-815.

Susser, M., 1966, 'Teaching social medicine in the United States', *Milbank mem. Fd. Quart*, 44, 389-410.

Zloczower, A., 1973, 'Konjunktur in der Forschung'. In: F. R. Pfetsch and A. Zloczower, *Innovation und Widerstände in der Wissenschaft*, 91-150, Bertelsmann, Düsseldorf.

PART FOUR

EDUCATIONAL OBJECTIVES

The previous section's evaluation of the current training programs in medical sociology against the work role expectations and perspectives of both medical sociologists and physicians is now logically extended into change-oriented reflection on training.

The attention given by the previous authors to professional futurology could create the impression that change-oriented reflection on training amounts to using training, for profit-maximizing motives, in the prognostics of societal trends. However, the training philosophy supporting the following contributions attributes a creative social function to training: being a co-derterminant for societal trends. In this philosophy, change in training may be the motor of social change. Therefore, after some attempts at projecting training in a future social perspective, a complementary reflection will follow on the training paradigms that proved desirable. Different training paradigms are believed to have a differential effect on expertise and other aspects of professional performance. This is the ultimate relevance of change-oriented intervention in training.

As an experiment, reflections on medical sociology training are taken from present-day educational thinking, i.e. from a frame of reference that systematically and purposefully constructs training paradigms aimed at educational objectives. This didactical method was actively tested in the workshop for its practicability. It is also elaborately discussed in this volume in 'Curriculum Construction: reflections on a workshop'.

M. Stacey and C.W. Aakster were among the first to explore the area of constructing educational objectives for training programs in medical sociology. The question of which subjects, skills and attitudes are desirable for incorporation into the medical sociology training process is dealt with by Stacey for sociology training and by Aakster for medical training.

Stacey presents a detailed description of her training program, specifying educational objectives. Sociology of medicine should be taught to sociology students because the institution of health care is such a central part of society that one can no longer pretend to understand modern social relations with medicine. 'No sociology department can really consider it is teaching sociology in the round if ignores the sociology of medicine'. One of the objectives to training medical sociology students to become sociologists is to make them observers of the health care system in which they are also participiants. The detachment thus developed by students conflicts some what with their need for commitment. The question of how to resolve this conflict is the question of the sociologist's role in society.

Aakster starts from the assumption that teaching medical sociology in medical training can yield results only if the intended objectives are incorporated as integral parts of the medical schools' training objectives. According to his system-theoretical description of medical schools, the latter are complex transformation systems in which objectives should be continually formulated keeping pace with the developments in this system and its socio-cultural environment. Aakster's suggestions for a reformed medical training are themselves an intervention in the transformation system of medical schools: the medical schools should be organized not along the line of the different medical specialisms (exemplified in the present department structure), but rather in view of the problem areas of health, illness and care. All health care services in the geographical area surrounding the medical schools should be made academic, i.e., provide some part of medical training.

8. Medical sociology training for sociologists

M. Stacey

8.1. Introduction

In this paper I propose to try to answer the questions: (a) why teach the sociology of medicine to sociology students?, and (b) how to do it and what are the problems? This paper is an extension and development of one which I submitted to a conference in Warsaw not too long ago (Stacey, 1973.) It reflects knowledge gained in those years from experience with the teaching of the sociology of medicine to sociology students in two different institutions; it reflects developments and maturation in the sociology of medicine itself and my own more mature understanding of the nature of sociology in general and the sub-discipline in particular.

8.1.1. Definition of the subject and the students

I shall start by reiterating some of the points from that earlier paper which are still relevant, for not everyone may be familiar with it. There I pointed out that I was a general sociologist of long standing who stumbled into the sociology of medicine from a consideration of a particular problem to do with the hospitalization of children (Stacey, Pill, Dearden, Robinson, 1970). When I speak of sociology students, I am referring to those who study social relations, social institutions, social interactions, social structure and culture. I am excluding those whose prime area of study is social administration or social policy or who are training to be social workers. The students I have in mind may go on later to train in these or other areas, but at present they are simply equipping themselves as sociologists, as students of society. For them, therefore, the sociology of medicine represents one specialism among many which they may study, others being, for example, the sociology of education, of industry, of the family, of social stratification, alongside sociological theory and methodology. When I speak of the sociology of medicine I also distinguish this subject from social medicine which I take to be a branch of medicine concerned with certain social aspects of health and illness. The sociology of medicine I take to be that discipline which looks upon medicine as a social institution. In saying 'medicine' here I wish to include the whole cluster of beliefs and practices associated with the ways in which a society deals with health and illness. I would, therefore, include not only the activities of doctors, but of all health care professionals and workers, and would also want to include alternative healing systems.

8.1.2. Its teaching in the U.K.

The number of scholars studying the sociology of medicine has grown considerably and the amount and sophistication of their scholarship has increased. In Britain, the Medical Sociology Section of the British Sociological Association is at present the largest and the most flourishing. In 1976, the entire Annual Conference of the Association was devoted to the sociology of health and illness and attraced a large audience. Nevertheless, the sociology of medicine is still relatively rarely taught to undergraduates, although it is spreading. In the United Kingdom there were three departments teaching it in 1973; there are now at least ten and it is also taught in a number of polytechnics. There is, however, a lack of textbooks on the sociology of medicine for sociologists, rather than medics or nurses. Richard Coe's recent book is unique among a recent spate of sociology texts and readers for practitioners (Coe, 1970; Cox and Mead, 1975; Robinson, 1973; Tuckett, 1976).

8.1.3. The sociology of medicine essential to sociology

To me, believing as I do that the way in which a society handles suffering, disease, birth and death is a crucial aspect of that society, it is strange that the sociology of medicine should have been so long neglected by sociologists. No major sociological theorist until Talcott Parsons had delved into the subject. It had been ignored by the classicists. What was the reason for this neglect, and why has it recently become more important? Social anthropologists have not neglected medicine in primitive societies to the extent that sociologists have neglected it in complex societies. Indeed, social anthropologists have recognized that the way in which a society deals with life-threatening episodes, the bodily discomforts of morbidity and the tortures of the mind, is crucial to an understanding of that society. The social anthropologist, of course, has the advantage of being a stranger in the society he is studying and of observing practices he does not believe in and services he does not intend to rely upon. He retains faith in, and uses, the services of his society of origin.

It is partly, I feel, the limitations which arise from studying a society in which one actually participates, that have led to the neglect of medicine. We all believe in the medicine of our own society. We need to believe in it the sense that we feel ourselves dependent on it. Our bellies may not contract with fear, as Anthony Forge reports his did, at the thought of the witch doctors in the next village (Forge, 1967), but they do contract with fear at the thought of offending or losing the services of our own doctors. Unlike the expatriot anthropologists, we are not in a position to draw back from our involvement, since, in studying our own society, we study a society in which we are already absorbed and in which we must stay while we learn the difficult lesson that there is nothing natural about the features we fear. Western sociologists were slow to learn this lesson. We have not seen medicine as a cultural or social institution, so much as a scientific discipline in which we believed. This scepticism and detachment is the first lesson we have to teach our sociology students.

8.1.4. Its previous neglect and the developing interest

The neglect of medicine by sociology may in part be explained culturally by the difficulty and discomfort of opening to question beliefs and practices in such profoundly emotive areas as illness and health, but the increasing interest of contemporary sociology in medicine has also to be explained. Impetus for the sociology of medicine has partly come from the doctors themselves who, increasingly recognizing the importance of sociological factors have encouraged sociological enquiry.

Rodney Coe has recently discussed what he sees as the convergence of interest between sociology and medicine with developments in each discipline leading to a mutual revival of interest and respect (Coe, 1970). Undoubtedly, the new problems posed by changed morbidity patterns, changed demographic patterns and by the limitations of the germ theory of disease and of the disease-cure model, have led practitioners of medicine to a renewed interest in the social sciences.

The interest of sociologists in the institutions of health care derive also, I believe, from the greater power which accrues to medicine today: unlike nineteenth century doctors, our contemporaries have powerful technology to aid them. They are the disbursors of the armoury of drugs provided by the pharmaceutical industry; they can command increasingly complex technologies to aid their therapies. Health care now constitutes a major industry of considerable economic and political consequence in all countries of the western world. In this industry doctors have been accorded a central place in all decision-making affecting health, a position reaffirmed in Britain in the reorganized national health service. In addition, doctors are increasingly appealed to for advice and decisions beyond the immediate areas of diagnosis and therapy to which their education and training is specifically directed. The claims made by comtemporary medicine and the status which it is today accorded, suggest to me that one can no longer pretend to understand comtemporary social relations without understanding those associated with medicine.

Part of the importance, power and potential of medicine is caused by the fact that increasingly large sections of the population have become involved in it. This has also led to an increased sociological interest. Requests have come to sociologists not only from the side of doctors and other health care workers, but also from the side of the patients. Thus, some sociologists have undertaken research flowing from their own involvement in health care and some because they have been commissioned by cause groups (e.g., Roth, 1963; Morris, 1969; Hewitt, 1970). We suggested above that the cultural involvement of sociologists in their own medical system could explain the slowness of sociologists to study the subject. It has also to be said that their involvement in a power system dominated by health care professionals is also relevant and goes some way to explain the development of sociology in medicine rather than the sociology of medicine. Herein lies the importance of teaching the sociology of medicine to sociology students and of teaching it oudside the medical school situation; that is in a situation, where the institution of medicine can be described and analyzed as just another set of social arrangements, albeit of major importance because of their central importance to the maintenance and regeneration of the society. The disadvantages of teaching outside the medical school derive from problems of access to health care situations (Coe, 1970) but these can usually be overcome.

To sum up this introduction then: my reasons for saying that the sociology of medicine should be taught to sociology students are principally that the institution of health care is so central and major a part of society that no sociology department can really consider it is teaching sociology in the round if it ignores it.

8.2. Objectives in teaching and learning

Why do undergraduate students read the sub-discipline which is usually offered as an option and is not seen as a core subject, as classical theory and methodology often are? Many read it from intrinsic interest, a fascination with the subject which they have acquired as participant observers in the health care system. They study it for enlightenment and for fun. Good reasons indeed. (I sometimes think we take much too serious and puritanical a view of our discipline.) Some read it because they have a concern to improve the world in some way and are attracted to the caring professions. Others may have an even clearer vocational interest. Some, of course, take it simply because they can't find a more congenial choice.

The question arises, therefore, of the way in which students are going to use their learning. For some it will be simply a matter of having graduated in sociology, of which the sociology of medicine is seen as a constituent part. Such students will constitute an informed and critical component among the intelligensia who are the recipients of health care and who perhaps influence policy decisions.

Some will proceed to careers where their knowledge of the health care system will be directly relevant, moving into health care research or administration or social work. The initial education, therefore, must be of a kind which will enable students to relate to the health care system as they find it, as well as having an ability to evaluate it critically. For those who are going on to research or administration, further training in the sociology of medicine will become essential, including direct experience of aspects of health care (Nuyens, 1973).

There may be some tension here in objectives between education and training. Education will lead to understanding, to criticism, to doubt. Training, on the other hand, must be based more on certainty about the correctness of procedures and clarity about role. Educational objectives are more diffuse and also more critical. In teaching the sociology of medicine to undergraduates, I believe the educational goals must be paramount, but one cannot be unmindful of the training component, for students must have a basis upon which to build their careers. At the same time, it is essential to remember that sociology can be made to serve any ends. As such, it does not give us the goal towards which the members of a society may wish to move. It is, therefore, important to convey to students that social engineering cannot be neutral. Any changes introduced into a society are likely to be more in the interests of some groups than of others.

8.3. Approaches to teaching

There are many ways in which one might set about teaching the subject. Mechanic's approach to medical sociology in his textbook is to take as his underlying assumption 'that much of human activity and the activity surrounding illness can be accounted for within a framework which views such behaviour as aspects and reactions to situations where persons are actively struggling to control their environment and life situation'. He sees behaviour of patients and practitioners in terms of the ways in which they define and respond to illness which 'can often be understood as a product of the problems they face in dealing with the social environment' (Mechanic, 1968).

Coe, on the other hand, orients his volume 'toward the contributions in the development of general sociology that can be made by studying sociological factors in a medical context'. Coe uses an interaction approach and divides his text into four parts: the first on health, illness and disease, the second on various health practices and practitioners, the third on the hospital and the fourth on medical organization and the financing of medical care. He bases his argument on what he believes to be the current convergence between sociology and medicine, rather than upon an overtly discussed model of society (Coe, 1970).

How do I set about teaching the subject and what problems have I encountered? In this period in sociology, when the 'thousand flowers' are in full bloom, one would not dare to be dogmatic. One can only say how one goes about the task and why. Yet, at the same time, the sociology of medicine offers a good opportunity for demonstrating the value and limitations of the various schools which are available for our students to choose from. Speaking personally, therefore, I start with the assumption that social institutions ('institutions' in the Ginsbergian or Parsonian sense) associated with health care are an integral part of the society in which they are found.

8.4. A main objective: to show interrelations between society and health care systems

The ways in which health care is handled both reflect and reinforce many of the central values and institutions of a society and are an integral part of its structure and culture. The way in which a society handles suffering and birth and death reflects intimately the essential values of that society and also reflects and reinforces its hierarchy of power and status, or modifies it, for the society is not static, nor are the practices of medicine. One, therefore, also needs to examine the interrelations between the society and the health care system. How are changes in the wider society affecting the health care system? What are the changes in the society to which health care practices and policies are contributing and what potential changes are being checked by these same practices?

In teaching sociology at all, a first task has to be to make students' perceptions about society overt. They must be encouraged to acquire a facility to question these assumptions about how society works and the values they have come to hold, assumptions with which they have grown up. In no other way can they learn to look at the social institutions and the social relations of their own society or other societies with anything approching the necessary detachment. In general, I would have thought that the final undergraduate year was soon enough to start teaching the sociology of medicine and by then this process of detachment should have already gone a considerable way. But beliefs and practices relating to health and illness are fundamental aspects of any society and, in addition, touch upon deeply felt matters associated with life and death. All students not only participate in these beliefs and attitudes, but have also been participants in the health care systems of their own societies, Part of their education as sociologists is to turn them into observers, as well as participators (Mills, 1959).

8.4.1. Cross-cultural study

Therefore, I start my course with a discussion of the variability of concepts of health and illness over space and time. Firstly, I introduce cross-cultural evidence which suggests that concepts of health and illness vary widely from culture to culture; that pain is felt differentially and that standards of behaviour in relation to pain are variable (e.g., Saunders, 1954; Paul, 1955; Kiev, 1955; Ablon, 1973).

At the same time, I show that resistances to change in medical practice, while they may be culturally rooted, may also be structurally based and may be not unrelated to vested interests (Lewis, 1955; Marriot, 1955; MacLean). Until they are introduced to this literature which discusses the variability of health and illness concepts and ways of handling morbidity, students are inclined to believe that illness, as taught in their families and as they have learned to experience it, is a physically objective phenomenon common to all mankind.

8.4.2. An historical approach

The next task, which helps in this detachment process, but which also lays the foundations for the understanding of contemporary western medicine, is to examine the history of concepts of health, medicine and health care organizations (clinics, practices, hospitals, professional bodies). Works as varied as Abel Smith's history of the hospitals, Glaser's *Social Settings and Medical Organizations*, and Foucault's *Birth of the Clinic* can contribute here (Smith, 1964; Foucault, 1973; Glaser, 1970). The sociology of medical knowledge, its production and reproduction can thus begin to be introduced historically and later used in an analysis of contemporary medicine, thereby contributing to the detachment which is so necessary to the student of the sociology of medicine, as well as to his understanding of what medicine is all about. [1]

8.4.3. Prevalence and incidence of disease

An area which continues to cause problems is the variability of the incidence of disease among and within populations. Clearly, a knowledge of the technicalities of the prevalence and incidence of disease, as these are understood in contemporary medicine, is necessary. Practices with regard to health and illness reflect not only the social structure and culture, but, in some sense, the illness state. At one and the same time one has to try to teach the scepticism about concepts and practices which is so essential and, at the same time, something about the senses in which there is 'really' suffering and how this is perceived to vary. A weakness in the theoretical approach and its relation to empirical data seems to make this knowledge quite difficult to integrate. Those works which deal well with this, such as that of Coe, do not deal adequately with the sociology of medical knowledge (Coe, 1970). I rate highly the work of Geo. Brown as an example of a study which links detailed statistical data with a structural approach to

1. It is interesting that a major contribution at the British Sociological Association Annual Conference was on the production and reproduction of medical knowledge, as will be reflected in the forthcoming volume. *Health Care and Health Knowledge,* Robert Dingwall, Christian Heath, Margaret Reid & Margaret Stacey (Ed.), Croom Helm.

sociology and to a recognition of suffering (Brown, Bhrolchain, Harris, 1975).

8.4.4. Knowledge of medicine

There are problems too about how much knowledge of medicine it might be thought necessary for a student of the sociology of medicine to acquire. At the undergraduate level this would not be much, I think. Familiarity with what health care practitioners are saying in certain areas of social concern may be as close as we can judge at this stage. In postgraduate work, on the other hand, greater familiarity with the medical topic area relevant to the subject of study may well become necessary.

8.5. General approach

Having completed the fundamental work on cross-cultural data, historical data and the minimum essentials of social medicine, the time is ripe to analyze contemporary western medicine. Here it is necessary to explain a little of my general sociological approach and what I consider to be important in society at large.

In sociological analysis I use a concept of structure which bears some relationship to a functionalist model, but perhaps more to a Marxist one. Any society I see as structured in the sense that members occupy positions of greater or less advantage, domination or subordination. Indeed, every member occupies several positions (statuses) which may well tend to cluster on a number of dimensions. How much this occurs affects greatly the overall characteristics of the society in question. Individuals in similar positions tend to form groups for common action, at the same time as some individuals may organize others in an exploitative relationship. I would not accept the functionalist notion of the 'needs of society', but rather see individuals or groups of members acting in their interests (which may include altruistic concerns). These interests may, of course, conflict and I, therefore, assume that some conflict is inevitable in society.

But my approach is also interactional, for I see this apparent structure emerging from constant interactions and negotiations and constantly changing. These interactions and negotiations take place within constraints as far as any one set of members is concerned. It is as if all negotiations took place within the constraints provided by negotiations which have already taken place elsewhere.

8.5.1. Major structural divisions

Among these constraints may be numbered those which are provided by the great divisions within contemporary western society: namely, the divisions based upon class and those based upon sex and gender. Therefore, in discussion of the health care system with students, I am concerned to examine how that system reflects, maintains or modifies those divisions. Thus, the division of labour in health care reflects the division of labour in society at large, recruitment to the medical profession in the west being remarkably classbased and male-dominated. Sources of and resistances to change in this pattern must be examined. The recent uprising of manual workers in hospitals in Britain and America is important in this regard.

8.5.1.1. Social class

Professions and occupations are, therefore, studied in their relation to the class system. The system of gender roles is also important and is also reflected in the division of labour. This can be looked at historically, as well as contemporarily, the supercession of wise women by male professionals being a focal point of the historical discussion (Ehrenreich, English, 1974).

8.5.1.2. Gender roles

The importance of gender roles can also be seen in differential illness patterns and treatment of men and women patients. Biologically – based sex differences must here be disentangled from socially – based differences associated with gender role. A particularly interesting example which can be examined in some detail is changing obstetric practice. This is a nice example which not only illustrates male-female relations in the wider society as reflected in medicine (both in the imposition of procedures upon women by male practitioners and also the consequent women's protest), but also doctor-patient relations and the place of technology in medicine.

It is characteristic of modern advanced industrial society that it is heavily reliant upon high technology medicine and the value of technology is tacitly assumed and symbolically reinforced from childbirth onwards, although the rational grounds for its use are not always as clear as its advocates assume (Cochrane, 1972; Chalmers, 1975).

In persuading women to accept high technology childbirth in the hospital location, doctors may be said to be reinforcing the values of a society which involve male domination and the crucial importance of technology. What it is they are doing when, as is happening in some parts of the United Kingdom, they recommend and practise the sterilization of women after their second child is more problematic. The implications are profound, not only for population, but for the institution of the family and the status of women. This constitutes an example of the ways in which doctors by their individual practice may be occasioning profound social and cultural changes.

8.5.2. The status of the patient

The status of the patient has been referred to in the context of obstetrics and gynaecology. This whole discussion has to take a place in its own right, for the patient must be included in the division of labour in the health service. The patient is an active participant in the production and maintenance of health. Yet, so often he/she is seen as a passive recipient. How and why this should be is an interesting sociological question and one which is only partly associated with the dependent status of the patient as an ill person and more associated with the dependent status of the patient as an ill person and more associated with imperatives of the health care professional's work situation. The discussion revolves around the conflict between the patient as work object and service object of the professionals. The whole question raises issues of domination, subordination and reciprocity central to sociology.

8.5.3. Cure and care

The problems that are associated with care where cure is not possible must be spelled out to students and the limitations of the disease-cure model enunciated. The low status accorded to these services can easily be illuminated by an understanding of the relationship of cure to the socio-economic system. Those who can contribute are valued. Those who cannot are at the 'bottom of the heap', be they mentally handicapped or geriatric. How else can we explain the relatively limited resources accorded to these groups? Can this be rectified within competitive economic systems? Indeed, what social circumstances would be necessary to accord high status and fair economic shares to the permanently non-productive?

8.5.3.1. The hospital

An analysis of the hospital as a social organization must clearly occupy a central position in any course, both the organization of the hospital as a whole and of the ward. Attention can be drawn to the various sociological approaches that have been used in the study of the hospital, from the Weberian to the phenomenological (e.g., Cartwright, 1964; Caudill, 1958; Davis, 1963; Roth, 1963; Goffman, 1961; Revans, 1971; Rosengren and Lefton, 1969; Straus et al, 1964; Freidson, 1963).

8.5.3.2. Macro and micro

One of the things which it is essential to do in sociology is to relate studies which deal with interactions on a small scale with studies of the larger society. It is clear that the larger society is only sustained by myriads of interpersonal interactions. The sociology of medicine should be a fruitful field for helping the student come to terms with these problems given the varied styles with which sociologists of medicine have approached their subject and the need to take account of interactionist as well as structuralist data. Perhaps it is in the study of the hospital that these relationships between approaches can best be seen.

8.5.3.3. Health care organization

As much as the organization of the hospital, so the organization of health care itself is important and treated as a central concern. Problems of financing and control, and, in the British situation, the contrast between the welfare, collectivist basis of the national health service and the oligopolistic, profit-making organization of the pharmaceutical industry is of particular interest. Here again is a specific example of a problem which is of central concern to mainstream sociology, issues of power, authority and control in economic and social organization.

8.5.4. Social order

There is a major problem in thinking and teaching about how to treat the institutions of medicine in relation to social order. As Ann Murcott has pointed out, Parsons' contribution has been taken up in a somewhat limited way with the emphasis being placed on the sick role and illness behaviour. Parsons' stress in Chapter Ten of *The Social System* was upon the importance and necessity of medical institutions for the maintenance of social order and the threat to that order which illness posed (Murcott, 1976).

Zola has drawn attention to another facet of the problem when he talks about medicine as an instrument of social control (Zola, 1975). What remains unclear in these so different accounts is what it is that is being controlled and on whose behalf? As Murcott suggests, an emphasis on collective medicine rather than individualized personal medicine is what flows logically from Parsons' functionalist account – a lesson which has only been taken in the west in war time. Zola seems to be complaining simply that the medicalization of morality is a threat to individual liberty.

8.6. Sociology and its application: detachment and environment   involvement

And here in these considerations some of the problems of teaching the applications of the sociology of medicine begin to emerge. I have spoken earlier about the question of teaching the students to be able to be sufficiently detached to perceive medicine sociologically. But there is also the question of involvement. Nuyens, following Sokolowska, talks in his Warsaw paper of the importance of social engineering (Nuyens, 1973). On whose behalf? In whose interest? What is the sociologist to see as his/her role? 'Engineering' cannot be neutral. Over the years I have been involved with various aspects of the running of the British health service. My involvement has not been neutral. It has been informed by my sociology, but has been directed to what I believed to be the best interests of patients or particular categories of patients. Surely, sociology students must be sufficiently sophisticated to see the partiality of any work involving social change which they undertake. An undergraduate training which would paralyze action or restrict it to particular sectors would deny health services valuable potential workers. How can this problem be resolved? Or is it again one that should be tackled at the postgraduate level? It touches the heart of the role of sociology and sociologists in society.

8.6.1. The meaning of health care practice

One of my unresolved problems is how to convey to the students some qualitative dimension of what it is to work in health care. All have some notion of what it is to be a patient: how does one convey the combinations of boredom, anxiety and frustration (of routinization and concurrent uncertainty) which may be involved in health care? How does one convey the meaning that the situations have for the participants? Phenomenological studies can help here. But there are not enough of these, nor do they cover a wide enough area.

Involvement in health care would seem to be one answer. Visits of observation seem too superficial and there are objections to intruding into the life of patients and staff. Occasionally, vacation work provides an answer, sometimes there is an ex-nurse or physiotherapist in the class. Visits from practitioners for discussion sessions can help. But a dimension seems to be missing. It is a dimension which seems particularly important for those who are going to work in health care or to do research on the sociology of medicine. Perhaps it is a dimension that can only be filled in at the postgraduate stage where, as Nuyens has pointed out, placements or attachments are important (Nuyens, 1973).

8.6.2. The problem of suffering

This problem may be close to another which I also feel is unresolved. It is the question of suffering. Medicine itself has ducked the issue of suffering to some extent by the adoption of the disease model. Its task is to identify disease and to cure disease. But the alleviation of suffering is what health care systems are all about. Sociology is poor at handling the feeling dimension. Sociological concepts are in their own way as abstract as medical concepts. Yet, much of what some sociologists are concerned about is the unintentional infliction of unnecessary suffering upon patients, or the failure to recognize and alleviate suffering (as, for example, in the work we have done on the unintended consequences of the hospitalization of children (Stacey, Pill, Dearden, Robinson, 1970). There is no doubt that students have feelings about what they learn in the sociology of medicine. How should these be dealt with? The work of Miller and Gwynne, *A Life Apart*, which deals with the young chronic sick in long term care, deals with this problem perhaps better than most sociological work (Miller, Gwynne, 1972).

An incident at the recent British Sociological Association Conference, when sociologists offended nurses and other professionals by laughing at certain passages in Wiseman's film, *The Hospital*, illustrates the point well. The nurses, as part of their socialization in the course of professional training, had learned methods for dealing with the combination of human tragedy, inadequacy and frustration portrayed by the film. These methods involved notions of proper behaviour and involved blocking certain emotions. The sociologists had not undergone this socialization and relieved their feelings by tragic-laughter (to their own bemusement sometimes). The nurses (who were also trained sociologists) were offended and upset by this reaction. Later discussion only partially eased the ensuing misunderstanding. In future, I propose to try and use film to see if in this way one can convey a further dimension of feeling and meaning to undergraduates, which is not conveyed by 'straight' sociological lecturing, seminars and reading.

8.6.3. Critics rather than sociologists

Although I see the analysis through which I take my students as one in which I try to look at health care as a social institution, there is no doubt that, judging from the work they submit for assessment, both essays and examinations, that I succeed better in teaching them to be critics of the contemporary health care system than in teaching them to be sociologists of it. This, must partly be a result of the absence of a satisfactory overarching theory which they can readily apply to all aspects of the service. But this would be a better explanation of a failure of their sociology to be consistent from one substantive area to another. Perhaps the problem arises partly from the enormity and complexity of seeing institutions associated with health and illness as part of the macro society. The problem may also arise because of a tendency for mainstream sociology still to regard the sociology of medicine as peripheral to, rather than integral in its concerns. The problem also has something to do with the lack of connection between some sociology in medicine and mainstream sociology.

8.7. Sociologists and workers

In teaching the sociology of medicine to sociology students, then, one has two main objectives: one is to educate them to be good general sociologists; the second is to prepare them for a life's work, to lay the foundations for their later training for specific occupations. In their general education it is important that students should learn, as I have argued, that any work involving the maintenance or the change of the social system is likely to be partial, to work to the advantage of one group rather than another. In becoming trained as sociologists of medicine, students may thinkingly or unthinkingly join the ranks of the elite who manipulate the majority of society, unless they learn to bear in mind and remain in constant touch with the patients and the public for whom health care systems exist. Herein lies a problem in the determination of our training objectives: it seems unlikely that there is one ideal model training programme because the tasks wich sociologists will do and for whom they do them will be so various.

Sociology has no way of showing what is the best way of organizing society and health care within it, although sociology can certainly help to inform the moral decisions by laying bare what is involved. Only when the goals have been decided on a moral basis can the sociologist help. It has to be part of our educational objectives to teach sociology students to understand this.

In conclusion, then, our educational objective should be to give students a critical and rounded understanding of their society and health care within it, so that they may not only understand the way the society works, but also grasp the implications for social maintenance or social change which their actions as trained personnel will have.

References

Ablon, Joan, 1973, 'Reactions of Samoan Burns Patients and Their Families to Severe Burns', *Social Science and Medicine,* vol. 7, pp. 167-178.

Brown, George W., 1975, Maire N. Bhrolchain and Tirril Harris 'Social Class and Psychiatric Disturbance Among Women in an Urban Population', *Sociology,* 9, 2, May 1975, pp. 225-254.

Cartwright, A., 1964, *Human Relations & Hospital Care,* Routledge and Kegan Paul.

Caudill, W., 1958, *The Psychiatric Hospital as a Small Society,* Harvard University Press.

Chalmers, Iain, 1975, Description and Evaluation of Different Approaches to the Management of Pregnancy and Labour in Cardiff 1965-1973. M. Sc. Thesis University of London.

Cochrane, A., 1972, *Effectiveness and Efficiency: Random Reflections on Health Services,* Oxford University Press for the Nuffield Provincial Hospitals Trust, London.

Coe, Rodney M., 1970, *Sociology of Medicine,* McGraw Hill.

Cox, C. and A. Mead, (Eds.), 1975, *A Sociology of Medical Practice,* Collier-MacMillan, London.

Dingwall, Robert and Christian Heath, Margaret Reid, Margaret Stacey, (Eds.) (forthcoming), *Health Care and Health Knowledge,* Croom Helm.

Davis, F., 1963, *Passage Through Crisis,* Bobbs Merrill.

Ehrenreich, B. and D. English, 1974, *Witches, Midwives and Nurses: A History of Women Healers,* Compendium.

Forge, Anthony, 1967, 'The Lonely Anthropologist', *New Society,* 17-8-67.

Foucault, M., 1973, *The Birth of the Clinic,* Tavistock.

Freidson, E., 1963, *The Hospital in Modern Society,* Free Press.

Goffman, E., 1961, *Asylums,* Doubleday.

Glaser, W., 1970, *Social Settings and Medical Organization,* Atherton.

Hewitt, Sheila, 1970, *The Family and the Handicapped Child,* Allen and Unwin.

Kiev, A., 1964, *Magic, Faith and Healing,* Free Press.

Lewis, Oscar, 1965, 'Medicine and Politics in a Mexican Village', in B. D. Paul, Health, Culture and Community.

MacLean, M. Una, 'Traditional Healers and Their Female Clients. Aspects of Nigerian Sickness Behaviour', *Journal of Health and Social Behaviour*, 10, pp. 172-186.

Marriott, McKim, 1965, 'Western Medicine in a Village in North India', in B.D. Paul, *Health, Culture and Community*.

Mechanic, D., 1968, *Medical Sociology: A Selective View*, Free Press, pp. 86-7.

Miller, E.J., and G.V. Gwynne, *A Life Apart*, Tavistock, 1972.

Mills, C. Wright, 1959, *The Sociological Imagination*, Oxford University Press, New York.

Morris, Pauline, 1969, *Put Away*, Routledge and Kegan Paul.

Murcott, Ann, 1976, 'Blind Alleys and Blinkers', paper presented to the British Sociological Association Conference, Cardiff mimeo.

Nuyens Yvo, 1973, 'Teaching Medical Sociology to Graduate Students in Sociology', paper given at Warsaw Conference, August, 1973.

Paul, B.D., 1955, *Health, Culture and Community*, Russell Sage.

Revans, R., 1971, *Hospitals Communication Choice and Change*, Tavistock.

Robinson, D., 1973, *Patients, Practitioners and Medical Care*, Heinemann.

Rosengren, W.R., and M. Lefton, 1969, *Hospitals and Patients*, Atherton.

Roth, Julius, 1963, *Timetables*, Bobbs Merrill.

Saunders, L., 1954, *Cultural Differences in Medical Care*, Russell Sage.

Smith, B. Abel, 1964, *The Hospitals, 1800-1948*, Heinemann, London,

Stacey, M., 1973, 'Teaching Medical Sociology to Sociology Students: A British View', paper given to International Conderence of Medical Sociology, Warsaw, August, 1973.

Stacey, M., R. Pill, R. Dearden and D. Robinson, 1970, *Hospitals, Children and Their Families*, Routledge and Kegan Paul.

Straus, A., et al, 1964, *Psychiatric Ideologies and Institutions*, Free Press, N.Y.

Tuckett, David, (Ed.) 1976, *An Introduction to Medical Sociology*, Tavistock.

Zobrowski, M., n.d., 'Cultural Components in Response to Pain', in Folta and Deck.

Zola, I., 1975, 'Medicine as an Institution of Social Control', reprinted in Cox and Mead, *A Sociology of Medical Practice*.

9. Medical sociology training for medical doctors

C.W. Aakster

9.1. Introductory remarks

From the title that the organizing committee of this Seminar choose for my presentation (educational objectives in medical schools), it is not clear whether the emphasis should be on educational objectives of medical schools as a whole, or on educational objectives of sociology-teaching within medical schools. But far from feeling unhappy about this seemingly ambiguous instruction, I am inclined to say that the committe should be praised for its wisdom. For we may safely assume that they themselves realize that teaching medical sociology to future physicians can only aspire to attain its goals if the sociological objectives are subsumed to and form an integral part of the educational objectives of medical schools in general. And this is exactly the stand that I shall take too.

9.2. Goals as dominant options

Before going into these objectives and goals as such, I should like to comment briefly on the social process by which objectives come to be accepted. My basic views in this respect may be summarized in the following statements. The objectives of any socio-cultural system should be seen as the outcome of a continuous interaction-process among individuals and subgroups within as well as without this system. The specific objectives that the system finally selects as its own, will be the objectives, interpretations, or options, of those individuals and subgroups that are highest in power and prestige within the system under consideration. In other words, objectives are not static descriptions of future desirable states, but they reflect power relations and value-patterns of the dominant subgroups. It follows that the formulation of objectives and the selection of dominant options in particular, is a continuous process, which parallels – be it at times with considerable delay– developments within medical schools and their sociocultural environment.

A second aspect of my approach to complex systems – and the traditional medical school in the Netherlands provides an excellent example of such a system – is that the subgroups and individuals which constitute the system and especially the way they are related to each other, should be considered, together with the technical base of the system as a transformationsystem. I would suggest that the too static term 'social structure' be replaced by 'transformation-system'. A medical school then becomes analyzable as a dynamic interaction-process in which inputs such as adolescents with loose motivations of becoming doctors, money, teachers etc., are transformed into outputs such as experts who are legitimately entitled to cure people of their ills, scientific publications, medical innovation etc.

It follows that not only the dominant options within medical schools, but also the allocation of money, of curriculum-hours, of recognition and acceptance, and of personnel, is the outcome of interaction-processes and thus of the existing influence and prestige-structure within as well as without medical schools. I believe that approaching medical objectives from this perspective, provides us with a more realistic view of the subject of our discussion, and especially of the present and not too successful struggle of the social sciences to gain acceptance of their options within medical educational systems.

9.3. The newly (re-)formulated objectives of medical schools in the Netherlands

As a next step I will discuss briefly the objectives that have been formulated and accepted as guidelines by the majority of medical faculties in the Netherlands (Raamplan, 1974).

The *first* of these five general objectives states that the physician should have at his disposal the knowledge, skills and attitudes, necessary for starting a professional career in medicine. The emphasis is on the word 'starting'.

The *second* objective is on the level of attitudes. It says that the physician should be sensitive, as far as his own responsibilities and limitations are concerned, to persons with whom he comes into contact during practice, to the society within which he functions as a physician, and to the sciences upon which his expertness has been based.

The *third* objective formulates necessary skills of the basic physician. They concern diagnosis, therapy, prevention, referral, cooperation with other health workers, judging own abilities and limitations, and the handling of relevant information from literature and other important sources.

The *fourth* objective concentrates on knowledge aspects. Main topics are knowledge of diseases, of symptomatology and diagnostics, of therapy and prognostics, of ecology, epidemiology and preventive medicine, of the health care system, and of their scientific backgrounds and methods.

The *fifth* and last objective is also a knowledge objective, but it concentrates on basic insights into normal somatic, psychic and social structures and functions of the human individual, their variability under changing situational conditions, causes and mechanisms of disturbances of this normal functioning, and of their scientific backgrounds.

These formulations are intentionally rather vague and general because it was realized that the same end-states can be reached along different lines. Each medical school should choose its idiosyncratic specifications and realizations of these general objectives. They differ in the following respects from earlier formulations: the addition of social skills, of attitudinal objectives, of knowledge of normal social and emotional functioning of the individual, of society generated disturbances, and of knowledge of the health care system as such. It is easy to see that these additions mainly stem from the area that is covered by the social disciplines including social medicine and epidemiology. In other words, the reformulation of objectives of medical schools, may be interpreted as an attempt of Dutch medical schools to socialize themselves, to restore the balance between form and content of medical education and societal resources and needs.

Personally I am completely satisfied with these objectives. I think that if physicians were to fulfil all of these requiremants – at least in the way I tend to interpret them –they would be able to respond adequately to societal health needs. The emphasis is, however, on the term 'if'. *If* medical students do fulfil all of these requirements they shall become good physicians, I assume. But *shall* they fulfil these requirements? To answer this question we will have to analyze the present situation and structure of medical schools a little deeper. In order to do so, I shall use the medical faculty of Leiden, where I have been working for about ten years, as my special frame of reference though many of the observations to be made, could apply equally well to other medical faculties in the Netherlands, as well as to those in other countries.

9.4. The relevant environments of medical schools

The next step in our analysis is to indicate some of the environmental conditions and their sources that set limits on the freedom of medical schools to select certain policies and activities at the expense of others.

A *first* source of environmental conditions is the national administration. It is relevant in at least three respects: providing funds, prescribing the number of students that are to be admitted, and structuring the educational process as such by formulating formal requirements concerning the content and duration of the medical study. It has been the policy of recent governments to slow down the growth rate of universities, by regulating the number of students, tightening the formal curricula, and limiting financial resources. This to very compact educational programs – especially in medicine – standardized for large numbers of students, with formal and distant teacher-student contacts.

A *second* environmental conditioning source is the university itself. The university was given the task of indicating priorities in allocating seriously reduced budgets fairly, to increasingly demanding sub-units (the faculties). At the same time funds had to be reserved for the erection of a body for the regulation and control, of this allocation of finance. As a practical consequence a formal contract was signed between university and medical faculty in which it was stipulated in detail how many physicians the medical faculty was to deliver within a fixed period of time in exchange for a certain amount of money. In order to attain a more acceptable student-teacher ratio however, the medical faculty had to surrender about ten percent of its formal positions for scientific, technical and administrative personnel.

Another consequence was that at a lower level of administration, the same procedure had to be repeated. The medical faculty's administration had to regulate and control the distribution of resources while the 32 departments of the medical faculty became competitors for the best share of these resources. The distribution of these limited resources was to be based mainly on the present number of curriculum hours which clearly favors the status quo. I will return to this aspect later on.

A *third* environmental condition stems from the Dutch health system in general. We mention the following features and their consequences for medical schools:

- a multitude of relatively autonomous health institutions and professionals; only a small proportion participates in the teaching of future physicians. This has at least two consequences: the morbiditypattern with which the medical student is confronted during his training is not representative of that for the total population, and: his teachers work within a sort of 'enclave' within the total health field.
- outside medical faculties, the salaries that may be earned by physicians are often considerably higher than within them, which does not guarantee that the most qualified physicians and teachers will remain within the educational system.
- an insurance system that favours curative intramural medicine by means of smooth retributions of treatment expenses, at the same time being hesitant in covering preventive measures
- an almost complete lack of feedback-mechanisms that relate effects of medical interventions to quality standards, manifest demands and health needs. This prevents a close and easy correspondence between curriculum content and actual health practice and health needs.

Other environmental conditions could have been mentioned, such as public opinion, the pharmaceutical and other industries, other health and welfare professions and agencies, patient organizations etc. but it will be clear that the environment may and usually does exert considerable influence upon goal formulations or interpretations, and upon their realization in terms of the allocation of sufficient resources.

9.5. The transformation system of medical schools

I will continue now with a short discussion of the transformation system of medical faculties in the Netherlands, excluding our newest faculty at Maastricht, which is quite a different story (see the contribution by Philipsen). Some of its striking features are the following:

I. A medical faculty is composed of many departments, about thirty-two in Leiden. Each department concentrates, so to speak, on a different part of the human individual with one or more professors at its head. The departments are not formally related to each other and may vary considerably in size, prestige, student-load, scientific climate or patient-orientation etc.

II. Since a new law was passed by the Dutch parliament prescribing some type of democratic participation and decision-making at the university, most medical schools have set up a sort of parliament, the so-called faculty-council. The prime responsibility for the realization of educational objectives and the approval of research programs, lies with these faculty-councils. They have, however, a few inherent problems. 1) the academic staff must always occupy at least half of the seats in these councils. 2) two features of the system are in-compatable; on the one hand, the individual council-member is encouraged to speak out openly, but on the other hand, in view of the formal assessments by superiors required to pass examinations, or to be promoted to higher positions, it does not always help to speak out openly... 3) the faculty council lacks – generally speaking – the means to enforce the execution of decisions that have been taken. This situation is gradually changing, thanks to the governmental policy of cutting the university budgets. The faculty-administration has been forced to formulate priorities, to withhold resources (for example for personnel) from the one department and 'inject' them into others. This takes us to a third aspect of the transformation system of medical faculties.

III. Each department specializes, more or less, in its own aspect of the human individual: his blood system, his brains, his extremities, his eyes or his genitals. In other words: each department has its own domain; there is a balance of claims to domains. Each department also has its own curriculum hours; sharing of curriculum hours is almost non-existent. It follows that the curriculum is discipline-oriented, not problem-oriented. The curriculum-hours are neatly distributed over the departments. The way they are distributed is the result of historical developments which will never end. Up till now we have observed a constant reshuffling of curriculum-hours as they were claimed by the different departments and the (sub-)disciplines within them. As long as there were no limitations on the duration of the study, or on the amount of money available, new claims could be honored by the creation of new departments, by the addition of more curriculum hours, by attracting new personnel; in other words, without upsetting the existing fragile but neat balance among the established departments. But, conditions have changed. In the last few years the curriculum has become so much more compact that any newcomer to the disciplines is considered with utmost suspicion. His claims not only threaten the neatly balanced division of curriculum hours as such, they also threaten the position as a whole of other departments: to realize his claims would imply that his share of the money-pie would increase at the expense of the share of others.

IV. Each socio-cultural system also has its own value-pattern. That is why we prefer the term 'socio-cultural system' to that of 'social system'. We assume that each socio-cultural system has more than just one such pattern, and that there will be one that will be especially dominating, this usually being the value-pattern of the most influential sub-group of this system. I do not want to suggest that each member of this dominant subgroup adheres equally to these dominant values, but they do seem to guide official decisions. Considering the dominant values within presentday medical schools, we notice that the emphasis is on quite different values from those that are advocated by social scientists. Medical schools adhere to individual treatment, technical and pharmaceutical interventions, physician-leadership, isolation of mind, body and society, and a morphological interpretation of disease. Social scientists usually take as their starting point whole-person conceptions, patient-participation, integrated treatment and so on. There is a danger of stereotyping however.

V. Medical schools are multi-level systems. The objectives of medical schools were formulated by a national committee consisting of representatives from seven medical faculties which existed at that moment. This is the first level. The second level is that of the separate medical faculties. Then we seen a differentiation: level 3A is that of four or five curriculum-commissions who are responsible for the organization and evaluation of a defined phase of the curriculum, for example the first propedeutic year of study. Level 3B is that of the separate thirty-two departments. Within these departments exist differentiations according to disciplines and year of the curriculum within which a given discipline or subject should be treated. The lowest (let us say the fourth) level of the educational system, is the level of the actual teaching process. It is my assumption that on each level of specification of general objectives, part of it fades away. The more the objectives are specified, in other words the closer we get to the lowest, actual teaching level, the stronger the tendency is to take into account perceptions of the taxability of the system of available resources of the individual preferences of teachers etc. In other words: in each step of specification, some of the newness of the general objectives, will be lost, so that at the lowest level of actual teaching, these new objectives are hardly recognizable. Objectives fade away like leaves in the autumn wind...

Clearly there are other important features of medical faculties that might have been mentioned, but this will suffice to present a picture of medical faculties as continuously changing, interacting complexities in which decisions and policies are very much dependent upon the mutual positions of departments within the existing balances of power and prestige. I will now attempt to formulate my ideas concerning the realization of the reformulated objectives of medical schools (as described in section 3 above), in particular of the objectives of the social disciplines within these schools.

9.6. The realization of social disciplines-based objectives in medical educational systems

The main problem with educational objectives is not their formulation and official acceptance, at least not on an abstract, general level, but in their application and realization on the level of actual teaching practice. Our analysis indicated the following problem areas:

- diminishing inputs, especially of money and personnel, with at the same time an increased student-load.
- the predominant position of curative intra-mural medicine within the health care system, with two important consequences: a non-representative morbididy- pattern in teaching institutions and an isolated position for teachers away from other health workers.
- a loosely integrated, highly differentiated structure of medical faculties, which does not stimulate cooperative, integrated and problem-oriented teaching.
- a scarce market-situation as far as the creation of new or the redistribution of existing curriculum hours is concerned, coupled to the underlying problem of resource-distribution
- conflicting value-patterns coupled to positions of higher or lower prestige and influence among departments and disciplines
- the fading-away of the newness of objectives at each further step in the specification process within a multi-level system like a medical faculty.

The question whether the newly reformulated objectives of medical schools in the Netherlands will be realized, should be projected against this background. Personally I am not optimistic about its chances for realization. This becomes clearer if we consider the present position of social disciplines within medical faculties. We notice three important features: 1) most medical schools have not yet established formal positions comparable to those of the natural and clinical sciences, for medical sociologists. 2) the number of regular curriculum-hours for social discipline teaching is usually very small and may not exceed 5 percent of available time in the clinical phase of the medical study. 3) the size of social discipline staff lags far behind that of other basic departments. In addition, communication among sociologists and clinicians remains at a rather low level, integrated teaching and research projects are almost non-existent and the clinic is hesistant about allowing the medical sociologist to 'stick his nose into *their* affairs'. Quite often the medical sociologist is criticized for his jargon, for his seemingly leftist orientation, and for his lack of insight into the practical problems of diagnosis and therapy. Indeed we may say that the introduction of medical sociology and medical psychology into medical schools, will not leave these schools unaffected. It is the task of medical sociology to study docters, medicine as a scientific system, doctor-patient relationships, and the effectiveness of health care systems, within a broader context. Medical sociology is not the descriptive study of diagnosis and treatment as such, which would be a purely medical affair, but its task is to analyze diagnosis and therapy (to mention just two arbitrarily chosen examples) as social processes. As medical sociologists we are interested in questions such as who diagnoses and cures whom for which reasons and with which effects? What does this mean to society and to the person and his social surrounding? Which structural variables and societal developments are at stake? Almost by definition he takes a critical stand, which by no means implies that the medical sociologist is of necessity negative or even destructive.

Let us return to our main topic. Taking the foregoing arguments into account, we conclude that the present condition of most medical faculties in the Netherlands is not conducive to attaining the recently reformulated official objectives. This is in the first place, because the new objectives will, in the course of their specification, be 'adjusted' to the established system and its corresponding balance of resource-distribution and in the second place because this distribution of resources is coupled to the existing balances of power and prestige, within which the social disciplines occupy only minor positions. These two aspects are, of course, interdependent, and therefore re-inforce each other.

To augment the changes for the realization of the reformulated objectives would require fundamental new structures as well. New objectives require new structures. Our final section will deal with this aspect.

9.7. Suggestions for a new education of doctors

Though the problem of selecting an optimal strategy for realizing a newer medical education is far too complex to be included in this presentation, I will put forward a few suggestions in order to stimulate thinking about this problem. These suggestions concern another transformation-system within medical schools, and the integration of medical schools into the health system as a whole.

In the *first* place I would suggest that the organization of medical schools should no longer be based upon disciplines which reflect differential interests in the body-system, but upon problem areas in relation to health, illness and care. This would involve a merging of basic and clinical disciplines and the formation of multidisciplinary research and educational teams.

In the *second* place all health institutions within a given area should be integrated into one inter-organizational network, within which each institution should accept responsibility for a certain part of the training of future physicians. The medical faculty should serve, in that case, as a sort of umbrella with prime responsibility for the quality of the teaching. In such a situation there would no longer be just one academic hospital, but all regional health institutions would be academic. The advantages would be that the morbidity pattern with which the future physician is confronted becomes more representative ; that the medical student comes into closer and earlier contact with patients and their social settings ; that the quality of health care in peripheral institutions may improve ; and that there will be a more direct and personal supervision of students by the teacher-practitioner.

In the *third* place, and this is especially relevant, as long as the two precedings suggestions have not been realized, the position of social disciplines in medicine, (encompassing not only sociology and psychology but social medicine and epidemiology as well) should receive special support – if not from the faculties then from national or local governments – in order to bridge at least partly the scientific gap between it and other basic departments within medical faculties.

* Due to the predominantly descriptive nature of Sand's contribution concerning the innovating elements in the Brussels medical training (which, though important, remain limited to didactical aspects of training), the text of his paper was not included in this publication.

PART FIVE

DESCRIPTION OF DIDACTICAL SITUATIONS

Teaching methods of, and practical training in medical sociology were discussed on a concrete level, i.e., from the basis of experience, by M. Jefferys for the medical sociology training of Bedford College, University of London, and by H. Philipsen and E. Sand for, respectively, the medical training at the Medical School of Maastricht and the Free University of Brussels.

Jefferys illustrates, in her description of the way in which selection and evaluation take place at Bedford College, the inevitability of subjective judgment in these matters. First, there is psychological inevitability – in trying to achieve their aims, or in other words, in trying to be role models, teachers implicity want to produce people in their own image. On the other hand, there is, as an external factor, the fact that the ever-growing number of applicants has resulted in a more 'severe' selection of appropriate student groups.

In his evaluation of the medical school in Maastricht – Europe's most valuable pendant of McMaster, where the integration of behavioral sciences in medical training is furthest advanced as compared to other similar medical training on the Continent – Philipsen states that, so far, problem-oriented methods, independant learning and learning in groups have been realized in the training program. He points out, however, the need for caution while evaluating such innovations. The Maastricht system has the following implications for the teaching of medical sociology. In problem-oriented learning actual health care problems are presented to the students. The assistance expected here from sociologists is mainly on the level of their competence in sociology *in* medicine. Sociology *of* medicine has fewer chances. Work with actual problems leads to individualization and lends itself better to formulation in somatic terms rather than in terms of social sciences.

In his paper on the medical training at the University of Brussels, E. Sand illustrates how, through maximum use of active training methods (e.g. epidemiological research as group work, i.e., 'social cases', in which students counsel families with medical and social problems), attempts to motivate students towards a comprehensive approach to the patient, illness, health education, prevention, epidemiological research and the field of public health.*

10. Teaching methods and practical training in sociology departments

Margot Jefferys

In this paper I will be discussing a selected number of *practical* problems which we in Bedford College have met in preparing our students for the research work they hope to do in the future. I shall start with our objectives, including our implicit objectives; what we want to do with students to give them an idea of what doing medical sociology, practising medical sociology, is and thus what being a medical sociologist actually means. Indeed, our objectives are often implicit rather than explicit. I suppose we could say that the main one is to give students a feeling of the intellectual excitement of trying to find out how social structure relates to the health care system, how the two interact at both the micro and the macro level.

Emphasis, particularly in the master's course, is on giving students some indication of what research in medical sociology involves, what it means in terms of looking for causality, and for interconnections, and in drawing conclusions about the nature of the relationships between the phenomena that we have studied.

I suppose that in a way what we are trying to do is to turn out students whom we would be proud to see entering on an intellectual exercise or on a career which we ourselves have enjoyed. Obviously, in our connections with students, we hope to get a considerable amount of personal gratification from our activities. This comes in many ways; for example we obviously feel gratified if the students feel satisfied, and feel that it has been an intellectually exciting, mind-extending exercise. We also feel gratified if people who subsequently employ our students feel that these students are well equipped to undertake the research or teaching tasks which they have been employed to do. These are our reasons for providing the course, its implicit but real objective.

However, although I feel we have been fairly successful at this stage I'm more aware of the problems than the successes. I would like to outline them here because I suspect that they are ones which will be mirrored elsewhere.

In trying to achieve our aims, in trying to act as role models, (because there is a certain degree of narcissism in teachers who want to produce people in their own image) our first problem arises during the selection process.

We have a number of people who want to come and study with us, and we have to choose a few from this pool. This activity is a time-consuming one if it is to be done with reasonable efficiency. What we do – through interviewing all those candidates who have the essential academic qualifications – is to explore the nature of the knowledge base wich they already possess, their imaginative capacity to handle ideas, and their motivation for wanting to take the course. For example, have they thought about a career? How does this application for a master's degree relate to their ideas of what they want to do in the future?

At this selection stage we obviously find many incompatibilities between the motivations of students and our motivations or disires. If we think that these are impossible to reconcile, that students have aims and objectives in taking the course and ideas about what it will give them, which we know we are not proposing to give, then we try to say to the student, 'This is not the course for you; you wouldn't achieve what you think, your expectations of us are unrealistic. You had better not come.' This may make rejection rather less traumatic for them than would the imputation of intellectual inadequacy. This raises the issue of student participation in the setting of objectives for academic courses. We are extraordinarily dictatorial in this regard. We modify our *specific* objectives from time to time in response to feed-back from students but on the whole we act as though we know best, that is, we feel that we have a knowledge of what research requires and what kinds of skills and knowledge have to be absorbed by a student to produce a good craftsman, i.e., to be able to use his or her sociological imagination. We are therefore fairly adamant that people who we feel are not likely to reach this standard. (our verdict is based on written work as well as on an interview), will not be included in our programme. We accept those we believe to have the potential to work on our lines.

There are all kinds of dilemmas of this sort. The question of how far students can profitably participate in an objective setting is an extremely difficult one. I'm not suggesting that our method is right: I am simply stating that there is a problem.

Again in the selection process we try to think of the mix of students who will come in any one year. It is not only the individual characteristics of the students which may be taken into account, therefore, but the extent to which the whole group that we're going to teach will or will not fit together. One problem here is that we have an increasingly large number of applications from students whose first language is not English, and sometimes from countries where our own knowledge of the social structure and of the health field is minimal. In these instances we feel we can give them very little help. So once again we take decisions which appear to be at odds with some educational principles and are certainly ones we do not like to take. We are conscious that in a group of twelve to sixteen students we can cope with two students who may have considerable language difficulties. We cannot cope with more because the burden on us and on other members of the group in helping individuals with a language barrier is great. Once again this is discriminatory in a way we do not like. Perhaps we have not solved this in the right way, but it is undoubtedly a problem which we have to face.

Having selected our students, we have to decide upon the curriculum. We have a pretty highly structured course with only a limited degree of flexibility and the possibilities for modifying the framework to permit changes brought about by student pressures are limited. Almost every year we get pressures from students to change the way or the form in which we teach, or to put into the course topics or methodology problems which they feel need more attention. We try to respond to these pressures, but normally we are faced with situations where the students do not form a united body against us. There are different groups of students some of whom want more input into one area and some less. These present very real difficulties that we are constantly having to consider.

At the beginning of each academic year we take a critical look at the presentation of the material and decide if it needs changing. We usually do change it since this prevents us from becoming bored, and keeps us alert. This is a problem because, as I think I indicated in the abstract, our whole ideological position – our philosophy – is that those people who are teaching ought to be engaged in current research in health problems of various kinds. We believe this helps us to understand the problems of trying to formulate the research questions we want to deal with. It also helps us to decide which form of research methodology is appropriate to answering which kinds of questions. It also enables us to look at the analytic frames we have produced and their adequacy for answering the research questions. So we are deeply engaged in research as well as in teaching. We are also – unfortunately in many respects because there are so few sociologists interested in the medical care field in Britain – constantly being requested by various governmental bodies and other research councils to adjudicate on research proposals, and do a hundred-and-one other things. Obviously it is tempting to put the students' interests at the bottom of the pile, priority-wise.

Becoming stale is a real problem after you've run a course for eight years. It is necessary to find devices to keep it alive, to keep ourselves alive and constantly to invigorate it.

I would also like to say a word about student pressures. We ask students to do a tremendous amount of work, and usually some of them feel that this is overdoing it – that they are under too much pressure. They complain and try to resist our pressures. The *Boys in White* study of Becker and his colleagues is very true of the situation in our faculty. Students resist us and try to reduce the pressures that we put on them. Another question which we have not solved satisfactorily is the relationships of the students with the research unit, that is with the paid staff who are working full-time on reseach. In theory it is supposed to be a close relationship; in practice we resent our research workers taking much time off to attend seminars and courses. As you can see we are very selfish people imbued with a large dose of the protestant ethic. We probably do not give our students or our research staff enough time for reflective consideration of the issues.

Another problem is our relationships with the external institutions in which we hope ultimately to place students to gain experience. This raises many problems for us. The students are often critical of the institutions into which they go. How can we then maintain a friendly relationship and access to data? What is needed is an enormous amount of tact and occasionally a bottle of alcohol or other kinds of emolient equipment to cope with the problem, so that doctors, nurses, social workers and others will continue to allow our students into their institutions to observe, to collect data, to interview them and their patients and so on.

The question of assessment is also a constant worry. Are our methods fair? How subjective are our judgements? We try to have a mix of assessments. We also regard every person who fails to reach our standards as our failure, because we are arrogant enough to think that our selection methods plus our curriculum ought to achieve one hundred percent success. But at the same time we are ambivalent even about this because failing student from time to time helps to maintain the idea among them that the work must be undertaken, that not everybody can automatically pass the examinations and obtain the degree just by being enrolled.

Finally we have problems with what I would call after-care or career development. Having taken on students to train them for research, to give them an idea of what a career in medical sociology could be, we feel that we have some responsibility to fit them into jobs where they can continue to acquire academic qualifications, and also satisfy their particular employers. We have many headaches in this respect particularly in situations where the job market is not good.

The above remarks should have made it clear that while we do feel we have something to offer and have a good deal of pride in some of the things we do, we're very conscious that we are often placed in positions of extreme ambiguity and ambivalence.

11. Teaching methods and practical training in medical schools: the case of Maastricht

H. Philipsen

11.1. The new faculty

In September 1974 the first fifty students were enrolled in the new medical faculty of the State University of Limburg at Maastricht, the most southern city of the Netherlands. This new medical faculty was not only established to increase the training and educating capacity of physicians. A main objective was to design a new curriculum which was more up to date, acknowledging the changes in medical care and its organization in modern society. To realize this objective, the initial staff had to specify the ideal characteristics of a new medical faculty contrary to the traditional type of medical faculty.

TRADITIONAL FACULTY	NEW FACULTY
– autonomous organization	– imbedded in regional health care
– limited to specialized care	– active participation in all elements of the health care system, including primary care
– a big academic hospital	– collaboration with several hospitals
– mainly curative	– preventive and curative

Although the other seven medical faculties in the Netherlands were at that moment already moving away from the traditional end of the continuum, they were still burdened with a characteristic faculty organization based on the more than a century-old traditional type. Maastricht had the opportunity to try to realize the main goals of the new ideals without this burden. The methods of organizing education, research and health care in the ideal types of traditional and new medical faculties can be summarized in the following aspects of organizational behaviour.

TRADITIONAL	NEW
– objectives stated by disciplines and departments	– objectives stated by community and faculty as a whole
– mono-disciplinary	– multi-disciplinary
– department-oriented	– project-oriented
– individual hobbyism	– team projects
– great variety of topics	– limited number of topics

Before entering into the details of the consequences of this global blueprint for a faculty-to-be, it has to be stated that the plans to start a new type of medical faculty were not simply motivated by the wish to be more modern than the somewhat conservative faculties; the change in objectives was also emphatically formulated in a positive way. In the 'Basic Philosophy of the Medical Faculty of Maastricht', an official document, a vision is given of the developments in society and medical care that make changes in medical education and research necessary.

The following aspects of society and health care developments were mentioned in the Basic Philosophy and related documents:

– acknowledgements of the interdependence of somatic and psychomatic disturbances;
– the need for society to have an open minded attitude to the vested interests in the health care system;
– the difficulty of developing health care quality standards in a discipline so fragmented into specialities and subdisciplines as medicine;
– the democratic and financial need for regionalization of health care and the obligation of a faculty to participate in the region;
– the desirability of medical faculties evaluating their educational designs continually from the viewpoint of contemporary and future health care problems.

11.2. The characteristics of the educational program

Starting from the global vision on a new type of faculty the following characteristics of the educational program were projected:

– problem orientation	vs.	discipline orientation
– independent learning	vs.	strongly structured learning
– including attitude development	vs.	primarily cognitive development
– formative evaluation	vs.	summative evaluation
– learning in groups	vs.	individual learning

Although none of these educational objectives will appear as strikingly revolutionary, to our knowledge the first two years' experience gained to date in Maastricht is in so far unique that the realization of the educational program has been ruthlessly dogmatic concerning the three elements problem-orientation, independent learning and learning in groups.

The other two elements, attitude development and evaluation of the students progress by his-self-assessment, were dominant characteristics in the planned curriculum but were not realized or not adequately realized during the first two years. I have no intention of dwelling in detail upon the issues of student evaluation and attitude development. In my opinion the problems and failures in these fields of educational design are not limited to medical faculties and are endemic in all education in contemporary society. More interesting to dwell upon are the three elements of educational innovation that have been introduced in our system.

The academic year is divided into ten four-weeks blocks. Six to eight of these blocks are organised around concrete problems the physician can encounter in his daily practice, e.g., the complaint of fatigue or tiredness in adults; or the range of normal, physical and personal development of babies. These problem fields presented in the form of individual cases, are obligatory objects for the students in certain stadia of their study. The other two to four blocks are used for periods of evaluation and themes which the individual student, in cooperation with the staff can choose for himself. The task of planning these problem-oriented blocks is given to a multi-disciplinary planning group of three professionals. E.g., the block fatigue or tiredness has been planned by staff members with a professional background in internal medicine, pharmacology and medical sociology. It is their responsibility to make an operational design which includes:

– four or more individual *cases* which the student must 'solve as health care problems';
– *educational material* such as books, papers, slides, films etc. which the students can use;
– *'hiring' other staff members* and outside specialists who can help the students professionally with the solving of the cases;
– creating opportunities for the students to have *contacts with actual health care situations* relevant to the problem being studied;
– training the students in *the skills they need* to solve the problems.

The planning group is not only responsible for the educational design but also for the realization of their plans. An important consequence of this system of planning is that the three staff members cannot pretend to possess all the skills and professional views necessary to solve the presented problems. They often have to coordinate with the contributions of other staff members. In this way they are forced to work in a multi-disciplinary fashion and not lapse into endless one-sided discussions.

In terms of division of labour necessary for the realization of the block design, a member of a planning group must divide activities according to two different roles:

– activities leading to an adequate coordination of multi-disciplinary efforts (*the staff member as planner*);
– activities leading to his own professional contribution to multi-disciplinary efforts as a whole (*the staff member as expert*).

For the realization of the designed block yet another staff role can be discerned. During the block period, students are divided into groups of eight, who have to work their way through the block and its working guide together. In order to reach this group-learning objective, obligatory group meetings are held twice weekly in the presence of the tutor of the group, a staff member or a senior student whose main task is to help the group choose the right procedures in their problem solving activities. A difficult part of this task can be to help the group survive when the group process itself stagnates. As most staff members are not trained in social-psychological aspects of group relations, the faculty is at present developing a training program on how to act as a tutor.

The consequences of the educational system as outlined above can be summarized from staff member and student viewpoints as follows:

The staff member:
- has to know at any moment what role he is playing: planner, expert, or tutor;
- has to subordinate his own discipline to a problem-oriented approach;
- has to compete with all staff members in deciding what concrete health care problems will be presented to the students.

The student:
- learns to solve problems, not to master disciplines;
- has to be active within his group in choosing the right means of solving problems; he cannot lean back passively and listen to the all-knowing expert;
- has to be able to work with all his peers.

The faculty's preference for this system is based on the following officially formulated advantages:
- integration of disciplines,
- integration of theory and practice,
- better motivation of students,
- improved relationship with medical practice,
- student-centred, not staff-centred education,
- emphasis on student responsibility,
- preparation for *'education permanente'*,
- emphasis on methods rather than contents,
- concentrated learning,

- training of team-work,
- peer learning and teaching,
- improved contacts with staff members,
- minimization of social isolation.

11.3. Bottlenecks in the education system

Although the faculty has been operating according to the above-mentioned educational system for the past two years and will continue to do so for at least another two years, certain difficulties are still present. These difficulties can be devided into four categories:

1. staff member inertia
2. student inertia
3. the risk of deprofessionalization
4. irritation with group learning

11.3.1. Staff member inertia

Almost every staff member brings his own background to the new system. This leads to three regrettable but unmistakable trends:

- staff members in universities are used to giving priority to research rather than to educational activities. The new educational system is rather time-consuming and is therefore more vulnerable than the old system to a staff member who prefers his own research grants to the less glamorous contacts with undergraduate students;
- staff members are traditionally trained in the role of expert. The art of being a planner or a tutor has to be learned from the beginning. The greatest danger the system seems to have to face is when a tutor steps out of his role and acts the expert;
- staff members always seem to be afraid of their own disciplines being underestamated, thus leading to more contribution per topic in the fields of biochemistry, anatomy or medical sociology necessary to the study of a particular problem.

These three problems may be part of the *'condition humane'* and are therefore quite understandable. Moreover, they can be discussed with most staff members. The danger of staff member inertia probably bears a more transitory character except perhaps for the more stubborn individuals and the more glamorous specialities.

11.3.2. Student inertia

Most students come to the faculty between their eighteenth and twentieth birthdays. The educational system in high schools is, in spite of massive changes in education, more of a structural than an autonomous nature. Prior to coming to the faculty the students have been surrounded by a very secure situation of being told what and when to learn. A situation of problem-oriented and independent learning is totally new. The student tries to conquer his insecurity by all kinds of tricks and methods that can induce a staff member given to vanity to play the role of expert and give the student the lecture he asks for.

Student inertia like staff member inertia is not really devastating for the system. In Maastricht about half of the student population have become convinced converts of independent nonstructured learning.

11.3.3. The risk of deprofessionalization

Almost all staff members and students agree upon the usefulness of problem-oriented blocks. Despite this important achievement one educational problem has not been solved by the faculty's system, i.e. is it possible to learn the fundamentals of any discipline simply by using those elements of a discipline that are needed for the solving of the concrete problems encountered somewhat arbitrarily during the study? The obvious answer of a convert of this system is that method and viewpoint are more important than content. It is not to be denied that only the future health care practice can show whether the problem-oriented physicians trained at Maastricht are more able to apply methods of biochemistry or medical sociology in their work than discipline-oriented doctors. The real danger at the moment is however that staff members and students under pressure of their fears and anxieties, use some blocks subversively as a means of giving systematic courses in supposedly important or difficult disciplines.

Up till now the faculty has not managed to eliminate this threat to problem-oriented education.

11.3.4. Irritation with group learning

Apart from some aspects of student evaluation, the only element the students have criticized heavily is the obligatory participation in group learning. After a period of about 1½ years it was felt that the majority of first generation students had for some time been frustrated by working in groups. Some wanted to choose their own groups for the rest of the study; others preferred to study individually. Although no one denies that group learning and peer-teaching have under certain circumstances clear advantages, the faculty may have to admit that the objectives, independent learning and group learning, are not really compatible. If a group of eight students has the freedom to decide how to tackle a problem for themselves why should not an individual student have the same right. This issue is sure to become vital in years to come. Important for the solution of the problem is how the faculty decides to define the issue. For many students and staff members the pros and cons of group learning are scientific questions: what is best for the system and the student. According to my more sociological and pessimistic vision the problem is not really scientific but political. He who really prefers independent learning cannot, over a period of time, give his support to group learning rather than individual learning. The principle of independent learning grants in the last instance the individual the right to choose his own means of education within the existing legal and material framework. This means that an obligation to learn in groups must be felt as an infringement upon the above-mentioned right.

The four bottlenecks discusses each have a different impact on the system. Phenomena of staff and student inertia will continue to exist, but are not really essential. The hypothesis that problem-oriented education is better than systematic introduction in many disciplines is highly probable but has to be proven by the doctors who graduate from the faculty. The one great problem to be solved within the existing system is the inconsistency of the objectives of group learning and independent learning.

11.4. Implications for the teaching of medical sociology

The superiority of the Maastricht educational system for the teaching of medical sociology is obvious. Sociology is accepted, at least formally, on an equal footing with other 'basis sciences' such as biochemistry, anatomy or physiology. In every problem-oriented system the sociologist can compete freely with other disciplines about the extent of his contribution. Notwithstanding this recognition there are some drawbacks in defining the material task of a medical sociologist. The main reason lies in the fact that the problems presented to the students during a block, are concrete health care problems. In the last two years we have found that the following difficulties may arise in an educational system as practised in Maastricht.

a. The concrete health care problems as presented in the blocks make demands on the sociologist's competence in his role as *sociologist-in-medicine*. He is asked to contribute to a more adequate daily practice. In this system it is very difficult to confront the students with the problems of *the sociology of medicine*. When a student tries to solve problems such as headache or tiredness in general practice, it is not so simple to give him a clear insight into the power relations in the national health care system.
b. Concrete health care problems are *individualized* problems. Until now we have failed as sociologists to present collective cases. For example, the student is confronted with an individual with suicidal tendencies not with the sociological problem that the suicide rates are rising explosively in the Limburg region.
c. Concrete health care problems are more easily defined in somatic terms than in social science terminology. It is much more difficult to draw attention to revalidation as a social problem as such than to present the student with a victim of a road accident or an atherosclerosis patient. The consequence may be that social sci-

ence knowledge is presented to the student in a fragmented way.
d. When students come fresh from secondary education to the
   university they have a basic knowledge of chemistry, physics and
   biology but in most cases they have no systematic knowledge
   whatsoever of sociology.

This gap in basic cognition between the social and natural sciences
cannot be closed in our educational system. The consequence is, in
our opinion, that the supposed unfamiliarity and vagueness of social
science knowledge is overestimated by students and other staff
members. One of the remedies should be the provision of good basic
texts in (medical) sociology. One of our main objectives must therefore be the production of educational media in cooperation with
others.

The educational system in Maastricht is not only a new start in
medical education but also a new opportunity for the teaching of
medical sociology. In order to make an optimal contribution, the
Medical Sociology Department in Maastricht has to be constantly
alert and must not lose sight of the importance of sociology of
medicine for collective behaviour. Something must also be done about
the regrettable lack of educational media.

PART SIX

EVALUATION METHODS
OF EDUCATIONAL PROCESSES

The general portrait of medical sociology depicted here shows it to be a rapidly expanding subfield of sociology whose training programs, however, are improvised too much and evaluated too little. As illustrations of the latter aspects, accounts from experience were, as always, very instructive. They confirmed both the difficulty and the necessity of evaluating in some systematic way the relevancy, results and effects obtained through the newly launched training programs in medical sociology.

Evaluation methods, as an essential part of the training process, are discussed by J. Daniels, Limburg University Center, Hasselt, and E. Nihoul, University of Ghent.

Daniëls deals with the possibilities of evaluation as an instrument in the improvement of courses and programs. Nihoul comments on a few effects of evaluation procedures on student learning and advocates a re-thinking of the use of evaluation procedures and their results in medical training.

12. Evaluation methods as instruments for improvement of courses and programs

J. Daniëls

12.1. Evaluation and the instructional process

The analysis of the nature of the instructional process clearly brings to light the relationship between evaluation and instruction. Basically, instruction is the process by which desirable changes are made in the behaviour of students. 'Behaviour' is used here in a broad sense and includes thinking, feeling and acting. Instruction is not effective unless some change in the behaviour of students has actually taken place. Thus, instruction in a particular science course, may be aiming at developing an understanding of certain important scientific principles, the ability to use these principles in explaining common scientific phenomena, and some skills in analysing scientific problems to determine what kinds of data are needed to solve them. Instruction in such a course of science will not be effective unless changes of the kind mentioned above actually take place in the students.

Unless instruction is to be merely a haphazard or intuitive process, it requires rational planning and implementation of the plans. Viewed in this way the design of instruction involves several decision-making steps.

The first of these is to decide which objectives to aim at or, stated more precisely, which changes in student behaviour to try to bring about.

The second step is to decide which content and learning experiences are likely to bring about the desired changes in student behaviour.

The third step is in accordance with a set of well-formulated constraints, to design an effective organization of these learning experiences so that their cumulative effect will bring about the desired behavioural changes in an efficient way.

The fourth and final step is to appraise the effects of the learning experiences to find out in what respects they have been effective and where they have failed to produce the desired results and, consequently, what changes are needed.

Obviously, this fourth step is educational measurement or, achievement testing or summative evaluation. Summative evaluation implies sharp decisions: a student is passed or failed on the basis of examinations; a course or educational program is started, continued or stopped, usually on the basis of faculty opinion about the need for it and its effectiveness. Summative evaluation is an essential part of instruction because without appraisal of results the instructor has no adequate way of checking the validity of judgements regarding the value of particular learning experiences and the effectiveness of their organization.

However, educational evaluation is not identical with the fourth phase of the instructional process or summative evaluation. Educational evaluation contributes to all phases of the instructional process for – as was mentioned above – the design and implementation of an instructional process is essentially a decision process. While planning and executing a teaching plan the educational practitioner must take several decisions on objectives, possible learning experiences and their effective organization. To perform this task of curriculum construction as well as the actual teaching task, a practitioner needs answers to several key questions:

- what is the social function I am training the students for? Or for which period in the total program am I preparing the students?
- Which goals do I therefore have to attain by my teaching?
- How can I best attain these goals and which alternative teaching methods are at my disposal?
- Which criteria determine my choice of teaching method?
- How effective are the methods chosen for the realisation of particular objectives?
- How can I optimalize my teaching?
- How does the student experience such an educational system and what are his specific study problems in the given system?

The answers to all these questions can be obtained through educational evaluation, or more precisely formative evaluation which aims at remediation, revision and gradual improvement of the educational system over a period of time.

12.2 The full context of evaluation (formative and summative evaluation)

Definition: 'Educational evaluation is the process of

- determining the kinds of decisions that have to be made,
- selecting, collecting and analyzing the useful information needed in making the decisions
- and reporting this information to appropriate decision makers for judging decision alternatives'.

This statement contains several key terms which require further elaboration and which will be found to have significant implications for the processes and techniques of evaluation.

First of all we defined educational evaluation as a *process*. This means a continuing activity of selecting, collecting and analysing useful information for judging decision alternatives during the planning and implementation of a course. At the same time educational evaluation is a sequential activity, each period of activity forming the basis for the next step of the construction process. Finally, educational evaluation is an iterative, recurrent or cyclic activity rather than a terminal activity or an activity of short duration.

Secondly, educational evaluation involves *'determining the kinds of decisions to be made'*. If evaluation is a process that provides information useful in guiding decision making, the first operational step is the identification of the most useful information. Consequently we need to know what decision alternatives are to be considered, for it is about these alternatives that information must be obtained. The design and implementation of an educational program or course necessitates many types of decisions on different levels and consequently many varieties of information are useful. We can distinguish three types of decisions for which evaluation is used:

1. decisions about individual students: identifying the needs of the student in order to plan his instruction or study activities, judging student merit for purposes of selection and grouping, acquainting the student with his own progress and deficiencies.
2. course improvement: deciding which instructional materials and methods are most suited to the goals of the course and where change is needed.
3. evolutionary adaptation: judging the need for and the effectiveness of an institution, an educational program or an individual course within the program.

Thirdly educational evaluation also means *selecting, collecting and analysing information* needed in making the decisions. When one considers the different types of decisions for which evaluation is used, it becomes apparent that evaluation is a diversified and multifaced activity and that no one set of principles will suffice for all situations but that many different methods and techniques will be involved. But specialists in educational measurement have concentrated to such an extent on one technique – the use of pencil – and – paper achievement tests for assigning scores to individual students – that the principles pertinent to that technique have somehow come to be seen as the very principles of evaluations. 'Tests', we are told, 'should fit the content of the curriculum, and only those evaluation procedures should be used that yield reliable scores'. These and other hallowed principles cannot be maintained in evaluation aimed at course improvement. We see, then, that in the practice of curriculum development the exclusive use of achievement scores is giving way to 'soft evaluation' or 'illuminative evaluation' where use is made of inventories, rating scales, etc... This points to a subtle change in the function that evaluation is expected to fulfil. The curriculum developer who produces student material is essentially a searcher, somebody who wants to keep possibilities open, who is out to discover new alternatives. After finishing the creative construction work he is willing to put his work to the test in practice. But during the construction, creativity and spontaneity dominate. In such a situation one has no need of a cold judgment, maintaining that the aims are not being reached, but omitting to say why they have not been reached and how this can be corrected. During the process of construction one needs a partner with whom to discuss the value of the work. The soft instruments fulfil this function better than the hard ones. They objectivate acts and motives and stimulate communication about the work as a whole.

We distinguished above between formative and summative evaluation, and between evaluation at the levels of the individual student, the course and the institution. We shall consider the different facets of evaluation, before concentrating on course evaluation. Figure 12.1

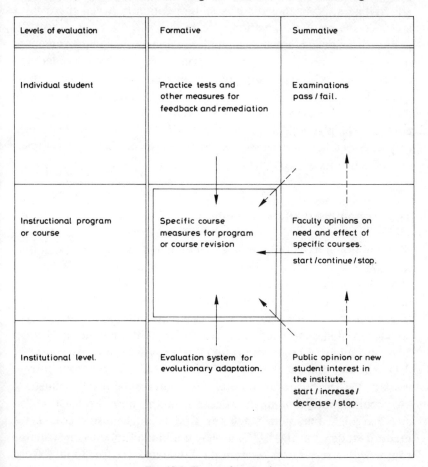

Levels of evaluation	Formative	Summative
Individual student	Practice tests and other measures for feedback and remediation	Examinations pass / fail.
Instructional program or course	Specific course measures for program or course revision	Faculty opinions on need and effect of specific courses. start / continue / stop.
Institutional level.	Evaluation system for evolutionary adaptation.	Public opinion or new student interest in the institute. start / increase / decrease / stop.

Fig. 12.1. Types of evaluation.

shows a 2 x 3 table in which each type and level of evaluation is identified. Also shown are the kind of data or information typically used in each cell and the kind of purpose or decision aimed at.

Summative evaluation aims at a rigid decision. A student is passed or failed on the basis of examinations. A course is started, continued or stopped, usually on the basis of faculty opinion concerning the need for it and its effectiveness. An institution or program is built, supported increasingly or decreasingly or suspended on the basis of public and governmental opinion concerning the need of it and its effectiveness. Note that there is some relation between these three levels of summative evaluations.

Formative evaluation aims at guidance and gradual improvement of the teaching process. The greatest service evaluation can render is to identify aspects of the course or teaching process where revision is desirable. But to be influential in course improvement evaluation, data must become available midway in curriculum development while the course is still pliable. And, as far a possible, evaluation should be used to understand how the course produces its effects; and what parameters influence its effectiveness.

12.3 Formative course evaluation

The traditional basis for course evaluation and, consequently, course revision has been faculty opinion. And this is an important source of ideas. But usually there was no empirical check on such revisions and faculty opinion is notoriously difficult to organize for change. Formative evaluation can perform both functions: check the value of a course revision empirically and stimulate faculty opinion for change. The most important indications for course revision come from student data: the two cells at the top of fig. 12.1. An example from current work at the Limburgs Universitair Centrum can be used to illustrate how course evaluation might proceed from this base. Prof. Dr. Gelan and Prof. Dr. Put, who teach the first year chemistry course for medical students at the LUC, designed a kind of modular-instruction course with a series of practice tests. Students were free to take these tests or not. Scoring was anonymous, so the scores were not used for

examination purposes. It was hoped that doing the practice tests
would promote more thorough work during the course and provide
feedback for students to use in improving their work.

Fig. 12.2. shows a plot of examination scores for the two parts of the
course. Each student is plotted as a number. This number indicates
the number of practice tests the student took during the course.
A circled number means that the student achieved a score of at least
10 out of 20 on 50 percent or more of the practice tests he took.

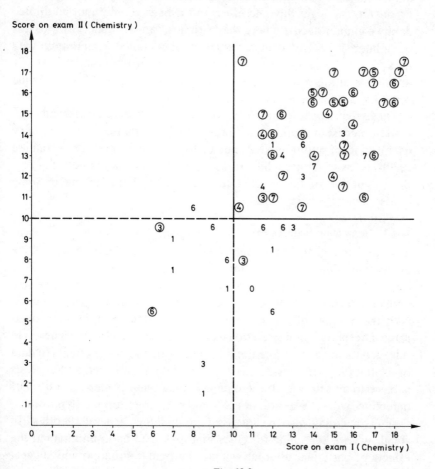

Fig. 12.2.

The students who passed both examinations took on the average about two more of the practice tests than the students who failed in one or both examinations. Note that every student who took all seven of the practice tests passed both examinations, even the two students who got consistently low scores on the practice tests.

The results are encouraging. They suggest, though they do not prove, that the practice tests help. An alternative explanation might be that the higher ability students tend to take more practice tests and get higher scores on examinations because of their superior abilities. The practice tests might have no effect in themselves. Without additional data we cannot decide where the truth lies, but we shall return to this point later. It is also clear that some students failed even though they took six of the seven practice tests. So even if the practice tests do help some of the students, they do not seem to help all of them. Some other kinds of course revision are also needed.

These figures show how formative evaluation data on students can help to suggest and guide course revision. The practice tests are a very useful kind of addition to a course, because they provide formative feedback to students, while at the same time providing both data for the evaluation of the practice-tests effects and the effects of some course characteristics.

12.3.1. Three main features of course evaluation

This example helps us to introduce three main features of course evaluation. These are: *description, comparison* and *interpretation* of effects. We described the present state of affairs in the chemistry course in terms of student data, we compared students' performances with the number of practice tests they had done and we developed some alternative interpretations of the observed effects. These, in turn, led us to seek a more detailed description of these effects in data of a later date. Of course, this process of data collection and analysis is basic to all science. But in course evaluation it is more of a form of detective work. We are not so much testing formal hypotheses, though that may also be involved, or building general theories. In stead, we are searching for clues that may help us to understand the effects of particular alternatives in a particular situation and suggest what further revisions might be worth trying in that situation.

12.3.1.1. *Description*

What do we mean by description?

Any course has many aspects and potentially many kinds of effects. The first goal of evaluation is to describe these as fully as possible. There are students, teachers, instructional materials, instructional procedures, and uses of support services like libraries, laboratories and audiovisual aids that need to be described. And there is an institutional context – a social climate and student subculture – as well as a social climate within the course and/or its subgroupings of students.

There are also many kinds of *possible* course outcomes: content knowledge, skills, attitudes, motivation to study more advanced content in this field, as well as more general abilities and problem-solving strategies useful in later learning and in performance in other fields. The emphasis here is on possible outcomes.

A course evaluation must be sensitive to unanticipated outcomes, and long-range effects, as well as to anticipated immediate outcomes. A course can be highly effective in producing content knowledge in chemistry for example, but if it produces a deep hatred for the study of science, or a tendency to use rote memory in learning, or a strong inhibition to think creatively about natural science problems, then the course needs improving. In other words we need a 'medical' model of course evaluation, in which we are sensitive to the possible side-effects as wel as the main objectives of our instructional treatment.

This is what is wrong with approaches to course evaluation that overemphasize the specification of objectives. The writings of Mager, Popham and others make it clear that it is important to know in some detail what the objectives of a course are. Instructional objectives are necessary. But university teachers have sometimes spent months specifying objectives in such fine detail, and at such great length, that afterwards there is no time or energy left to do the evaluation. And inevitably there will be little thought given to the measurement of the many possible side-effects.

In other words, achievement testing, based on instructional objectives are too narrow or insufficient as course evaluation. But we should add at least a few other criterion measures, using questionnaires or interviews for example to obtain students' attitudes about the course, the teacher, themselves as learners, or interest in the subject-matter, etc... These are called *exit measures* : they are used to describe student performance on completion of a course. But exit measures are only one category of measures concerned in course evaluation.

Fig. 12.3. shows a hypothetical course 'X' in medical sociology which is part of a total educational program for medicine. *Exit measures* are obtained at the end of the course as shown.

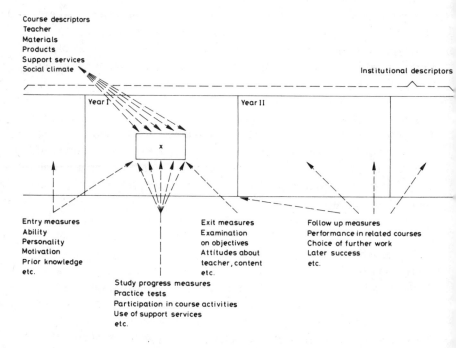

Course descriptors
Teacher
Materials
Products
Support services
Social climate

Institutional descriptors

Year I

Year II

x

Entry measures
Ability
Personality
Motivation
Prior knowledge
etc.

Exit measures
Examination
on objectives
Attitudes about
teacher, content
etc.

Follow up measures
Performance in related courses
Choice of further work
Later success
etc.

Study progress measures
Practice tests
Participation in course activities
Use of support services
etc.

Fig. 12.3. Course 'X', medical sociology.

Five other categories of measures are also identified. These are *entry measures, study progress measures, follow-up measures, course descriptors*, and *institutional descriptors*. Aldo listed are examples of some of the measures possible in each category.

Entry measures describe student characteristics at the start of the course. They show individual differences in knowledge and educational background relevant to the course, but also the mental abilities, personality characteristics and motivations of the students. Having some measures available from this category is extremely useful for evaluation, as will be shown in some further examples. These measures allow an analysis of the exit data to determine which kinds of students do well or poorly under particular instructional conditions. This gives clues about course effects and can suggest further revisions aimed at individualization of instruction.

Study progress measures are intermediate assessments of course progress. The practice tests mentioned above provide a good example of these, but one can also measure student participation is exercises and discussions, and their use of the library and other support services, through systematic observations and unobtrusive record keeping. With questionnaires or interviews one can also assess each student's study habits in the course etc...

Follow-up measures cover the possible long-range effects of the course. In addition to retention and transfer tests, one can record choices made by students, or their succes in more advanced work, in the same or related disciplines.

Course descriptors are not so much quantitative measures as they are narrative accounts by the teacher or other observers of what actually went on in the course, together with the actual materials used. Every course should have a 'course memory' in which all the many details about procedure are recorded each time the course is given. This would show just what happened, what the teacher tried to do, what unforeseen events occured that might have had some effects on student learning, etc...

There may also be an attempt to describe the social climate in the student group – do they help one another or are they competitive, is the group dominated by a few leaders, what is the collective view of the teacher and the course, etc...

Institutional descriptors provide a similar description of the institution as a whole and indicate what relation this course has to others in the same and later years. This is perhaps more important for some kinds of programs, like medicine, than for others, but it usually helps to interpret results if some sense of the institutional context is available.

Now clearly no single course evaluation can be expected to collect and analyze all this descriptive information. Those concerned with evaluating course 'X' will probably concentrate only on course descriptors of study progress and exit measures. One cannot have every course in an institution taking its own measures of initial ability; the students would soon rebel at the excessive amount of testing, even if the budget allowed all this. Here the institute should accept an 'evaluation system' which obtains entry measures, follow-up measures; and institutional descriptors. These data are then available to support individual course evaluation. We can now see how some of this information might be useful in our practice test example.

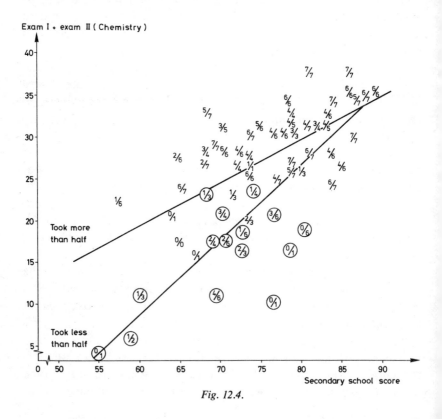

Fig. 12.4.

Earlier we said that an alternative interpretation might be that student ability determined both the taking of practice tests and the passing of examinations in this case; practice tests might not influence examination scores at all. Now if we use the students 'scores' from secondary school performance as a measure of student mental ability, we get the results shown in fig. 12.4. Here the two examination scores have been added to form the ordinate, secondary-school scores are on the abscissa, and each student is shown by a fraction indicating 'number of practice tests passed over the number taken'.

Those students who are circled failed the year.

Clearly, initial ability predicts examination performance because the trend of the data points is linear and positively sloped. That is, on average the higher the entry score the higher the examination score. More importantly, for any given vertical slice, the higher examination scores seems to be associated with the taking and passing of more practice tests or at least with a higher ratio of tests passed to tests taken.

We can show this more clearly by fitting two linear regression slopes, one for students who took less than half of the practice tests another for the students who took more of the practice tests. We see that the best fitting line is for students who did more of the practice tests. Two students with the same low initial score will, on the average, get different examination scores as a function of practice tests. The student who takes more pratice tests will do better in the examination than the one who takes fewer practice tests. And this seems to be true for all students who have secondary-school scores below about 75.

Above this level of initial ability, it does not matter whether a student takes the practice tests or not; he still does well in the examinations.

12.3.1.2. Comparison

This introduces the second feature of data analysis for course evaluation: comparison. We distinguished two groups of students in terms of study progress in the course, and we compared them in terms of the relation between an entry measure and an exit measure. We found that some students benefit from practice tests and some do not need them.

This result could be used in the course in the future; we might tell
students with secondary-school scores below 75 that the practice tests
are especially important for them. We could also go further with our
comparison study. Some students did six practice tests and still failed.
Others at the same initial ability levels did six tests and passed. If we
had other descriptive information on these students, perhaps personality or motivation or study habit measures, we could check to see if any
of these variables differed greatly between the two groups. Perhaps
those who passed in this group had higher achievement motivation
and studied practice test material after each test while those who
failed did not. This might lead to further suggestions for student
counselling.

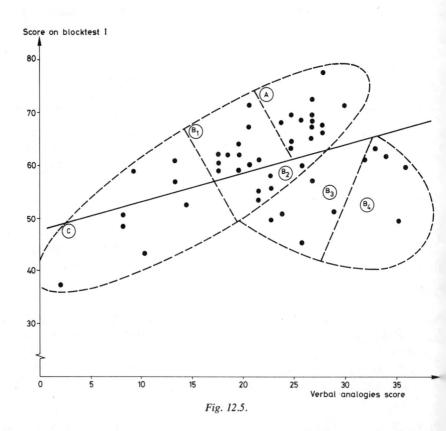

Fig. 12.5.

Another example comes from the Medical Faculty, Maastricht, in the Netherlands. Instruction in this program proceeds by problem-oriented discussion in small groups; there are no lectures. Fig. 12.5. shows the relation between entering mental ability – the verbal analogies test score – and the achievement test given at the end of the first 4-week block of instruction. Each student is one point on this graph. This scatterplot is unusual: for many students we find that there is a strong relation between initial ability and achievement, but some high ability students still do poorly: Groups A, B1, C show a strong positive ability-achievement relation. Groups B1, B2, B3 and B4 show a negative relation between ability and achievement.

When these subgroups are compared on personality and motivation measures it appears that the high ability students nearer to B4 were more highly motivated towards achievement than those near B1 *but* they were also much more in need of *independence* and *task orientation*. They were much less oriented toward social interaction than those near B1. Some high ability students seem to have trouble adapting to the social group process which is the basic method of instruction in this program. These students, may need to be given a more individualized program where they can work on their own, or perhaps something can be done to help them adapt more quickly to the group discussion method.

12.4. Recommendations for course evaluation

These are only simple examples, without much detail. They are only isolated moments in the continuing process of course revision and evaluation. And, of course, in any given situation much more work needs to be done to be sure that interpretations and subsequent course changes were the best ones. But it should be clear from these examples how description comparison and interpretation, and critical consideration of entry measures, progress measures, exit measures and course descriptors, can lead to course improvement.

Throughout the above, we have assumed that entry measures are based on information obtained from psychological tests, and exit measures on achievement tests and examinations. These are perhaps the principal methods, since they have been most frequently used in the past. But it is important to note that there are other methods for gathering information useful in course evaluation. Let us consider some of these.

Student questionnaires and/or interviews can be used to provide study progress information on study habits. They also can be directed at teacher behavior, instructional procedures and materials, and support services, reflecting both aspects of study progress during the course and attitudinal outcomes after the course. They provide a unique kind of course description, from the student point of view. And they are the only means of assessing the social climate operating in the course. Given the variety of information obtainable from student opinion questionnaires, it is recommended that course evaluations should always make use of this technique. Students are after all the consumers of instruction and their views on a course may give uniquely valuable clues as to its improvement.

Teacher questionnaires and interviews provide unique information for course description, because much of what goes into a course – the planning, the choice of materials, and the frustrations, etc. – is often not observable by others. After all, teachers are the ones with the most experience in a given course. They too may provide unique clues for course improvement. In many cases of course the teacher *is* the evaluator. Here the teacher-evaluator should really not trust himself completely. Often, fresh insights into what is working and what is not working in a course come from outside observers. Classroom observation by a trained person or a colleague can often provide measures of student performances of which the teacher is unaware, as well as a more objective view of teacher performance and other course characteristics. As an adjunct to this, expert judgments are also valuable in evaluating the quality of materials, texts, films, etc., in a course.

Finally a little-known and little-used but potentially powerful technique is the use of unobtrusive measures. These are indicators of what occurs naturally in the course of instruction, and they do not intrude on the students or teachers in the course because the administration of questionnaires, interviews, observations, etc., is not needed.

Examples are visits to the library, volunteers for extra assignments, requests for extra or supplementary readings, absences, breakage of laboratory equipment, choice of work in later courses or pursuit of advanced degrees, etc.

None of these measures alone means much. But they can be added up at times to show important positive or negative course effects.

We can conclude by listing a few recommendations to be considered for course evaluations in the future.

1. Obtain as full a description of the course and its students as possible. We should at least obtain:
   A. entry measures of general mental ability and prior knowledge of content;
   B. study progress measures of practice tests, performance and participation in other course activities;
   C. exit measures of content knowledge and skills and student attitudes toward the course, the teacher and the content;
   D. a course description by the teacher and a file of all materials used.
2. Consider possible side effects as well as principal objectives of the course.
3. Pursue any and all forms of data analysis that might give clues about course effects. But always produce scatterplots such as those shown earlier to relate entry and exit measures, and compute regression slopes for these. Do not rely only on test averages to describe course effects, since averages do not display individual student performance.
4. Use whatever comparisons among students are available. Groups to be compared can be defined by entry measures, or study progress measures.
5. Be persistent in keeping records of data from year to year. Any course revision that is worth evaluating is worth pursuing over several years. Improvements are often obtained gradually.
6. Try out interpretations. Think of counter-interpretations. Form further data analyses to pursue these counter-interpretations and add measures the next year to clarify the choice between alternative interpretations.
7. Support the construction of an evaluation system in the institution, so that fuller description of students at entry, at exit, and in follow-up years will be possible in future course evaluations.

Finally, those who wish to try some of these techniques should be encouraged by their faculties to do so, for courses can be improved systematically only through improved course evaluation.

References

Creemers, B. and P. Weeda, 1974, *Amerikaanse Reiservaringen,* (voorstudie Curriculumonderzoek), Utrecht, Instituut voor Pedagogische en Andragogische Wetenschappen, p. 55.

Cohen, D., 1973, *New Approaches to the process of developing and evaluating Chemistry curricula.* Paper presented at the Intern. Congress on Improvement of Chemistry Education, Wroclaw, Poland, p. 38.

Cronbach, L.J., 1963, Course improvement through evaluation, *Teachers Coll. Rec.,* (64), p. 672-683.

Hastings, J.Th., 1966, Curriculum evaluation. The why of the Outcomes, *J. of Educ. Meas.,* (3), No. 1, p. 27-32.

Meuwese, W., 1971, Evaluation Mechanisms for Educational Systems, *British J. of Educ. Techn.,* (2), No. 1, p. 57-63.

Snow, R.E., *Approaches to course evaluation.* Colloquium Didactiek van de Natuurwetenschappen, Diepenbeek, L.U.C., p. 10. 1975.

Snow, R.E., 1973, *An Evaluation System for Medical Education,* Leiden, p. 46.

Snow, R.E. and H.F.W. Wijnen, 1975, *Implementing an Evaluation System for Medical Education,* (Technical Report No. 1), Maastricht, M.F.M. p. 43.

Suchman, E.A., 1969, The Role of Evaluative Research. In: *Proceedings of the 1969 international conference on testing problems,* Princeton, N.J., Educ. Testing Service, p. 93-103.

Tyler, R.W., 1950. The Function of Measurement in improving Instruction. In: Lindquist, E.F. (ed.) 1950, *Educational Measurement,* Washington, A.C.E., p. 47-67.

Tyler, R.W., 1942, General statement an evaluation, *J. Educ. Res.,* (35), p. 492-501.

13. Evaluation methods as part of training programs

E. Nihoul

During the past 150 years, the demands of society for quality in professional training and performance have grown steadily.

In medicine, a complex educational structure and organization aiming at modern methods, quality and certified competence have put an increasing pressure on faculty and students alike. At the time of certification, the graduating M.D. can take a deep breath and enter the field of practice. The community, the faculty and the physician himself can then be confident that M.D.'s are able to respond adequately to the need for health and disease care. However, for years now, dissonant voices are being heard more and more frequently and audibly, from the community, the government, professional societies and even from medical faculties. Something is probably going wrong in the Kingdom of Medicine. The latest therapeutic measure aimed at remediating revealed deficiences in medical practice is *continuing education*. There is no space or time here to develop the hypothesis that the effects of *continuing education* as conceived at present could even cause the situation to worsen rather than improve.

The cherished reassuring principle of equating a certified degree with competence was chiefly developed after the French revolution by a rising industrial and production minded middle class. It opened the schools doors to a larger number of learners and at the same time, with the purpose of assuring competence, managed to impose a common currciculum for each profession and to try to achieve uniformity in education, as they do in some countries with the production of cheese of a constant quality. Exception being made for 'animals of pure race' and for 'Brave New World' this conception is in contradiction with modern findings in educational and behavioral sciences.

If attention is focused on the medical student certain questions may arise. Is he more able to function in the present situation where he has to fit a standardized mould of education, or in a system where he could achieve a self chosen set of objectives and be allowed to perform subsequently at his own level of competence? Is he more satisfied and rewarded in the present system than he could be in a competence-based practice of medicine? Reactions to medicine and physicians growing at present, may cast doubts on this hypothesis. To suggest answers to these questions is, however beyond the scope of this paper, but with respect to the educational process the second situation, does look more sound and satisfactory.

Revised concepts about the results of education more in keeping with the facts and less with unverified assumptions could lead, to quote a well-known sociologist to the view that: 'It could be desirable to move from: to each according to his degree to: to each according to his abilities'.

Teaching is not an end but just one of the means that (should) facilitate the learning of pre-set and carefully defined objectives. Learning is the process by which new behaviours are developed and old ones are readjusted and the occurence of learning can be ascertained only if a change in observable behaviour between entry and exit of a learning experience can be established.

Teaching becomes, then, the organization of learning experiences in such a way that learning is facilitated.

The aim of evaluation is to gather data about the learning and teaching process. This information should serve and help learners and teachers alike. It should allow them to assess how they fare towards the goals they have set and if necessary to correct the course of this process.

In the preceding paper, J. Daniëls has presented evaluation as a tool to improve programs and courses at a departmental or institutional level. The present paper intends to consider some effects of evaluation procedures on the learning of the students and to present some arguments that may lead to reconsideration of the use of evaluation procedures and its results in medical education.

An important part of evaluation on medical education is the accumulation of data about individual student achievements not only at the cognitive level but also at the attitudinal level, e.g. attitudes towards: health and disease, patients, colleagues and other categories of health workers, and also towards own learning. The way these data are used during the educational process is of paramount importance to the learning of the student. Flexner wrote: 'However the teachers teach, the way in which the student studies is largely influenced by the examinations'.

The assessment of the final competence of the graduating M.D. is a necessity derived from the commitment and the responsibility of the faculty towards the community who expects, asks and pays for an adequate response to its needs in the health and disease area. Incidentally, these needs should be considered as priorities for the definition of the desirable competence of physicians, for the construction of the curriculum and the content of evaluation.[1]

The finality of certifying and of pass-or-fail examinations is to guarantee the quality of the final product. In this function, assessment data are used to pass a judgement on individuals.

In many medical schools, this is the most frequent and often the only function of evaluation. If any system may have unfavorable and disagreable consequences for the future of the learner, it is reasonable to expect him to do what he can to avoid these consequences. And that is why so many disappointed teachers complain that students are learning 'only for the examinations' and that examinations have become a goal in themselves. A quick look at the examinations systems prevalent in many medical schools even leads us to suspect that they are an impediment rather than a help for the learning and that they act negatively on the achievement of the objectives the teachers say they want the students to achieve.

'Examinations are among the least understood and most misused tools of education. They are used mainly to certify that the student has learned an acceptable amount of what he has been taught and to provide a grade representing that attainment. While the announced objectives of the institution may be to develop the knowledge, skills, and attitudes necessary to being a good physician or nurse, the examinations seldom measure more than the simple recall of isolated pieces of information. The student's grade is usually determined by comparing his performance with the class as a whole, that is grading on the curve, rather than grading according to standards carefully developed by the Faculty... The examination system is a dominant force in the setting for learning'. (Bryant, 1969)

Medical faculties and teachers profess that they are committed to educate 'good' physicians able to respond adequately to the needs for health care and that they want to help the students to be able:

1. *To acquire the desirable competence at the cognitive, skills and attitude levels and to use discrimination and judgement to solve health and disease problems.* Analysis of the content of examinations reveals that they chiefly (70-90 percent and more) measure the recall of isolated information. Few questions test the ability to generalize and interpret. There is little or no measurement of abilities in analysis, judgement and solution of familiar and unfamiliar problems. Pass or fail decisions: to be based upon an assumption that individual examiners without explicit criteria or predetermined performance standards and using data derived from a very limited sample of candidate behaviour, can make sound judgements about his qualification for... practice' (Miller, 1969).

2. *To consider the patient in health or disease as a whole and not as a collection of systems and organs.* Gynecology, endocrinology, psychiatry and social medicine are taught in separated disciplines as separated piece of a puzzle, and if dysmenorrhea comes up at the examination, the student is advised to consider first whom he is going to answer. He may never be able to solve dysmenorrhea problems correctly, but he can demonstrate the ability to direct his mind immediately to the characteristic 'profile' of the typical woman with psychogenic pain and the next day with the same alertness to describe the effects of dysmenorrhea in occupational health. Nevertheless additional learning has taken place: the student has developed strategies and tactics to pass his examinations successfully. This was not one of the objectives of the faculty.

3. *To function independently and to become a life-long self-learner.* Content, timing, frequency of teaching and examinations are identical for all students. No or very little allowance is made for individual differences among students: in their background, objectives, motivation, profile of interests and pace of learning. Even teachers in medical schools have learned and still learn as unique individuals. Learning demands that the learner feels a need and a desire to know and to become competent. The recognition and acception of ignorance then becomes a potent motor of learning. During learning the student wants to assess for himself what he can and what he cannot do. He is ready to expose his ignorance and to

say: 'I cannot do that, show me'. But *not* in the situation of a judgmental pass-or-fail evaluation. At such examinations the skill of concealing ignorance is rewarded by grades or marks! G. Miller (1969) has concluded: 'Students discover very early how to play this shabby game in which the goal is not learning but some arbitrary and meaningless symbol called a grade'.

Such a situation is hardly reconcilable with the goals of medical education. Neither does it help to fulfil the social commitment of the faculty, which is the acquirement by the students of a defined adequate competence. L.S. Shulman describes the outcome of such a system:

'Consider the analogy of a race. Imagine the mile run if it began with the firing of a gun and ended at the end of four minutes when another gun went off and everyone had to stop wherever they were. It would be even more ludicrous if about five minutes later another gun went off for the next race and everyone began the next race at the point from which they had ended the previous one. We fould find it rather laughable, and yet we run our educational programs in precisely this manner. Ostensibly, our purposes in education, especially in medical education, are to see to it that a certain minimal level of competence is established for each learner. Therefore, we should logically set levels of achievement as constants and let time act as a variable. Instead, we do exactly the opposite. We set time as a constant and have students run until their time is up. The grades we give reflect how far they have gotten in the race within the time span we have allocated (Shulman, 1970)'.

Setting the level of achieved competence as a constant to be attained by almost all students and considering the time for achievement as a variable has led to the concept of learning for mastery, with as corollaries: independent study, competence-based – not discipline-centered – learning and formative evaluation.

Patient centered problems become the recognized objectives instead of the content of separate disciplines e.g.: digestive problems and jaundice are objectives, not gastro-enterology; cough, chest pain, short breathing, not pneumology. This does not imply that pneumology disappears from the cuuriculum, but the discipline is just one resource among many others, that can be used to solve a patient's problem. [2]

Mastery learning requires:

2. See appendix 3.

- Clear and communicative description of competence levels.
- Definition of the successive steps of learning.
- Supply of adequate learning situations.
- Construction of self-evaluation tools testing the professed competence objectives, not merely recall. Each test is constructed to assess specifically each step of the progression towards competence. This implies a great variety of testing situations and of testing devices.

If these conditions are fulfilled, the student knows *before* passing the summative examination whether he has or has not achieved the objectives.

Learning for mastery can be visualized, as in Fig. 13.1. as a staircase leading to competence.

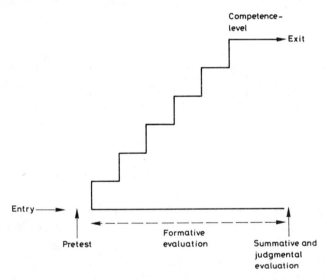

Fig. 13.1. Learning for mastery.

Evaluation procedures that fulfil both the requirements of the learning process and of certification belong in such a progression. The difference between them resides in *when* and *for what purposes* they are used.

Entry evaluation

If students are considered as individuals and if, therefore, allowance is made for individual differences among students, then differences in abilities at the starting point should *make* a difference in the path, the timing and the content of their learning activities.

A child of 6, starting elementary school, brings with him what he has already learned, his past experiences, even his view on dependency – independency in learning.

A medical student starting at the age of 18-22 is accompanied by even more asserted abilities, motivation, attitudes and personal goals. If the purpose is to help him to achieve a defined competence, then his entry abilities and attitudes should be taken into account during the successive steps of his medical education.

Moreover, the assessment of the entry knowledge and abilities allows the teacher to correct and to redirect his teaching.

If some students in the class have already acquired some abilities before starting the course, it is pointless and wasteful to force them to go through the same learning situation again and 'learn' what they already know. And if some students have not yet achieved prerequisities of certain abilities, it will be useless to attempt to build up their knowledge if there is no foundation.

Formative evaluation

If somebody starts sailing from England to Buenos Aires, he has to check frequently that he stays on the correct course. Without charts, navigation instruments and radio, he can only guess that he is sailing in a vague direction between West and South. He will probably realize that he has missed his goal only when, if ever, he anchors off a desolated coast in South America or perhaps in Africa. On the other hand, however, frequent and accurate feedback about his course, would allow him to proceed efficiently towards his objective. Any deviation from his route could be then corrected in time.

The student often ploughs laboriously through the waters of medical education with shabby, antiquated navigational aids, incomplete and ambiguous charts. And like the sailor, he will know only after the final examination that he has missed his goal, with no further opportunity to correct deficiencies.

Such a learning system is often ineffective and certainly inefficient. Economically and socially unsound, it is a waste of time, energy and what is worse, a waste of enthusiasm and motivation.

Formative evaluation is nothing else than a guidance system. The message to the student is very simple: 'at certain points on the route, if you *believe* you know enough, ascertain if you really do.

The presented tests are truly representative of the objectives. Correct answers to questions and acceptable solutions to problems are a sign you have achieved the objectives. So don't worry. Before the final examination you already know that you will pass.

It is the duty and the responsibility of the faculty to develop accurate charts and navigational aids, to beacon the course with directions, check points and evaluation timing.

These check points in the course of the program refer to the successive steps leading to achievement of the educational objectives. For the formative evaluation, a vast array of testing methods are used. They are constructed according to the behaviors that are to be demonstrated by the students.

The data of formative evaluation are used for different purposes than those gathered after entry or summative examination.

If these data are intended to be used as a guidance and as an incentive to correct deficiencies, they may not be used for grades or marks. Mistakes, ignorance and inabilities revealed by the tests *during* the learning may not lead to a judgement of the students. If they do, such an evaluation at this stage of their progression will impede their learning.

Therefore results of the tests are communicated personally and confidentially to the student to give him an idea of what he has already achieved and what he has yet to achieve.

If the students are to believe that formative evaluation leads to facilitation of their learning and not to a potential black spot on their record, then its application must be fair.[3] After a diagnostic examina-

3. See appendix 2.

tion of your car, you don't expect the mechanic to tell you that you are a negligent driver and to report you to the Driving Licence commission. Instead you expect him to say: you may drive this car further if you correct this and take care of that. If they accept this function and are willing to provide the help needed some teachers may revise their role in the learning process.

Summative evaluation

At entry, competence-based objectives have been clearly communicated to the students. Adequate learning resources are made available: books, people, audio-visuals media, situations for learning skills and a rich variety of self-testing devices.

If the faculty creates an environment favorable to learning and if the student makes use of the learning situations provided then very few of them will be unable to pass the judgmental examinations. Summative evaluation should be made with a frequency that allows the assessment of a comprehensive and logical sum of competencies, not just of discipline centered knowledge.

Periods between summative examinations should be long enough to allow the learner to cover the program, to make frequent use of the formative evaluation aids and to have time to correct deficiencies.

Provided the faculty has offered clear and realistic objectives, adequate learning situations and resources, and corresponding self-evaluation devices, the responsibility of learning rests on the student. If he does not reach the assigned competence level he must be failed.

In a society where the placement of professionals in the hierarchical scale of competence and responsibility still depends greatly on degrees it is pointless to produce cut-rate physicians.

References

Bryant, J., 1969, Health and the Developing World. Cornell University Press, quoted by McGaghie, W.C., et al., (1976) in *Competency Based Curriculum Development.* Center for Educational Development, Univ. Illniois, Chicago.

Flexner, A., 1925, Medical Education: A Comparative Study, Macmillan, New York, quoted by M. Simpson in *Medical Education*, 1973. Butterworths, London.

Miller, G.E., 1976, *Mec. Educ. 10*, 81.

Miller, G.E., 1969, 'The Study of Medical Education', *Brit. J. Med. Educ. 3*, 5.

Shulman, L.S., 1970, 'Cognitive Learings and the Educational Process', *J. Med. Educ. 45, 90*.

APPENDIX 1

If it is postulated that the priority function of physicians is to acquire and maintain that competence which allows them to deliver adequate health care, then the main sources from which educational objectives can be derived are to be found in the areas of community needs and of provision of health care. Fig. 13.2. reproduces the social cybernetic relations between community, physicians and medical school.

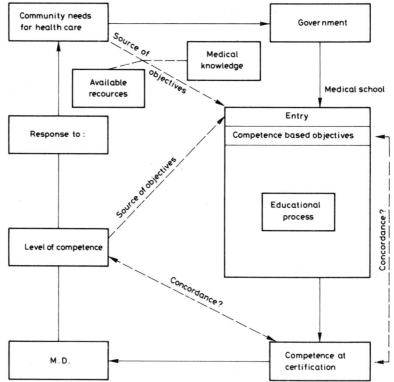

Fig. 13.2. Social cybernetic relations between community, physicians and medical school.

Available medical resources are different in different countries. Biomedical knowledge, already a huge body, is still expanding exponentially. A great part of of this knowledge can explain the sufferings of patients, but cannot yet cure or even alleviate them. Physicians are effective in some areas of patient care, but deficiencies still exist in other areas. These deficiencies, when identified, then become educational needs, which in turn should influence the educational goals and process in the medical school, as shown in fig. 13.3.

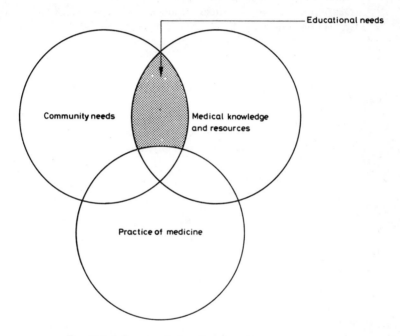

Fig. 13.3. Influence of educational needs.

An analogous mechanism of feedback can function inside the medical school. Once educational needs have been identified, they are translated into training objectives that condition the teaching methodology and the learning experience.

The competence assessed during the process and at certification provides a valuable feedback to evaluate the training program.

APPENDIX 2

The use of formative evaluation in a course of medical microbiology

Up till 5-6 years ago, the course of Medical Microbiology (University of Ghent-Belgium) was taught during lectures, with the help of traditional aids such as books, illustrations and practical exercises. End-of-the-year M.C.Q. examinations were taken, followed by an oral examination for the students with marginal or insufficient scores.

There was no in-course testing.

Distribution of scores at final examinations is described by curve A of the graph. in fig. 13.4.

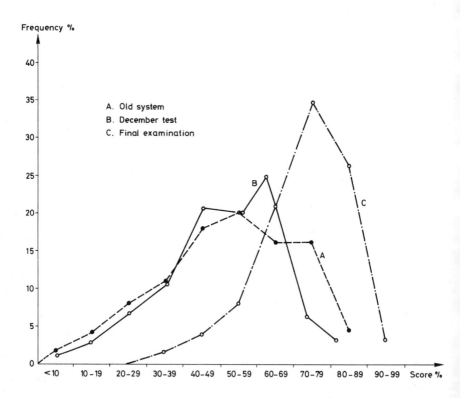

Fig. 13.4. Distribution of scores in a course of medical microbiology.

Three years ago the system was revised.

1. Students start with following materials:
   - a standard book of medical microbiology
   - a mimeographed course consisting in learning packages constructed around groups of infections e.g. urinary, respiratory, digestive infections, etc...
   - for each package a set of sequential learning objectives is presented.

   The program makes no provision for differences in pace of learning. Instructional objectives and final examinations are identical for all students.

   The students are advised to cover a learning package by themselves using the objectives as guidelines. Lectures are restricted as much as the reaction of students allows.

   Scheduled class hours are frequently spent on formative evaluation. Areas of testing are announced well in advance. Questions are presented on an overhead projector. The students can answer anonymously with the aid of an electrical push button system.

   A panel with lighted spots displays the correct and erroneous answers. Feedback is provided immediately for each question.

2. Half of the time scheduled for practical exercices is spent on the solving of patient management problems on a level compatible with their abilities at this stage of their training (comparable with the 2nd year in U.S. Medical School).

   Students, arranged in groups of 10, are presented with an initial situation of an infection. They make use of any books they want. The instructor in each group has received a programmed written simulation with all data necessary to solve the problem.

   The group receives an answer to every question it asks but no information is given that is not specifically asked for.

   The exercise finishes when the group has presented a diagnosis, prosals of treatment, proposals.

   Feedback is given immediately about the course of action chosen, formulation and checking of hypotheses, sources of information, interpretation of information, final conclusions.

3. After the first trimester (in December), students have to pass an M.C.Q. examination. Results of this test have no influence on the fianl examination.

   Item analysis and scoring are done by computer. Feedback for each item is given in the class room.

   Results are communicated to the individual student by placing him on the distribution curve of the class and by providing him with a temporary and tentative prognosis of his achievements.

   This can be expressed as:
   a) 'you are on the right road to succeed easily at the final examination'.

b) 'risk of failing is small. A few corrections in your progression should easily take care of that'.

c) 'risks are evident. You should change something in the way you work. Staff members are available for consultation'.

A typical distribution curve of such a half term examination is represented by curve B on the graph and is similar to the final results of the previous system.

For the last three years results of the final examination have consistently produced higher scores (curve C).

The conclusion is that exposing the students to written objectives, frequent anonymous tests and problems correlated with the objectives and a simulation of a final examination have definitely facilitated learning to some extent. The system does not claim however that these learning experiences lead to mastery of the medical practice. One of the main reasons is that they are still predominantly discipline centered.

APPENDIX 3

Discipline centered versus patient oriented teaching

The following case story has been borrowed from a book intended as a learning aid to hematology. Italics are mine and meant here as an aid in understanding the comments presented.

Initial history and physical examination

This *18 year-old married female* was atmitted to University Hospital on January 6, 1970 with chief complaints of increasing *tiredness* over the past two weeks, spontaneous *epistaxis* during the past four weeks and *easy bruising* over the last eight weeks.

She had been well until about eight weeks prior to admission when she had *'flu-like' symptoms*. For eight days she was *febrile,* had severe headaches, was extremely tired and had a non-productive cough. She had had ten attacks of *epistaxis* during the preceding several weeks. One week prior to admission she had an attack of pruritus; after scratching, she noticed red, *bruised areas*. Three days prior to admission she climbed several flights of stairs and became quite dyspneic with substernal pain. The dyspnea and pain disappeared with rest.

For the past *three years* she had been taking *isoniazid* 100 mgm three times a day (she had been exposed to *tuberculosis* and had a *positive P.P.D.(*. She had taken *Librium* 10 mgm at *bedtime* for the past *two years*. In November 1969 (two months prior to admission) she took *diet pills* (disbutal gradumet) for eight days, however, these made her *excessively nervous* and were discontinued.

Physical examination revealed a moderately *obese young adult female* who did not appear acutely or chronically ill. A few *petechiae* were present over the extremities, *ecchymotic* areas were noted on the wrist, the left breast and in both popliteal areas. Bilateral anterior cervical nodes 2.5 cm in diameter and slightly tender were present. *Splenic dullness was increased.*

Initial laboratory data

Hemoglobin:	13.2 gm%
Hematocrit:	39.0%
Leukocytes:	5,600/cu mm
	Bands: 1%
	Seg. Neutrophils: 46%
	Lymphocytes: 51%
	Monocytes: 2%

About 25% of the lymphocytes appeared to be atypical.

Platelets:	9,000/cu mm
Urinalysis:	Within normal limits
B.U.N.:	11 mgm%
SGOT:	15 I.U. (Normal 30-80 I.U.)
Total bilirubin:	0.2 mgm%
Total serum protein:	6.6 gm% with normal electrophoretic pattern
L.E. preparation:	Negative x 3
Bone Marrow Aspiration:	Hypercellular marrow.
Myeloblasts:	0.4%
Promyelocytes:	4.0%
Neutrophils:	
Myelocytes:	6.8%
Metamyelocytes:	7.4%
Bands and segmented:	36.8%
Eosinophils:	1.2%
Lymphocytes:	17.0%
Plasmacytes:	0.8%
Normoblasts:	25.6%
M:E ratio:	2.1

A normoblastic, sequential maturation was present. Marked hyperplasia of the granulocytic series was present, but the development was sequential.

Megakaryocytes ware markedly increased and appeared in clumps. Many immature forms were seen. Some granulation of the cytoplasm. *Platelet formation was decreased.*

A few scattered atypical moninuclear cells, morphologically similar to those present in the peripheral blood were seen.

Monospot test:	Positive

Heterophile:
  Presumptive: 1: 896
  Guinea pig kidney absorption: 1: 448
  Beef red blood cell absorption: 1: 14
Impression: Infectious mononucleosis with secondary thrombocytopenia.

Problems
  1. Thrombocytopenia
  2. Infectious monocucleosis.

Solution of problems
  When this patient was admitted the immediate *problem* was the correction of the thrombecytopenia. At the time of admission possible causes of the severe thrombocytopenia considered were: acute I.T.P., chronic I.T.P., drug induced I.T.P., T.T.P., hypersplenism and thrombocytopenia secondary to disease process involving bone marrow, i.e., leukemia, myelofibrosis, aplastic anemia. Immediately a bone marrow aspiration was performed and showed a markedly increase in the number of megakaryocytes. The megakaryocytes had a very distinct cellular membrane, the so-called hard shell megakaryocytes: it appeared as if no platelets were being produced. The unanswered question is whether these megakaryocytes have been depleted of platelets or wheter platelet production is suppressed by a humoral effect. The immediate fact that must be ascertained is that the committed cell or the uncommitted cell is at fault. If the committed cell compartment is depleted or suppressed, removal or control of the offending agent should result in recovery in a matter of days. In druginduced thrombocytopenia where the drug acts as a haptene, in acute I.T.P. where the virus acts as a haptene, in chronic I.T.P. where platelet antibodies are present – in all of these cases if the offending agent can be eliminated, suppressed or interfered with then the thrombocytopenia should correct itself. The patient was immediately started on prednisone in an effort to block the antigenantibody reaction regardless of the basic etiology. After four days of prednisone 20 mgm every six hours, the platelet count was 61,000/cu mm, after six days 146,000/cu mm. Over the next two weeks the dose of prednisone was gradually decreased to 20 mgm q. 8: 00 a.m. and 5 mgm q. 4: 00 p.m. At this point the platelet count was 97,000. The *patient was discharged* and during the next several months the prednisone was discontinued and the platelet count remained at normal levels.
  The case history goes on with a long and erudite discussion about possible etiology of thrombocytopenia and the probable relation with infectious mononucleosis.

Comments (on the process, not on the content)

This piece of teaching aims at and succeeds in the realistic presentation of a riddle – not a patient – in hematology. The presentation is well documented with data of laboratory investigations, their interpretation and with information from recent scientific literature.

The patient was discharged after three weeks in hospital and subsequently 'the platelet count remained at normal levels'.

At this time, it would have been interesting to ask the patient 'How is your health, do you feel well?' and to listen to her answer.

The student who learns how the expert solves this problem and who aims at the *same kind* of expertise may miss some of the needs of the patient.

Twice the word 'problem' was used.

The first time it was used to mean diagnosis: thrombocytopenia and infectious mononucleosis.

The second time, it meant how the physician will treat the condition. But each time, it refers to problems – real ones – of the physician, not to the problems of the patient.

Indeed the initial description of the patient's condition mentions:
- 18 year-old married female
- for the past three years, she takes isoniazid (after exposure to tuberculosis and positive tuberculine reaction)
- for the past two years, takes librium for insomnia
- moderate obesity. Patient took diet pills for short time. She felt excessively nervous and stopped with these pills.

So, after being discharged from the hospital this young woman – having been through a period of acute infection with some infrequent complications – is still facing her old problems or so this piece of teaching allows us to suppose.

14. Curriculum construction: reflections on a workshop

J. Vansteenkiste

14.1. Introduction

The workshop on medical sociology curriculum construction, both for the training of sociologists and physicians, was organized as an experimental counterpart to the theoretical foundation of the seminar.

The workshop was originally intended to challenge the approximately 140 participants in this international conference, consisting mostly of sociologists and medical doctors, to use the insights gathered from the exchange of reflections, evaluations and wishful thinking as the basis for training programs in medical sociology. With the avowed pragmatic intention of elaborating a listing of educational objectives and subsequently converting these objectives into curriculum contents, the participants divided into small work groups. Half of the groups were oriented towards medical sociology training for future physicians, the other half towards sociology training.

Two educational scientists, S. Maes and M. Goyvaerts-Boekaert, University of Antwerp, had prepared a didactical work method for this experiment. They elaborately explained this procedure in their paper, 'Indications for curriculum construction featuring the formulation of objectives and the selection of content'. [1] An abridged version of this paper is given below.

Medical sociology curriculum construction, according to the proposed method, appeared to be relatively practical for the groups dealing with training for future physicians, although the recollected objectives seemed arbitrary and showed little consistency. In the groups dealing with sociology training, however, the same curriculum construction

1. S. Maes, M. Goyvaerts-Boekaerts, Department of Education, Univ. of Antwerp (U.I.A.), Belgium, 'Indications for Curriculum Construction featuring the formulation of objectives and the selection of content,' First Draft Copy, 1976.

exercise proved to be unworkable and caused vehement contestation of what was labeled 'a medical, artifical and behavioristic treatment of the teaching-learning process'.

The workshop provoked a wave of criticism, aggravating both the pros and cons on the didactical approach. Yet the discomfort underlying this criticism, which was worded rather vaguely, pertained mainly to the inadequacy of behavioristic principles for grounding medical sociology.

The most meaningful way of reflecting on the workshop's experiment, perhaps, is to attempt an interpretation of this intuitive suspicion and the rather superficial labeling of the didactical processing of training programs, rather than to report the proceedings of the workshop in a more formal manner. Therefore, we will not evaluate here the actual outcome of the workgroups' activities but examine why the didactical method seemed to be more applicable to the elaboration of objectives for a medical sociology program for medical training than for sociology training. This element deserves our attention because it concerns a phenomenon that was recurrent throughout the workshop.

Restating the participants' overall evaluation of the workshop, we may say that an incompatibility was felt between a pragmatic approach according to the didactic instructions of curriculum construction and the essence of what happens in a training process. The decision-making process of behavioristically determined educational objectives (see section 2) was felt to be a programmed instruction method referring to a paradigm of conditioning concerning learning.

The reflections below (see sections 3, 4 and 5) aim at finding an explanation for this alleged inadequacy of the didactical method. By way of introduction, a condensed but complete account[2] of the method's instructions will be given.

2. To this end the original paper has been abridged.

14.2. Indications for curriculum construction featuring the formulation of objectives and the selection of content.

14.2.1. Curriculum construction: a sequential decision process.

Any teaching situation is created so as to make learners acquire some knowledge, skills or attitudes. Any educational scientist, however, would have great difficulty explaining the basic concepts 'learning' and 'teaching', for there are as many definitions of these concepts as there are scholars in the field. Nevertheless, most educational psychologists and educational scientists agree that *learning* means a relatively permanent change in the behavior of the learner and that efficient *teaching* implies that the teacher or lecturer is able to change the behavioral repertoire of the learner in the intended way.

This approach to the teaching-learning process puts the emphasis on the behavioral changes in the learner rather than on the contents of the learning process. Consequently, a mere listing of subject matter to be learned is not an adequate basis for constructing a curriculum or teaching unit. Indeed, the basic building block of any curriculum should be the listing of all intended behavioral changes in the learner. Put in another way: the curriculum should be based on a listing of objectives which one wants the students to attain at the end of the curriculum.

It is a fact, however, that most university courses do not have adequately defined goals. When asked the purpose of their courses, lecturers may give the vague answer that they aim at providing their students with a well-integrated general background in their subject. But on the whole they have no clear conception of the goals they are trying to attain. It is obvious, however, that in a teaching situation where the goals and more important, the objectives are lacking, the lecturer is not in a position to analyse adequately the students' entering behavior in selecting the content of the teaching units, in choosing the instructional procedures and in devising an adequate evaluation procedure. All these components really depend on the general aims and objectives of the course. These components can be viewed as sequential steps in the decision-making process of curriculum construction and outlined as follows in fig. 14.1:

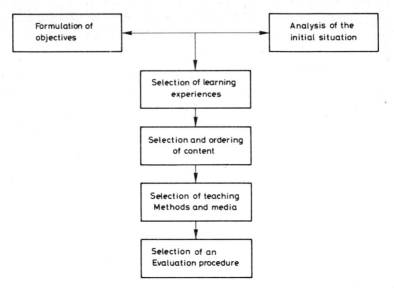

Figure 14.1. The six sequential components in the decision-making process (Synthesis of various models such as De Corte *et al*, Glaser, Meuwese, Van Gelder, Wheeler).

14.2.2. Curriculum construction: components

The first component of the sequential decision process represents the formulation of general and concrete objectives, the starting point or the basic building block of the whole curriculum process. This component will be elaborated on in section 2.3. after the presentation of the model's other components. It will suffice to say here that objectives are statements about the behavior which the students should display when they have finished the curriculum or teaching unit. These objectives, originating as rather imprecise and vague general aims, must be made progressively more specific and must be ultimately formulated in terms of concrete observable student behavior.

The first component of the decision process, viz., *the formulation of the objectives*, is closely linked to the second component, viz., *the analysis of the students' initial or entering behavior.* The latter is quintessential in the sequential decision process because it provides the necessary information about the students' existing knowledge, skills and attitudes. If this aspect of the curriculum construction process is ignored, the lecturer or the curriculum-constructor runs the risk of selecting and formulating objectives which are either redundant, inadequate or impossible to attain. In addition to the analysis of the students' initial behavior, other aspects ought to be investigated in the initial stages of the curriculum construction process, viz., (i) the educational system, or, in a wider context, the social scene within which the training program is situated, (ii) the social subgroup the students are members of, (iii) the characteristic features of the lecturers who will be involved in the training program, etc. All these factors influence the first component, the formulation of objectives, to a large extent. For it stands to reason that the formulation of the ultimate behavioral objectives, i.e. the intended behavioral changes which the lecturer wants his students to achieve, depends on the existing knowledge, skills and attitudes of the students, to a large extent, as well as on their potentials, interests, needs and on the overall teaching environment. When the objectives have been formulated – obviously in close connection with the conclusions of the analysis process – the lecturer must *select a number of relevant experiences*, which will help his students to acquire the intended behavioral change.

There are a number of ways in which the lecturer may provide his students with the relevant information about this objective. But the student has the best chance of changing his attitude or behavior when he is confronted with a concrete practical case.

The next component in the decision chain is the selection of content. The selection of content must be based on the formulated objectives and not the other way around.

It should not be the aim of any educational program that students learn merely subject matter.

The content of the teaching unit is nothing more than a means of realizing the intended behavioral change. Component five of the decision process is labelled 'selection of teaching methods and media'.

In the training of medical sociology, as in other university courses, the emphasis is still too much on lectures and seminars.

The last component in the decision process is *the design of the evaluation procedure.* In this last stage a procedure should be developed which checks whether the intended objectives have been attained. In order to be able to decide unequivocally whether the students' behavior has indeed altered in the intended direction, it is of the utmost importance that the lecturer has formulated the objectives in terms of measurable behavioral patterns.

14.2.3. The formulation of objectives.

As mentioned above, objectives are statements about the required terminal behavior which the students must display when they have finished a teaching unit. It is necessary, at this point, to make a distinction between several kinds of objectives.

14.2.3.1. General objectives versus concrete objectives.

First, a distinction is made between general objectives and concrete objectives. General objectives, though absolutely essential in constructing the curriculum, are insufficient as guidelines for directing the teaching-learning process. They are too vague and imprecise and have no concrete meanings attached to them.

If general objections do not clearly specify the type of behavioral change the lecturer must aim at obtaining, it follows that the lecturer will not be able to decide, unequivocally, whether his students have indeed acquired the expected behavior at the end of the course or teaching unit.

On the contrary, concrete objectives are more specific and precise in nature and allow the lecturer to evaluate whether his students have acquired the desired terminal behavior. It may be concluded then, that general objectives are valuable to the lecturer but are in need of further specification, i.e. they need to be formulated in terms of concrete observable student behavior.

What is meant by concrete, observable behavior and how precisely should goals be formulated? In this respect, some criteria with which the goals should comply as far as possible can be supplied.

The first of these criteria specifies that goals should be *stated in terms of the behavior of the students.*

The second criterion is an elaboration of the first. It refers to the specific skill or behavior which the students should display at the end of the course or teaching unit. These specific behavioral patterns are best described by the auxiliary verb 'to be able to' followed by a series of verbs which *specify the observable behavior*, e.g., 'to be able to draw...', 'to be able to underline...' 'to be able to specify in a sentence', 'to be able to list...' 'to be able to calculate...', 'to be able to demonstrate...', etc.[3]

The third criterion relates to the *content of the objectives*. It is obvious that in order to be adequately formulated, objectives must specify accurately the content to which the formulated objective must be applied.

The next criterion concerns *the conditions under which the students must be able to demonstrate the specified behavior.*

A final criterion is the degree to which a given behavior must be mastered. The lecturer must *decide beforehand how well the students are to be able to perform the terminal behavior*. This decision or norm must be reflected in the objective.

14.2.3.2. Objectives relating to knowledge, skills and attitudes.

A further distinction has to be made between objectives relating to *knowledge*, objectives relating to *skills* and objectives relating to *attitudes*.

It should be noted that 'knowledge' can only be measured if the objective is stated in a 'be able to' form, i.e., in terms of a specific behavioral skill. Attitudes, on the other hand, consist equally of a skill plus the willingness to use this skill at the right time. Hence, one could subdivide objectives into two basic categories, viz. skills and attitudes.

In order to provide a useful frame of reference against which objectives can be formulated, one must classify the different kinds of objectives according to their basic components. This classification is intended only as an aid in formulating the objectives and, as such, is, incomplete.

3. As an illustration, the authors, Maes and Goyvaerts-Boekaert added Deno and Jenkins' list of a series of 99 verbs which have been arranged along a continuum ranging from more observalbe to less observalbe. (Deno, Jenkins, Rank Order Distribution of Means and Variances for 99 Verbs Ratings, 1969).

A. KNOWLEDGE

Comprehension and recall of:

1. specific facts, events, symbols, and referents
   e.g., to be acquainted with the regulations concerning medical repayments
2. ways and means of dealing with specific facts, events, symbols, and their referents
   e.g., to be able to summarize and discuss a book on medical sociology
3. universals and abstractions in a field
   e.g., to be able to explain the structure of the Belgian Public Health Service

B. SKILLS

1. intellectual skills:
   e.g. to be able to report a conversation with a patient
2. social skills:
   e.g. to be able to analyse the non-verbal communication of a patient
3. psychomotor skills:
   this skill is less relevant for the training program in medical sociology

C. ATTITUDES

= feelings, sensitivities, beliefs, and values. It will suffice to refer to the example quoted by Aakster: 'What is especially stressed in medical education is: being independent and autonomous, taking quick action, reliance on own judgement and relevance...'

Finally attention must be drawn to the fact that, when formulating an attitude, one should take care that the necessary knowledge and skill underlying this attitude are also taken into account.

14.2.4. The selection of content

As mentioned earlier, teaching subject matter is not the ultimate aim of the teaching-learning process; the subject matter must serve as a means of acquiring the formulated objectives, and has, as such, a mediatory role. In order to assist the lecturer in selecting the subject matter which will serve this mediatory role, a number of criteria are supplied. The following two major and three minor criteria, taken from Wheeler (1972), are not intended as absolute requirements but rather as a basis for selection.

The two major criteria are: the validity of content and the significance of content. The former specifies that the content which has been selected to realize a particular objective must enable students to perform the terminal behavior. The second criterion specifies that the content must be significant. It stands to reason that the content selected for the realization of a particular objective, or set of objectives, should include the basic subject matter; in this case, the subject matter of medical sociology.

The three minor criteria are: the needs and interests of the students, the utility criterion, and learnability. The first specifies that the subject matter must be in accordance with the needs and interest of the students following the course. Although one should pay attention to this requirement mainly when formulating the objectives, it should also be kept in mind when selecting the contents of a course.

The second minor criterion, viz., the utility criterion, relates to the social efficiency and the social relevance of the subject matter. The contents of a course may not seem socially relevant or useful at first sight to students; nevertheless, it is recommended that lectures in medical sociology see to it that their students pay attention to the social relevance and the practical value of the knowledge and skills which they are teaching.

The last minor criterion is learnability. This implies that the level of the subject matter must be adapted to the level of the students.

All the components of the sequential decision process are intrinsically related; one ought to take each of them into account when planning to construct a curriculum.

14.3. Situating the didactical method for curriculum construction.

In general, both opinions on, and the pedagogic-didactic approach to, training in academic circles are based more on casual and superficial impressions than on systematic investigation and reflection. Historically, this may result from the fact that scholarship in western universities was originally a private concern. This tradition underwent a revolution as a result of two social processes which are roughly and generally designated as massification and democratization of training. These notions refer to the heightening in the population's general educational level and the quantitative expansion of the student population. These processes began around the turn of the century, starting at lower educational levels and continuing at the university level after World War II.

This structural change in the training situation compelled the universities to institutionalize the scholarship of academic circles into an academic system, grafted to the value pattern of cognitive rationality. [4] The organizational problems of an expanding academic system necessitated a concern with the problems of educating.

The manner in which this concern was expressed has also evolved. What looked like, at the beginning, from a scientific point of view, a kind of empiricist attitude, later developed into scientific concern.

Medical training is a good example of this development. This may be explained, on the one hand, by the seniority of its institutionalization process (extending from medical apprenticeship to the present-day organization of medical instruction), on the other hand, by the social weight accorded to the profession, which is partly shaped by medical training. The latter element, in view of the fact that the practice of this profession is felt to be problematic (both internally by the professionals and externally by society) becomes an incentive for paying attention to training.

Both factors play a comparatively less important role for sociology,

---

4. Referring to Parsons' definition, we mean here: the development, the manipulation and the tranference of bodies of knowledge judged in terms of empirical validity.

which is a much less institutionalized discipline. One reason for this is suggested by its genesis: sociology is a relatively young science, but, more importantly, its institutionalization process has been impeded because it runs parallel to a process in a parent discipline. In the European universities, an internal slowing-down factor in the evolution of human science forces sociology, in the first phase of its autonomous development, to grow away from either philosophy, law or economics. Moreover, societal claims involving the social usefulness of the various sociological professions are less specific than for the medical profession.

If sociologists themselves feel this to be a problem, they have so far given free rein to their sociological speculation about their own training rather than make this the object of their research activities. On the other hand, a sociology of the profession and a sociology of education have been developed for other trainings and professions. Medical sociology, for example, has shown vivid interest in medical training.

In order to situate the didactical method for curriculum construction in the context of the changes in concern in academic training, this evolution should be researched more extensively than is possible here. Here only a brief outline can be given of the interest social-scientific research has shown in academic teaching. Moreover, the outline focuses on medical training. Such an overview is a minimal support for the thesis that a scientific method for the didactic processing of training, as presented by Maes and Goyvaerts, is consistent with what will be called the 'recent offshoots of social research on training'.

Medical training is very appropriate as an example not only for the above-mentioned reasons of advanced institutionalization and social relevance, but also because a great deal of research has been done in the field of medical training in comparison with training programs in other fields.

A major impulse to this research came from several medical schools in the U.S.A. in the 1950's. This was an incubation period for new initiatives, changes and reforms of the medical training situation, which was considered to be problematic. The medical trainers themselves felt the need, after trial and error concerning the medical training situation, to collect systematically-analyzed scientific knowledge in this field.

This was also American sociology's golden era of research on professional socialization. Social-scientific research on medical training then led to works such as *Boys in White* and *The Student-Physician*.[5]

Both projects were scientific in-depth analyses and examined the process of becoming a physician as an extensive process, thereby relying largely on qualitative research methods and several years of field work. Consequently, these studies provided an original body of knowledge, supported by an abundance of rich insights.

After this onset, however, a stagnation of projects with comparable span and depth could be observed in the U.S., while in Europe such projects were neither developed nor duplicated. This observed stagnation calls for elucidation. R.C. Fox, in the cited paper, page 2, formulates the problem as:

---

5. The following review has been taken from R.C. Fox, *The Process of Professional Socialization, Is there A 'New' Medical Student? A Comparative View of Medical Socialization in the 1950's* and *the 1970's*. Paper, published in Laurence R. Tancredi, ed. Ethics of Health Care. Washington, D.C.: National Academy of Sciences, 1974, pp. 197-227.

Major publications based on these studies include: Howard S. Becker, Blanche Geer, Evertt C. Hughes and Anselm L. Strauss, *Boys in White: Student Culture in Medical School*, Chicago (the University of Chicago Press 1961); Kenneth R. Hammond and Fred Kern, Jr., *Teaching Comprehensive Medical Care*, Cambridge, Mass (Harvard University Press, for the Commonweatlh Fund, 1956); Milton J. Horowitz, *Educating Tomorrow's Doctors*, New York (Appleton-Century-Crofts, 1964); Robert K. Merton, George Reader and Patricia L. Kendall, eds., *The Student-Physician: Introductory Studies in the Sociology of Medical Education*, Cambridge, Mass. (Harvard University Press, for the Commonwealth Fund, 1957); George E. Miller, *Teaching and Learning in Medical School*, Cambridge, Mass. (Harvard University Press, for the Commonweatlh Fund, 1961). In addition, at least two major books on the house officership phase of medical training came out of that period: Stephen J. Miller, *Prescription for Leadership: Training for the Medical Elite*, Chicago (Aldine Publishing Co., 1970) and Emily Mumford, *Interns: From Students to Physicians*, Cambridge, Mass. (Harvard University Press, for the Commonwealth Fund, 1970). For a state of the field review of these and other sociology of medical education studies, see Samuel W. Bloom, 'The Sociology of Medical Education: Some Comments on the State of the Field', *Milbank Memorial Fund Quarterly*, Vol. XLIII, n° 2, April 1965, pp. 143-184.

'Why the current paucity of work on medical socialization exists is a subject for study in and on itself. Its explanation is intricately associated with the stage of development and the collective mood both of social science and medicine, and with more general cultural, economic and political trends in the society that affect these disciplines'.

Fox gives the following elements for an explanation (page 34-35):

'This is as much a consequence of social scientists' brand of ambivalence towards the socialization process as it is a question of medical schools' receptivity to such undertakings or availability of funds to carry them out. ... They [sociologists of medicine] are not enthusiastic about launching studies of becoming a physician in the 1970's, and even less disposed to cast them in the conceptual framework of the 1950's. Insofar as they would be at all willing to conduct research in medical schools rather than in medical practice settings, these sociologists would lay greater stress on studying the faculty, the social organization of the medical school, and especially its organization of power, than on inquiring into student attitudes, experiences and culture. They seem to be more interested in political and economic facets of the medical school than sociologists were in the fifties, and more intent on doing research that will have policy implications. One detects in their orientation a certain undercurrent of disappointment over the fact that the sociology of medical school inquiries carried out twenty years ago did not lead to reforms in the educational process which significantly improved the way that medicine is organized and practiced in our society. These activist yearnings and regrets on the part of sociologists, along with their increased social structural determinism, are not conducive to their undertaking studies of medical socialization in the seventies'.

In other words, to explain the stagnation of research modeled on the original projects, Fox points out two elements associated with social science practice. First, general sociology's conceptualization has been characterized by a shift from in-depth research on a primarily cultural-analysis level to a more structural analysis, focusing primarily on organizational aspects. Furthermore, in association with the structural analysis level, quantitative research methods and techniques have been replacing the qualitative ones. Secondly, the social scientists increasingly develop activist expectations about the immediate and practical reforming impact of their research, while social research of the socialization-study type provides little outlook for this.

The latter type of research is no longer desired by medical trainers either. They have more and more instrumental expectations about social research, particularly since innovations and experiments have begun in medical training in the last two decades. In other words, medical trainers expect more practical results from the scientific contribution of evaluative types of research. The problems involving training which they want researched are restricted and specific in nature.

Regarding social-scientific research into medical training, these two patterns of expectations, from the 'demand' side (the medical schools) as well as from the 'supply' side (the social scientists), are the current background against which the reduction of the broadly-encompassing exploratory investigations of the 1950's to the more narrowly-conceptualized recent investigations should be seen. The recent studies, as they are reported regularly in professional journals, are of a partial and evaluative conception, dealing with such aspects as 'evaluation systems for medical training', 'training of medical students in interpersonal relationship skills', 'constructing a new course for the teaching of general practice', 'student expectations and reactions towards behavioral science', 'changes in physician attitudes towards reform in medical education', etc. These studies usually construct a field experimental design on a limited research population or setting and are conducted with the highly sophisticated research techniques of the quantitative social survey methods.

Systematic reading of such research reports gives rise to several remarks: Is it possible that, in social research on medical training, a Kuhnian phenomenon of a narrowing of scope is taking place – the recent studies being only fillers in a field opened up by the pioneering studies? Has the recent trend of social research into medical training been contaminated by the positive scientific orientation of the setting it studies? Or have the medical trainers transferred the scientific point of view, typical for their own field of knowledge, to the research approach of the training process? If this is true, it seems that the medical nemesis has stricken social research as well, and that because of cultural iatrogenesis, the social sciences' specificity is threatened.

These reflections confirm the suggestions in the above-mentioned elements explaining the shift in the nature of social scientific research; for a complete explanation, an approach from the point of view of the sociology of knowledge is indispensable. But, for research into medical training, additional explanatory elements should be sought which may play a role in the specific interplay of supply and demand involving this research field. Such an investigation, however, is outside the limits of a descriptive outline of social scientific research into medical training.

In rounding off this outline, one may conclude that recent social-scientific research on medical training confines its scientific approach to partial aspects of the process of medical training. In the line of this approach, the research has immediate, practical objectives. One of these is the research design's orientation towards discovering how well medical training attains its propagated (traditional and/or experimental) objectives. Complementing this is the attempt to determine which factors and circumstances affect, or possibly promote, the completion of these objectives.

The factors and variables that are evaluated in these offshoots of social research constitute the foundation on which the didactical approach constructs its frame of reference. They are collected to constitute the initial situation. The method then consists of programming them for the desired training output. This output is divided into objectives. These objectives are drafted in monitorable behavior categories which have to be realized in the students' behavior by the end of the training.

Determining these objectives amounts ultimately to laying out the factors and variables affecting the behavior categories. These include elements present in the initial situation as well as any new imputable factors found to be relevant by scientific research and enabling adjustment of the training process.

These reflections were aimed at enabling a better understanding of the scientific nature claimed by the didactic method presented. The conclusion that can be drawn: the content of this method essentially amounts to a derivation of research results from the most recent trend of scientific research into training. Concerning the quality of this research, it can be observed that it more and more reaches the level of 'empiricism at its worst'.

It seems paradoxical that academic open-ness to a scientific approach to training, developing from the feeling of discomfort about the traditional intuitively-empiristic attitude, results in substituting scientific empiricism for this attitude.

14.4. Analysis of the didactical method for hidden assumptions

14.4.1. One dimensionality with respect to behavior-determinants

An analysis of the training process that is as systematic and as rational as that in which the didactical method is framed is, indeed, scientifically-empiricist in nature: it is a scientific empiricism to assume a correlation between measurable qualities and characteristics of individual students and subsequent academic performance at the end of the training, as measured by grades and similar evaluation criteria.

This has to do with the affinity of the didactical method's analysis of the training process with predominantly psychological theories on learning behavior. Under the influence of these theories, trained capacities are believed to be determining for the successful-ness of student behavior, and this successful-ness is further extrapolized towards professional behavior.

In this respect, the didactical method is guilty of being incomplete by not sufficiently taking sociological insights into account in addition to psychological insights. It is unsociological to ignore the importance of the sustaining value-environment for behavior, thus overlooking the sociological premise 'that motivations are characteristically translated into corresponding behavior only when the social context provides for this'.[6]

Insufficient consideration of environment determinants with respect to behavior explains the fact that the didactical method automatically relates professional behavior to performance during training. This has, *a fortiori*, consequences when it suggests the projection of the medical student's successful academic performance into his professional behavior. Precisely with regard to professions, institutional elements act strongly on behavior as environment determinants.

In E. Freidson's theory of the profession elaborated for the medical profession, he points out the crucial influence on professional be-

---

6. R.K. Merton, *The Student-Physician. Introductory Studies in the Sociology of Medical Education,* Cambridge, Harvard University Press, 1957, p. 12.

havior inherent in features of practice organization and division of labor.

'Such elements are critical because they deal with facets of professional occupations that are independent of individual motivation or intention, and... that may minimize the importance to behavior of the personal qualities of intelligence, ethicality, and trained skill imputed to professionals...'.[7]

14.4.2. One-dimensionality in the conceptualization of training

The same one-dimensionality (behavior not viewed as influenced, on the one hand, by personal qualities and, on the other, by the social and cultural environment, i.e., not viewed as the result of the inter-action between the individual and his personal qualities[8] and patterned situations) is also present in the way in which the training process is conceptualized by the didactical method. Indeed, both dimensions are closely connected in training; they may be called, respectively, the psychology and the sociology of learning. The didactical method, however, adopts primarily the psychology of learning. This is a simplification of the complexity of learning, which is the essence of training, as it is with any socialization process. Complex learning is not only a function of intelligence and aptitude, of motivations and self-images it is also a function of the social environments in which learning and performance take place.

14.4.3. Reductionistic conceptualization of socialization

The incompleteness of the didactical method as described in sections 4.1. and 4.2. appears in the narrowed socialization concept underlying this method.

To clarify this, 'socialization' will first be defined in its broad

---

7. E. Freidson, *Professional Dominance: The Social Structure of Medical Care*, N.Y., Atherton Press, 1970, p. 133.
8. See R.K. Merton, *The Student Physician*, p. 62. In this paragraph the author discusses the possibilities and limitations of psychological and sociological research on selected problems in medical education. He points out that in these research projects, the theoretical problems are still larger than the technical ones: '...theoretical problems which have to do with the conceptual framework adopted in these inquiries.'

conceptualization, using sociological insights of, among others, structural functionalism. This definition will then serve as a frame of reference against which the socialization concept of the didactical method can be revealed.

In a comprehensive general formula, the socialization process is understood to be 'the process through which individuals are inducted into their culture. It involves the acquisition of attitudes and values, of skills and behavior patterns making up social roles established in the social structure'.[9]

This program continues throughout the life cycle as 'a progressive series of differentiations, each subsequent level numerically more inclusive and structurally more complex than the last. Socialization can be analyzed with respect to the differentiation of the personality and with respect to increasing complexity of the social structures and normative patterns in which the personality participates and to which it becomes committed'.[10]

The socialization process is observed to have phases and, therefore, can be differentiated with respect to various social-structural levels, each one of which involves ontogenetic elements.

Socialization takes place in two types of role acquisition processes.

The first type concerns more direct learning, i.e., learning guided by explicitly didactical intentions. The second one, which might be called' 'moral socialization', takes place through more indirect learning: the individual acquires values, attitudes and behavior patterns not as a result of explicit intervention but rather as a side-effect of personal growth through life events, as a 'by-product' of life itself.

Direct socialization processes easily lend themselves to formal instruction and transference of knowledge and skills; in other words, to what may be labeled, from another conceptualization, specific and technical learning as opposed to diffuse socialization.[11] The notion of

---

9. R.K. Merton, *The Student Physician*, p. 40.
10. T. Parsons, G.M. Platt, Age, 'Social structure and socialization in higher education', in Sociology of Education, 43 (1970) 1, p. 7
11. The conceptualization of diffuse socialization versus specific and technical learning is taken from: J.W. Meyer, 'The Charter: Conditions of diffuse socialization in schools', in W.R. Scott, *Social Process and Social Structures, an Introduction to Sociology*, N.Y., Holt, Rinehart and Winston, 1970, pp. 564-578.

diffuse socialization refers to 'the acquisition by individuals of qualities which will guide a considerable range of their behavior – behavior in differing contexts and *vis-à-vis* different social others'. [12]

Direct socialization processes cover a whole range: they may focus on either the diffuse or the very techincal dimension; nevertheless, they always include elements of both. Education is to be catalogued under the heading: direct socialization towards processes.

The didactical method, because it is being marooned in the psychological dimension of learning, views training as socialization from the perspective of structuring the students' individual personalities. Because of the method's belief in the behavioristic trend of learning psychology, this means a structuring of personality observable by behavior.

Since environmental influence, for the didactical method, has in itself only secondary importance in learning, the method attributes socializing relevance only to those aspects of the training situation which it acknowledges have an impact on behavior. The most obvious impact-having factors are located in the immediate vicinity; in other words, in the organizational features of the training situation.

These reflections on socialization, associated with the presumptions of the didactical method, may explain why the method conceptualizes socialization from an angle that is restricted to what might be called organizational socialization. This implies a two-fold restriction of the socialization process in its broad meaning. The first restriction is that one socialization phase is abstracted, viz., that of training itself, which is more or less amputated from the overall process developing throughout the individual's life cycle.

This phase makes a rupture with what precedes it. This means that the socializing effect of training is attributed to the intervention in the students' experience of their present life situation. This is a rupture between the training phase and the post-training phase. It strips the training's socialization phase of its anticipatory reality.

The second restriction is the reduction of socialization to a process taking place within the well-defined locus of the training institution. This means that training is viewed as a socially-isolated event, and

12. J. W. Meyer, a bove, p. 566.

that institutionalized training is separated from its social grounding.

The organizational socialization concept supporting the didactical method views training as a socialization phase that is fixed with regard to phasing and localization.

In reference to the instructions about the nature of the objectives that are to be realized, the didactical method, bases these instructions on the following ambiguity: The content and relevance of the educational objectives for their expected socializing effect are on the level of diffuse socialization. They represent qualities that should be acquired through training in order to guide later social functioning; in other words, they are the moral substratum of training. This moral substratum, however, is fixed or imputed on objectives that must be concretely formulated. This means that moral values and other diffusely socializable qualities are methodologically translated to the level of specific and technical learning. Thus, basic values of training are programmed as context-specific values. Irregardless of desirability, the practicability of the internalization and reinforcement of basic values as socializing effects, aimed at by means of formalized instruction, may surely be questioned.

14.4.4. Societal implications

As has been suggested in the exposition of the socialization concept implicity used by the didactical method, attention should be given to the social repercussions of processing training using this method.

The didactical method presumes that training takes place in a rather hermetic subsystem within society. Within the limits of such a model, the didactical construction of the training is accomplished as a closed-circuit programming of the training.

This implies the theoretical negation of the adage, voiced in all forms of institutionalized direct socialization, that every institutionalized system is, structurally and culturally, part of the wider social system and is influenced by changing societal needs and expectations. This perspective, of dialectical interplay between training and society, is lacking in the approach to training as organizational socialization. As a result, several processes that can be observed in this interplay are overlooked. Nevertheless:

'Schools affect graduates through several other processes [than small socialization effects of organizational arrangements on student attitudes and behavior] which have been largely overlooked due to the exclusive attention given to locating socialization effects of different organizational conditions. Schools affect individuals and society in the following ways, independently of any impacts they have on individuals. First they are used to construct categories of membership in society, to which important job and other rights and social meanings are attached. Second, schools legitimate these rights by institutionalizing ideas about the qualities and abilities of graduates versus non-graduates. Third, schools are the agencies that ritually certify graduates as members of social status groups to whose privileges they are entitled. All of these processes operate independently of any direct socialization effect schools have on students.'[13]

'... Interaction between socializers and socializees in these settings [schools] is enormously conditioned by the understanding both parties have of the wider standing of the institution in society – what social position it can guarantee its clients in society, or what future it can hold out to them.'[14]

The impact attributed by the didactical method to the socialization it aims at through training should be relativized as follows: the socializing effect resulting from the organizational structure of training should be weighed against the socializing effect resulting from the interaction between society and the organization of training, and the manner in which the organization of training is being defined by society. The latter socializing effect is the one that depends upon the social charter of the training organization. This charter may be defined as 'the agreed-on social definition of its products'[15] and is 'an attribute of an organization's relation to its environmental context, not its internal structure'.[16]

By concentrating on the training problem and attempting to give it an adequate solution through curriculum construction, the didactical method implies the risk of either ignoring the social charter of university training or preventing it from being questioned. It is difficult to minimize this risk, since the didactical method employs the instrument of curriculum construction without questioning which symbolic function a curriculum (in its organization context of a certain

13. D. H. Kamens, Legitimating Myths and Educational Organization: The Relationship between Organizational Ideology and Formal Structure, in: *American Sociological Review*, 42 (1977) April, p. 209.
14. J. W. Meyer, p. 567.
15. J. W. Meyer, p. 565.
16. J. W. Meyer, p. 567.

training) represents for the nature of the socialization that is offered and/or aimed at. On the other hand, when taking into account the social charter of training, the organizational structure – notably the form and content of the curriculum – are considered as indicators of the nature and objectives of the socialization offered.

Considering the negation of the charter of training by the didactical method, it may be hypothesized that it acknowledges exclusively the socially-manifest function of the training's socialization process, i.e., the function of transferring the basic value of training itself – the socialization of the cognitive rationality by training for excellence in the mastery of knowledge and skills.

The latent function of university training, i.e. its recruitment function for specific membership categories is society, is left out of scope. Such a perspective lends itself perfectly to the ideological disguise of the socially-stratifying effect of the recruitment function. The supply by the university of a so-called intellectual elite is indeed moored in the dialectic between training and society. This implies that both training and social canalization of university graduates have connections with interest groups in society.

It is in the socio-cultural and economic field of interests interacting between university and society that the stratifying function of university training should be situated: simultaneously with the intellectual flow from the university towards society is the flow of power and privileges that are to be distributed, dealt within society.

14.5. Beyond the evident explanation of a workshop's experiment...

The above evaluation of the societal implications of the didactical method leads to the conclusion that this method, presenting itself as an aid for structuring training in a more scientific manner, is in fact an instrument that makes it possible to intervene in the interaction between training and society.

On the basis of this observation, the fact that the didactical method proved to be more applicable to medical training than to sociological training will now be re-examined.

Two obvious, interrelated, explanations can be given for this phenomenon. First, there are the different natures of the socialization processes within the two training types. Within the socialization process in medical training, emphasis is put on specific and technical learning; whereas sociology training is characterized more by diffuse socialization.

Secondly, as has already been suggested in the paragraph situating the didactical method, medical training is preparation for a profession that shows a very avowed institutionalization in society, whereas sociology training provides a competence that as yet has no correspondence with a marked functional differentiation of professional roles.

This professional vagueness of sociology confirms the desirability of a diffuse training of competence, personal qualities, values and norms that can be applied flexibly to various professional situations. This contradicts the idea of giving training priority to training for specific behavior, which would obviously hamper the formulation of concrete, specific, preferably behavioral, educational objectives.

Constructing training on the basis of such objectives as described above is basically the incorporating of professional objectives into training. In specialized medical professional roles professional objectives can, indeed, be incorporated.

Exploring this evident explanation further, the fact that the didactical method is better suited to medical training than to sociology training is actually an indicator of the stability of the mechanisms of social connection concerning training. As to the nature of the connection between medical training and the medical profession, some insights from Freidson's profession theory have been mentioned already above. The aim in doing so was to point out, as a feature of the medical profession, the institutional influence of the practice organization, and the division of labor, on professional performance. The explanation which this theory offers for the strong institutional influence of a profession is professional autonomy, or the profession's self-directiveness *vis-à-vis* its own expertise. The medical profession displays this self-directiveness on different levels. The most important of these, perhaps is, the creation of a legally- or politically-privileged social status for its own professional practice. Here, however, a second level is relevant: a basic part of self-directiveness is the exclusive control over 'the production and over the application of knowledge and skills in the work it [the profession] performs'. [17] In controlling medical training, the medical profession has direct interests related to regulating and safeguarding the labor market.

No further evidence is needed to see that the didactical method is an adequate means of establishing control over training, by way of training construction.

If, in academic and other medical settings, this method is valorized (and there seems to be a trend in this direction [18]) or even concretely applied, notably in experimental training programs, the situating and analyzing of this method may hopefully raise some justified questions about the nature of the educational concern warranted by the didactical method. Moreover, the trend for valorization takes place in a period in which both the medical profession and the training are considered social problems and qualify for re-definition and modification – for the many reasons given in the previous chapters. The case of medical training shows how a didactical approach to training, presented in the name of scientific efficiency, allows itself to be ideologically encapsulated in a configuration between training and interest-groups in order to make training controllable.

For sociology, such social impulses to make training controllable are less strong.

The degree to which social connection concerning this training is real, as well as the connection mechanisms themselves, are liable for discussion. A thorough questioning of the charter of sociology in society is required before conclusions can be drawn about the opportunity for stabilized connections.

17. E. Freidson, *Professional Dominance: The Social Structure of Medical Care*, N.Y., Atherton Press, 1970, p. 134.
18. See, for example, the instructions for the reform of medical training, published by the W.H.O., *Educational Handbook* (Guide Pédagogique), 1976.

PART SEVEN

EVALUATION OF THE SEMINAR

15. Critical evaluation of the seminar

Derek Gill

The conference was opened by Professor Yvo Nuyens, the Chairman of the Planning Committee, with a brief account of the genesis of the seminar. Reference was made to the international conference on sociology held in Yablona, Poland, in 1973, under the auspices of Professor Magdalena Sokolowska and her colleagues from the Polish Academy of Sciences, and to the meetings of the Medical Sociology Research Committee of the International Sociological Association in Toronto in 1974, both of which included papers on the training of medical sociologists and their roles in medical education. Professor Nuyens went on to state that these two meetings had generated such discussion and interest in the subject that the decision emerged to hold an international conference devoted to these particular themes and in the past few days, we have been engaged here in an enterprise which might best be described as the development of a sociology of medical sciology. Nuyens, in his introduction, emphasized that the discussion should focus upon future training programs and how these might be changed or enlarged to accommodate the increasing demands being made upon medical sociology and medical sociologists – demands for involvement in the operation of health care programs, health care planning, policy-making and the involvement of sociologists in the activities of various pressure groups ranging from consumer representative organizations through action groups to participation in a variety of bodies representing the interests and activities of the medical profession and other health care practitioners – as well as the increasingly important contribution which medical sociologists make towards the training of medical students. Professor Mark Field, the President of the Research Committee for the Sociology of Medecine of ISA, then thanked, on behalf of the committee, the persons and institutions responsible for the organization and convening of these meetings. Field summarized the objectives of the Medical Sociology Committee, which amongst other things, tries to act as a catalyst for the genesis of international meetings, where medical scociologists from all over the world can meet with their colleagues from other countries. Mark Field introduced a ringing note into the proceedings, although as far as I am aware he is not a campanologist, by reminding the audience of the apostolic, even priestly, function of medicine, both contemporaneously and historically. Professor H. Janssens of Antwerp University, the Chairman of the Belgium Inter-University Consultation Board for General Practitioner Training, then welcomed the delegates to the conference on behalf of the Belgium medical profession. Dr. Janssens went on to describe a new development in the teaching of general practioners in some Belgium institutions. Future generations of general practioners are being taught jointly in seminars by experienced general practitioners and medical sociologists. This innovation in general practitioner training is an attempt to provide students with an approach to and an understanding of the inextricable mix of medical, sociological and biological factors which relate to the incidence of illness and disease and the development of a prospective approach to the problems of primary care. In this way, future generations of general practitioners are being taught to treat their patients in the context of their family, community and societal relationships – in short, to treat the whole patient rather than the illness or disease episode or general disquiet or discomfort which motivated the doctor-patient interaction. Dr. Woudenberg, the Regional Officer for Health Education and Social Sciences, World Health Organization, European Division in Copenhagen, then welcomed the delegates on behalf of WHO. Dr. Woudenberg, himself a health educator, emphasized the need to focus upon preventive health measures by persuading populations to take more responsibility for their own health care. In this way, Woudenberg argued, by the inculcation of habits leading to more healthy lifestyles, health education programs have the potential for considerably improving the health status of populations.

Rather than continuing with a sequential account of the conference proceedings and papers presented, I have chosen to group the papers under three broad headings; Developments in Medical Education; Teaching Medical Sociology in Medical Schools, and The Discipline of Medical Sociology. Not all papers fit neatly into this three-fold classification. Professor Sokolowska, for example, in her article on the teaching of medical sociology to sociologists also commented upon the need to prepare medical sociologists specifically for the tasks that they face when teaching medical students. Nevertheless, I have allocated her paper to the third category since it seemed to me she dealt most thoroughly with that topic in her paper. The presentation described in the previous chapter by Maes and Goyvaerts-Boekaerts on educational objectives and the subsequent small group sessions devoted to attempts to formulate educational objectives for the teaching of medical sociologist or for the application of medical sociology in medical schools are also dealt with separately. Moreover, many of the papers dealt with issues outside the sections to which I have allocated them, but when this is the case, reference has been made to their contribution in other areas.

15.1. New developments in medical education

The papers by Thiadens, Thung, Aakster, Philipsen, Daniëls and Nihoul all seem to reflect a common theme: the changing nature of medical practice today compared with the features that characterized medicine during the inter-war years. Specialization in medicine did not start in the period immediately following World War II, nor indeed in the twentieth century, since some medical specialities and even sub-specialities had been established by 1900. Nevertheless further rapid growth of specialization and subdivision within meical specialities reached its most rapid rate of growth in the years following World War II, just at the time when socio-demographic changes and a new pattern in the incidence of illness and disease was beginning to emerge. Today, high proportions of the population are surviving into middle and old age and advances in scientific medicine and medical technology have eliminated many of the life-threatening acute conditions which, in previous years, absorbed so much of the currently available medical resources. Today it is the chronic and degenerative diseases that are the major focus of concern, where care rather than cure becomes the major orientation of medical activity. This in turn seems to have led many countries to focus more upon primary care, since the chronic and degenerative diseases are frequently dealt with outside, rather than inside, the hospital setting. In Thiadens' paper, «The Patient as an Ally of the Doctor and the Nurse», these themes are reflected in arguments in favor of involving the patient as an equal and active partner in the triad of doctor, patient and nurse in which all three may contribute, almost in equal measure, to the treatment, or amelioration of a chronic condition. The patient becomes an active rather than a passive component of the triadic interaction and the hierarchial relationship between doctor, nurse and patient, perhaps in that order, is construed as inappropriate as a modus operandi for providing health care services. Thung, as well as referring to changes in the nature of disease, also takes into account the increasing political demand for an equitable distribution of health care resources. He stresses the need for a radical alteration in the basic value system within the medical profession in which it, the profession, should attempt to lower, or even eradicate, the social distance, high status and prestige gap which exists between doctor and patient. These forces together call for a radical re-structuring of the medical curriculum and the atmosphere in which medicine is taught in medical schools; Thung appeals to medical sociologists to join with other forces bent on curriculum reform and change. Aakster's paper represents an exceedingly comprehensive and broad survey of the multiplicity of forces which, together, are changing the face of medical practice and, therefore, which call in question the relevance of traditional methods of medical education for the training of future generations of medical practitioners. Thung concludes that medical education should shift to a problem-oriented approach for the training of new generations of practitioners. While he advocates this approach across the board for both basic sciences and clinical disciplines, he nevertheless emphasizes the need for behavioral scientists to incorporate theoretical and conceptual issues into the problem-oriented approach. This dilemma is neatly focused upon by Dr. Philipsen when he states... «when a student tries to solve problems such as headaches or tiredness in general practice it is not so simple to give the student a clear insight into the power relations in the national health care system». Philipsen stresses the tendency for problems to be individualized in medical school settings. The professional-patient interaction is almost always defined as a one-to-one relationship and a problem-orientation might tend to emphasize even further a dualistic relationship. In fact many, perhaps most, doctor-patient interactions involve more than two participants in the interaction. In secondary and tertiary care facilities the team concept is only too obvious. In the operating theater, in spinal cord injury teams, in burn teams for the treatment of severely injured patients and in primary care the team will often include doctors, nurse practitioners, social workers, physicians' assistants, physicians' extenders, as well as receptionists, clerical workers and other support personnel who will include outreach workers such as health visitors, district nurses and so on. The problem-oriented approach may be a great advance on the 'telephone-directory-type' learning that has characterized so much of medical education in the past but it must not be viewed as the panacea for all ills since there is a need to encourage students to view health care problems from a collective as well as from an individualistic orientation.

Alongside the change in curriculum content and methods of teaching in medical schools, Daniëls and Nihoul both stress the need for changes in assessment and evaluation systems. Their emphasis upon the time element in evaluation and assessment situations seems as logical as it appears humane. In the past, we have required medical students to jump over hurdles and leap through hoops at intervals and to accumulate sufficient information to cross examination barriers which may or may not bear any relation to the future tasks they will be called upon to accomplish either as medical students in later stages of training or subsequently as practitioners. The advantage of the positions taken by Nihoul and Daniëls seem to me to emphasize the dynamic nature of the educational process. Daniëls proposes that students should first be tested as they enter a course, an entry measure followed by practical measures of their performance and participation during the course as well as tests available to the students as they themselves feel a need for them during the course and, finally, exit measures which can then be contrasted with the initial entry measure to demonstrate to the student what he has indeed learned. At each stage the assessment and evaluation instrument is a learning procedure since it incorporates feedback to the student on his or her progress. Alongside this the instructors are required to keep careful course descriptions in all facets and then, if student difficulties arise, the course content and method of teaching can be examined to see if any changes may be implemented to aid and assist the students to learn more adequately. In this way the student passes through medical school by a step-by-step evaluation process in which learning and assessment are integrated rather than separated. The papers in this section are representative of some of the most exciting developments in medical education which are currently being examined in a number of progressive medical schools. Similar changes may be noted in a number of American medical schools, such as the Docent system introduced at the University of Missouri-Kansas City medical school which is very similar to that described by Philipsen for Maastricht. Nevertheless, we should be well aware of the entrenched conservatism of many of the older and highly prestigious medical schools in Europe and Britain and in the United States. Many of us, perhaps most, who work in a medical school setting, cannot expect changes of the kind discussed in this section in our own medical schools for many a long year; perhaps not until the turn of the century.

15.2. Teaching medical sociology in medical schools

The papers and presentations in this section, tended not unnaturally, to reflect the different situations in the various authors' countries as well as the author's personal experience at their own universities or teaching institutions. Professor Sand's description of the teaching programs in medical sociology at the University of Brussels reflects very strongly the influence of Professor René Sand, himself a pioneer in social medicine, who had instituted a teaching program in this field before World War II. Today, medical sociology is taught in this university by means of a combination of seminars and practical work stressing the relationships between illness, disease, environmental conditions and patterns of human behavior. The course retains a strong epidemiological focus, reflecting its origins in a department of social medicine. In a rational world, one might have expected much greater collaboration between departments of social work and medical sociology. Pflanz and Siegrist state in their paper that:

'Social medicine, public health and preventive medicine could be powerful allies of medical sociology. It is a pity that competition and struggle between social medicine and medical sociology have paralyzed this cooperation in our country. There are no clear distinctions in the context of work, no jurisdictional boundaries of both specialities in the division of labor.'

Indeed, in some institutions, a healthy marriage between social medicine and medical sociology has occurred. At Hanover, Professor Pflanz»S Institute for Epidemiology and Social Medicine houses medical sociologists and epidemiologists in a congenial and cooperative collegiate relationship. The same is true of Professor Holst's Institute of Social Medicine at the University of Copenhagen. Similar conditions of collaboration and mutual respect between social medicine specialists and medical sociologists can be observed in a number of british medical schools, but the converse is also true and schism and conflict between the disciplines can be observed in Britain, Europe and America. Where cooperation does exist it is difficult to avoid the conclusion that the reciprocity and exchange stems from the vision and insight of key individuals. Where cooperation is absent or conflict is very apparent, one can usually detect an element of fear in the perceptions of the members of each discipline towards their opposite numbers. To my mind, it is fear which underlies the distinction between the sociology *of* and the sociology *in* medicine. Medical sociologists fear a lack of autonomy, a lack of academic freedom, if they are incorporated into departments of social medicine. On the other hand, social medical practitioners perceive medical sociology as a threat as it begins to expand its areas of interest into concerns which traditionally characterize social medicine – investigations of the etiology and epidemiology of disease, the analysis of health care delivery systems and the evaluation of medical procedures and practices. Antipathy between social medicine and medical sociology is probably exacerbated when the former discipline is located in a School of Public Health, isolated from mainstream medicine. In the developed world, some attempt is being made to introduce medical sociology and other behavioral sciences into the curriculum for medical education, within a variety of administrative arrangements, often locating the medical sociologists in the medical school or affiliated with it in some way; whereas Schools of Public Health have tended to remain somewhat isolated from the medical school *per se*. In Great Britain, the new specialty of Community Physician has emerged, partly in response to the reorganization of the National Health Service in 1974. Community Physicians are charged with the responsibility of identifying the health care needs of communities and assessing the extent to which current service provisions do or do not meet those needs. Many medical sociologists perceive themselves as being involved in a very similar task. It would be hazardous indeed to predict the ultimate nature of the relationship between medical sociology and social medicine but the next decade might see the establishment of closer relationships between the two disciplines by focusing attention upon the identification and assessment of community health care needs.

Professor Pattishall's paper reflects a mode of development of medical sociology on the North American continent very different from that in Britain and Europe. At Hershey, the teaching of medical sociology is integrated with other behavioral science disciplines – economics, anthropology, psychology, social psychology and so on. British and European medical sociology incorporates a tradition of critical evaluation of the health care system. Moreover, as I shall contend later, the roots of medical sociology are much older in Europe than in America. In Great-Britain, the accountability of the medical profession to the body politic and the public in general is greater than in America where the medical profession enjoys a very considerable functional autonomy. Accordingly Professor Pattishall warns us against an over-emphasis by medical sociologists of social ills. He emphasizes that it should be the responsibility of the total medical profession to address the problems of inequity and maldistribution of scarce medical resources. Professor Pattishall and his colleagues at Hershey also have long experience in the challenging and difficult task of teaching behavioral sciences to medical students. Most of us with any experience in this area know that medical students, by and large, are most reluctant to devote time and effort to the study of the behavioral sciences. To counteract this problem Pattishall and his colleagues have devoted much time and energy to developing a behavioral science curriculum which covers the mix of social and medical concerns which impinge upon illness and disease. In this way the behavioral scientists at Hershey have probably been more successful than most in directing the attention of medical students to the inextricable mix of biological and social factors which relate to the practice of medicine. In America, the behavioral sciences are now being examined in the National Boards Medical Examination, Part I. The medical students at Hershey are probably better prepared than any other students in American medical schools to achieve high levels of success in this examination.

In a paper not presented at the conference but circulated to the participants by Guz, Ostrowska and Titkow, the authors report on an interesting experiment in which medical sociology students and medical students are taught together. Sociology students from the third, fourth and fifth years of their program of study are taught alongside medical students in their third year. This innovation was initiated in an attempt to break the stereotypes which prevail in the minds of both medical students and medical sociologists concerning their opposite numbers. The authors go on to describe the course content and the method of teaching but the program has been underway for too short a time for there to be any informed evaluation of its relative merits and demerits. This seems to me to be a very exciting venture. At some future international conference we should certainly encourage the authors to report more extensively on this attempt to integrate and coordinate two apparently disparate disciplines.

15.3. The development of educational objectives

Midway through the conference, an interesting experiment was attempted. As described by J. Vansteenkiste in the preceding chapter, Stan Maes and Monique Goyvaerts-Boekaerts of the Department of Education of the University of Antwerp discussed the formulation of educational objectives and the subsequent selection of course content. Subsequently, the participants were divided into small discussion groups, charged with the responsibility of developing educational objectives for the teaching of sociology to medical students or for the teaching of medical sociology to sociology students. Although the discussion groups included a healthy, interdisciplinary mix, there was a marked tendency for the sociologists to gravitate to the groups developing educational objectives for the training of medical sociologists and for the medical practitioners to join those groups dealing with the development of educational objectives as they applied to the education of medical students in the behavioral sciences. By and large the medical groups were more successful than the sociological groups. The medical groups raised the least number of objections to the whole process, persisted with their task throughout the allocated time period and were drmatically more successful than the sociologists, in that they produced longer lists of educational objectives for the application of social science information to medical student education programs. The relative lack of 'success' of the sociology groups seemed to be related to the greater diversity of the medical sociology enterprise in different countries. Medical procedures, at least in the developed world, vary relatively little from country to country. Rates of appendectomy may vary considerably from country to country as Professor Pflanz has shown, but the operation for appendicitis is more or less identical in London, New York, Paris and Hamburg. On the other hand, the organization and structure of the health care system is very different from country to country or may vary considerably within countries in different geographic regions. In this sense, the sociologists were presented with a task which was by nature more situationally specific. The application of behavioral science teaching techniques in medical student education is likely to be very different in a London medical school than in a school in Boston or Brussels or in Amsterdam. Moreover, the behavioral sciences are necessarily discursive disciplines where the emphasis is upon dynamic changes in the social structure as it pertains to the health care system. In this sense, educational objectives are constantly in a process of flux and change. But above all, the development of educational objectives is a time-consuming procedure. First of all, the group must get to know each other and develop a pattern of communication and interaction which facilitates the exchange of information. All scientists tend to approach the teaching situation in accordance with their own particular brand of expert knowledge. Clearly, some subjects in which medical sociologists are interested are less relevant to the process of medical education than others. The development of educational objectives therefore becomes a gradual evaluation and selection of priorities from a range of potential subjects to be taught and teachers to teach them. These situations vary from one society to antoher and the outcomes in terms of educational objectives are likely to reflect the different circumstances of each country. Much the same reasoning applies to the teaching of medical sociology to medical students, where the overall goals are likely to reflect the societally specific ideologies and value positions of each nation. Indeed as we shall see in the next section, the development of medical sociology in Great Britain and Europe differs greatly from that in the United States. This is probably because of the different etiology of the predominant values and ideological systems, reflected in the distinctions between the cultures of the New and the Old World. The sociologists, therefore, were prepared to be much less dogmatic in the development of educational objectives for the training of both medical sociologists and medical students in the behavioral sciences. Their objectives tended to be very much broader and more general, presumably to facilitate subsequent refinement in accordance with the needs of specific institutions. Indeed the sociologists seemed to want to question the basic process; they were suspicious of the reliability of the exercise, at least in the conference setting. The sociologists wanted to question the assumptions underlying the development of educational objectives rather than attempt to develop them.

15.4. The teaching and development of medical sociology

In many sociology departments, the teaching of medical sociology is restricted to post-graduate education. To my mind, Margaret Stacey challenged this situation very effectively and argued very convincingly for the need to teach medical sociology to students at the undergraduate level in sociology departments when she stated that:

'The ways in which health care is handled both reflect and reinforce many of the central values and institutions of a society and are an integral part of its structure and culture. The way in which a society handles suffering and birth and death reflects intimately the essential values of that society and also reflects and reinforces its hierarchy of power and status, or modifies it, for the society is not static, nor are the practices of medicine. One therefore also needs to examine the interrelationships between the society and the health care system. How are changes in the wider society affecting the health care system? What are the changes in the society to which health care practices and policies are contributing and what potential changes are being checked by these same practices?'

The academic training of any sociologist should therefore encompass some introduction to the sociology of medicine since the institutions of medicine and health care are so central to the total structure of any given society. Whatever their subsequent specialty or subspecialty, sociologists should have some basic understanding of the health care institutions of their own and other societies.

Margaret Stacey goes on to analyze a number of other very significant problems in the process of teaching the sociology of medicine, to which only brief reference can be made because of the constraints of time. Both Professors Sokolowska and Pattishall suggest that medical sociologists, particularly if they are to work in medical settings, need to develop some familiarity with medical practitioners and the practice of medicine and the biological basis of health and illness. Stacey takes the view that, at least at the undergraduate level, the student need not develop much awareness of the technology of medicine since the focus is upon the cultural and societal interrelationships between the health care industry and the broader social system. Indeed, she argues that one of the problems for teachers of the sociology of medicine is to provide students with a degree of social distance between the practice of medicine and sociological analysis. On the other hand, she argues, again very convincingly, that it is difficult to provide medical sociology students with an understanding of the pain and suffering which is so often either the intentional or unintentional consequence of certain medical procedures and practices. Stacey goes on to describe an incident which occured at the recent British Sociological Association conference in Manchester when 'sociologists offended nurses and other professionals by laughing at Wiseman's film, *The Hospital*'. The nurses had apparently developed, through their professional training, mechanisms for handling suffering, stress and the frustrations depicted in the film, whereas the sociologists' response was to relieve their feelings by nervous, self-conscious, even embarassed laughter. I have observed the same reaction among first-year medical students exposed to this film, a most interesting reaction. The first-year medical students, perhaps like the sociology students, had had no opportunity to come to terms with human suffering and the stresses and frustrations that characterized hospital medicine. My own observations would suggest that M.D.'' tend to deal with this kind of situation by engineering a degree of social distance between themselves and their patients. This then enables the professional to limit the extent to which the pain and suffering of his patients impinges upon his own emotions and social space.

Professor Magdalena Sokolowska, in her presentation, provoked considerable supportive applause when she argued that attempts to teach medical sociology from a too narrow perspective almost always ended with failure. Perspectives as different as social stratification theory and symbolic interactionism, when used as the basic focus for the application of medical sociology to medical student teaching, were almost always disastrous failures. In part, this reflected the concern that Professor Pattishall expressed over sociological experts being invited to address students in medical schools. As a solution to this problem, Professor Sokolowska proposed that medical sociologists who are going to undertake the teaching of medical students need a specific training for this task. She suggested that courses specifically designed to introduce medical sociologists to the major topics of medicine and the modes of thought characteristic of health care professionals would do much to ameliorate the situation. She also argued that medical sociology had done much to contribute to the development of general sociological theory. A similar theme is reflected in Professor Stacey's paper when she emphasizes the central role that the study of medicine and health care needs to play in the training of sociologists at all levels of their academic development. Certainly, in the areas of both theory and method development, medical sociologists have, in recent years made some very significant contributions to the development of the basic discipline. Glaser's and

Strauss'work on grounded theory immediately comes to mind, as does
Friedson's major contribution to our understanding of the concept of
profession. Parsons' work, although increasingly subject to criticism
and re-evaluation, has unquestionably made very significant contributions to our knowledge of society. Sokolowska also argued vigorously
in favor of some training in economics for sociologists and went on to
state that such training was a basic requirement for the development
of medical sociology. This view tends to attract immediate support
amongst European sociologists. As I shall argue later, the origins of
both sociology and medical sociology owe much to the critical and
reformist tradition in European intellectual thought which often
entailed an analysis and subsequent challenge of basic socio-economic
structures. In a much over-simplified form this challenge centered
upon the fundamental criticism of the philosophical beliefs and value
systems that underlay both laissez-faire capitalism and crude Bentha-
mite utilitarianism. The European intellectual tradition of criticism of
the establishment, a tradition whose foundations were laid in the
nineteenth century Reformist Movement and whose expression and
development continues in the twentieth century, generated an overall
climate of opinion in which many of the social sciences subsequently
developed, expanded and became increasingly important factors in
the process of social change.

Professor Bloom, charged with the responsibility of preparing a
paper on 'The Profession of Medical Sociology in the Future: Implications for Training Programs' commenced with a very personal statement of his participation in the Yablona meetings and the opportunity
this created for him to begin to get to know his Eastern European as
well as Western European colleagues in medical sociology. Bloom's
paper contains some very valuable ideas on the recent history of the
development of medical sociology and I am more than grateful for the
opportunity to comment upon them. On the situation of medical
sociology in 1973, Bloom states:

'Another striking feature of the time for the United States was the pressure for change
toward policy science. Medical sociology appeared to emerge from one identity to
assume another: from a scholarly profession, it was becoming more applied. At the
same time, Europe presented a picture of quite different development, essentially the
reverse. From origins in policy and planning, the medical sociology of Europe seemed
to be moving toward a more academic balance.'

Bloom then goes on to present a succinct outline of the development of American medical sociology from the period immed day, but before so doing, he presents in summary form the trends in American medical sociology to which he referred in his Warsaw paper of 1973. I reproduce this schematic presentation here, although it is available in Bloom's text, because it is so central to the argument that I wish to cevelop.

FROM	TO
a social psychological frame of reference	institutional analysis
small-scale social relations as subjects of research	large social systems
role analysis in specifically limited settings	complex organizational analysis
basic theoretical concerns with classic social analysis of behavior	policy science directed toward systematic translation of basic knowledge into decision-making
a perspective of human relations and communication	power structure analysis

As mentioned above Bloom suggests that the growth of European and British medical sociology reflects trends almost the reverse of the American situation. This contrast in the development of American and European medical sociology suggests to me another question, namely, are we yet in a position to define exactly what medical sociology is. Having answered, or attempted to answer that question, we could then ask when, in point of historical fact, people began to address issues which we would now accept as being medical sociological in emphasis or content. A clue to the resolution of both problems is to be found in the first paragraph of Pflanz's and Siegrist's paper:

'Although the term 'medical sociology' was not used in Germany before 1955, the idea itself has a long tradition in German medical thinking. We shall not attempt to delineate the whole development of thinking in an area which today we would call medical sociology, but we must mention two classics of medical sociology: the writings of Virchow and Saloman Neumann (around 1848) the book by Mueller-Lyer, of 1914, about the sociology of suffering. About the same time a more pragmatic approach was chosen by Alfred Grotjahn, the great man of German social hygiene, who emphasized the necessity of a union between social hygiene, sociology and economics. The Swiss H. E. Sigerist was already using the sociological approach to the history of medicine

when he was teaching at Leipzig, just as he did later in the United States. The most
influential figure for an entire generation was probably Viktor von Weizsäcker, one of
the most important promoters of medical sociology and psychomatics in Germany from
the early thirties until the years after World War II.'

In essence, Pflanz and Siegrist are suggesting that medical sociology is
very much older than it would seem to be. How should we characterize Sir Edwin Chadwick's report on the sanitary conditions of the
laboring class in England in 1842? Today, I suppose, we would call
Chadwick's work a carefully designed statement of the health care
needs of specific urban communities and of the nation, based upon
empirical research. If the medical sociology section of the Britisch
Sociological Association had existed in 1906, the architects of the
Education (School Meals) Act of that year might have been invited to
become founder members. Had the section existed in 1909, Sidney
and Beatrice Webb might have been invited to become president and
vice-president. Had the section existed in 1911 or in 1948, Lloyd
George and Bevan might have been invited to become honorary
vice-presidents. In the period 1866-1872, the sessional proceedings of
the National Association for the Promotion of Social Science frequently dealt with issues concerning health care needs and the
extension and development of medical provision. Earlier, in the
1850's, the papers of the Social Science Association often devoted
much attention to similar concerns. But above all, the principle
gradually became established that it was the responsibility of at least
some members of the intelligentsia to take on the duty of challenging
the values and ideological assumptions of the establishment and its
policy. This seems to me to be what Robert Day meant, when
referring to the future of medical sociology:

'That our future prospects as a discipline and a specialty area can be greatly enhanced
by returning to the critical, reflexive posture which evolved in large part from the
European tradition of social science.'

Day's analysis of the career structure and affiliation of leading
American medical sociologists clearly identifies their 'respectable'
origins in terms of academic sociology. Most of the individuals whose
careers Day describes, when they have criticized the American health

care system, have done so implicitly rather than explicitly. Until very recently it was difficult indeed to identify critics of the health care system such as those so characteristic of European and British medical sociology.

This difference in orientation in medical sociology between the two continents clearly reflects the different development of the intellectual tradition in North American and European cultures. Herbert Spencer, a Social Darwinist and an advocate of unbridled competition and laissez-faire capitalism, was actively teaching and giving guest lectures on the American university circuit long after his work had been rejected and forgotten in Europe. Herbert Spencer's teachings were much more compatible with the individualistic orientation and value system of American society than they were with the beginnings of the collectivist philosopy which emerged in European society about 185 years ago, promoted first by the events of 1789 and gradually developing increasing support throughout the nineteenth and twentieth centuries. It is also worth recalling that the America of the early 1950's enabled McCarthyism to develop and attain a grip on American social and political institutions. McCarty was able to destroy the careers of individuals as divers as obstetricians/gynecologists and film stars simply by labeling them as Communists. More generally, any radical or even mildly reformist position could be destroyed by invoking the label communist or fellow traveller. Without a strong tradition of intellectual challenge of establishment thought and policies, what were early American medical sociologists to do? In such a situation, American medical sociologists, together with other social scientists, were not in a position to conduct policy-based research except indirectly. Consequently they concentrated, in both teaching and research activities, upon 'safer' academic issues in medical sociology.

This analysis of trends and tendencies across the two continents can only be highly speculative here. Much more work needs to be done if these ideas are to be developed to the level of even a very preliminary hypothesis. Moreover, alternative explanations immediately come to mind. Medical sociology may have to develop professional credibility as an academic discipline before it can even begin to address issues such as those associated with social policy concerns. One could hypothesise that medical sociologists initially attached themselves to a highly prestigious profession, that of medicine, in an effort to develop academic credibility and respectability. Only when this was achieved could they begin to develop autonomously and to pose questions out of their own disciplinary perspective that were pertinent to broader social issues. Nevertheless, it is interesting to note that in recent years, a critical and reflexive sociology, perhaps based on Marxist or neo-Marxist principles of analysis, is ermerging in America. The origin of this movement is perhaps to be found in the agitations and protest movements that characterized the late 1960's in America; the emergence of a counter-culture, the Kent State shootings, the discovery of poverty, the growth of women's liberation and the protest movement against the war in Vietnam. While Theodore Roszak and Charles A. Reich can hardly be called sociologists or Marxists, their work clearly clarifies and begins to document the protest movement in general. In medical sociology these trends are immediately recognizable in the 1970's in the work of people such as Waitzkin and Waterman, Navarro, Bodenheimer, *et al.*, to mention just a few names which immediately come to mind. The founding of the *International Journal of Health Services* in 1971 under the editorship of Vincente Navarro provided a vehicle in which critical reviews and research on the American health care system have subsequently been published.

15.5. The future of medical sociology

In terms of its place in general sociology, medical sociology has now come of age. The discipline has made significant contributions to the development of general sociological theory and has practical and social policy implications. With rare exceptions, however, medical sociology has not devoted much attention to the problems of the development of health care services in the Third World. Some Third World countries are intent upon developing a high technology-based form of Western health care services, which are often irrelevant to their real health care needs. China, aware that its resources are insufficient to introduce high technology medicine across the total country, has opted for the development of a health care system based on hygience, public health and preventive medicine. The World Health Organization is placing considerable emphasis upon attempts to understand the needs of the Third World countries and to contribute to the resolution of service to meet those needs and actively seeks the collaboration, cooperation and assistance of medical sociologists in this enterprise. It is to be hoped that medical sociologists interested in the distinctions between high and low technology medicine and their application in different countries' situations will soon emerge.

While one of the new challenges may indeed be in Third World settings, Professor Jefferys in het 1974 paper, which incidentally was first presented in Yablona, draws our attention to the problem of high and low technology medicine in the developed world:

'Which of these roles is the medical profession most likely to fill in the future, that of technologist, concerned primarily with physiology, or that of applied behavioral scientists, concerned with the psycho-social as much as with the physiologic. I do not know the answer to this question. The odds are evenly balanced. There are pressures in both directions, and the outcome will depend not only on decisions taken by the medical profession itself which, in any case, is not a monolithic body speaking with a single voice. While some of the highly prestigious super-specialists are likely to line up for a restriction of concern, new specialty groups within medicine, such as the psychiatrists and the community physicians as well as revitalized general practitioners, are determined to broaden their medical horizons but remain within the medical world.'

The practioners of high technology medicine may see the behavioral sciences as totally irrelevant to their day-to-day practices and procedures. In this sense, they may withdraw from the current interaction between medicine and the behavioral sciences. On the other hand, primary care practitioners may turn increasingly to the behavioral sciences for help and assistance in meeting the different health care needs of a changing society and the changing incidence of illness and disease. The shortage of primary care practitioners in America, where in 1973, twenty-four percent of M.D.'s described themselves as generalists and seventy-six percent as specialists, has resulted in a situation where alternatives are being considered for the provision of primary health care. Physicians' assistants, physicians' extenders, nurse practioners, medex personnel are all currently being trained with a view to these new varieties of health care professionals taking on more and more responsibility for providing primary health care needs. The medical profession is trying to increase the proportion of what are now described as family physicians, whose major, although not exclusive, orientation is towards primary health care needs. Nevertheless, it still takes eleven years to train a family physician in the American system of medical education, a procedure that is both lengthy and expensive. A few studies have suggested that populations, particularly those living in areas currently undersupplied with doctors, are very happy to utilize the total scale of physician extenders as their primary source of health care provision. Medical sociologists would do well to concern themselves with these kinds of innovations in health care delivery systems and to generate research projects which are capable of evaluating this form of medical care.

Professor Nuyens challenged us, in his opening remarks at this conference, to consider further applications of the discipline to the new forces and situations which are currently impinging upon the practice of medicine. The professions of health services management and health education are growing in importance and significance as society begins to acknowledge the need for more efficient management of health care services and the need to ensure, among the public, a greater awareness of the contribution that good health habits in terms of lifestyles can play in maintaining health. What role should medical sociologists play in the training of health educators and health service managers? In many complex industrialized social systems, consumers now play an active role in the health care system. In Great Britain, the community health councils are now responsible for the evaluation, on the part of the public in general, of the 'effectiveness and efficiency of health care services', to steal a phrase from Professor Cochrane. Some of the community health councils have medical sociologists among their members appointed presumably because of their knowledge of the health care system. What should their role and responsibilities be in this situation? Clearly, medical sociology in the foreseeable future can expand and extend into areas which present a variety of opportunities as yet ill-defined. One of our major priorities might be to prepare future generations of sociologists to be capable of reacting to these opportunities and new needs. If governmental support for the training of medical sociologists continues to decline, as Bloom's paper suggests, at least in the American Setting, then perhaps we should focus more directly upon Professor Stacey's approach, the introduction of medical sociology into the undergraduate curricula of sociology departments.

References

Bodenheimer, T., S. Cummings and E. Harding, 1974, 'Capitalizing an illness: the health insurance industry', *Int. J. Hlth. Serv.*, *4*, no. 4, 589-598.

Jefferys, M., 1974, 'Social science and medical education in Britain: a sociological analysis of their relationship'. *Int. J. Hlth. Serv.*, *4*, No. 3, 549-565.

Navarro, Y., 1975, 'The industrialization of fetishism or the fetishism of industrialization: a critique of Ivan Illich'. *Soc. Sci. and Med.*, *9*, No. 7, 351-365.

Reich, C.A., 1971, *The Greening of America*, Bantam Books, Inc., New York.

Roszak, T., 1969, *The Making of a Counter Culture*, Doubleday and Co., Inc., New York.

Waitzkin, H., and B. Waterman, 1974, *The Exploitation of Illness in Capitalist Society*, Bobbs-Merrill, Indianapolis.

PART EIGHT

BIBLIOGRAPHY

16. A selected bibliography of recent articles

J. Vansteenkiste

This bibliography consists exclusively of recent articles with immediate relevance to the subject of the seminar: training programs in medical sociology for behavioral scientists and physicians, evaluations of existing initiatives, theses, ideologies and wishful thinking about the future of medical sociology (particularly within the medical setting.)[1]

An extensive and international selection of journals has been scrutinized. The following references, however are restricted in quantity and the list is not intended to be exhaustive.

The intention was to provide a usable instrument. For the same reason, a very brief indication of the contents is added most of the time.

Coe, R.M., Teaching Behavioral Sciences in schools of medicine: observations on some Latin-American schools, *Soc. Sci and Med.,* 9 (1975) 4/5, 221-225.

> This paper discusses the conceptualization and implementation of teaching behavioral sciences in schools of medicine. Observations in ten schools of medicine in Latin-America lead to a conceptual clarification of the terms social medicine and community medicine. Consideration of variations in scope and sequence of curricula programming leads to a tentative identification of three 'types' of curricula: traditional, expanded and integrated.
> Recommendations are made for changes in curricula to enhance the teaching of behavioral sciences in other schools of medicine.

Counte, M.A., Kimberly, J.R., Change in physician attitudes toward

---

1. Handbooks are omitted because it is assumed that they are sufficiently known.

reform in medical education: the results of a field experiment, *Soc. Sci and Med.,* 10 (1976) 11/12, 547-552.

The study reported in this article uses a field experimental design to assess the impact of participation in an innovative program in medical education on the attitudes of practicing physicians.

The new program's aims are to show the clinical relevancy of basic sciences to students; enable them to define their own learning process; and develop an illness-oriented curriculum instead of a discipline-oriented one.

Two problems studied are:
– Are physicians who participate in such programs likely to become more favorably disposed toward changing the structure of medical education than those who do not?
– Will restructuring of their roles to include participation in such experiments result in positive changes in their attitudes toward the need for reform?

Johnson, M. L., Medical Sociology and Sociological Theory, *Soc. Sci and Med.,* 9 (1975) 4/5, 227-232.

Medical sociology has grown at an exponential rate during the past two decades. As a consequence, its development has been inevitably uneven in the sense that some skills and competences have advanced more rapidly than others.

The sub-discipline is theoretically impoverished, not only through its failure to contribute significantly to sociology's conceptual stock, but also through its shyness in utilizing theoretical constructs in its research.

Assertions of this type have been made about other areas of sociology at a similar stage, but by the very nature of the interface of sociology and its subject areas, each case merits separate attention.

Gleghorn, R. A., Gleghorn, J. M., Lowy, F. H., Contributions of Behavioral Sciences to Health Care. *The Milbank Memorial Fund Quarterly,* XLIX (1971) 2, 133-174.

An historical perspective.

Hannay, D. R., Linked appointments for medical sociologists, *Medical Education,* 10 (1976) 3, 213-214.

Linked appointments are one way of complementing the two approaches, viz. sociology in medicine and sociology of medicine. The teaching of sociology to medical students in Britain shows a considerable variation, which can be ascribed to the ambivalent position of the medical sociology teaching staff: there are, on the one hand, medical sociologists located within the medical schools and, on the other hand, medical sociologists located within departments of sociology.

Hollingshead A. B., Medical Sociology: A Brief Review, *The Milbank Memorial Fund Quarterly,* Health and Society, 51 (1973) 4, pp. 531-544.

A brief history of the development of medical sociology (in the U.S.A.) is presented here. In the first three decades of the twentieth century medical sociology was identified first with the field of social work and later with the field of public health. Not until the 1930's and the 1040's did the interrelations between society and the health sciences become of interest to sociologists.

After the close of World War II, the expansion of the National Institutes of Health and the interest of private foundations in interdisciplinary research stimulated and supported the growth of medical sociology as an area of research and teaching. During the 1950's, the field developed in two directions: sociology of medicine, centered in departments of sociology in universities, and sociology in medicine, concentrated in schools of medicine and health care facilities.

As training programs proliferated through the 1960's, the market for books on the subject grew quickly. Five textbooks on medical sociology are reviewed, and some suggestions are made about issues in need of study for the future development of the field.

Irwin, W. G., Bamber, J. H., Henneman, J., Constructing a new course for undergraduate teaching of general practice, *Medical Education,* 10 (1976) 4, 302-308. This paper outlines in Part I the method used to analyse and redefine a set of educational objectives on which a new course of teaching of general practice in the later clinical years is based, at the Department of General Practice, Queen's University, Belfast. Part II describes the course (limited to contributions on behavioral sciences from a psychological viewpoint), the learning methods, behavioral attainments and the techniques of evaluation to be implemented.

Kemper, Th. D., Fritz, H., Kelner, M., Social Science in Schools of Medicine, *The Milbank Memorial Fund Quarterly*, XLIX, (1971) 2, 244-271.

A review of some of the reasons for the introduction of social science into medicine, some of the difficulties social scientists have encountered, particularly in the course of teaching medical students, and the specific program in behavioral science recently introduced in the Faculty of Medicine at the University of Toronto.

Kinch, R. A. H., et al., Teaching of Behavior, Growth and Development in the Preclinical Years, *The Milbank Memorial Fund Quarterly*, XLIX, (1971) 2, 228-243.

Special attention is given to the organization, orientation and application of specific teaching methods for a behavior course in the medical curriculum.

Larsen, D. E., Behavioral Science in the Faculty of Medicine, University of Alberta (Canada), *The Milbank Memorial Fund Quarterly,* XLIX, (1971) 2, 219-227.

This paper provides a brief description of the behavioral science subjects that are formally offered in the curriculum of the Faculty of Medicine at the University of Alberta and a discussion of the problems and issues that behavioral scientists have faced in attempting to participate in the education of medical students at this institution.

Among the problems dealt with are:
- the relevancy of behavioral scientists teaching in medicine
- problems in relation to team-teaching
- specifying a relatively clear and potent teaching role for the behavioral scientist
- problems of administrative nature: a reduction of the behavioral scientists' autonomy (confusion of professional identity) as a result of being under the administrative control of physicians.

Levine, D.M. and Bonito, A.J., Impact of clinical training on attitudes of medical students: self-perpetuating barrier to change in the system, *Brit. Journal of Med. Education,* 8 (1974) 1, 13-16.

An analysis of a study about the attitudes of a sample of students and teachers in a medical school toward changes in the organization of medical practice.

Nuyens, Y., Teaching medical sociology to graduate students in sociology: a three-year experience, in Sokolowska, M. *Health, Medicine, Society,* Dordrecht, D. Reidel Publishing Company, 1976, 471-501.

This paper gives a detailed description of a training program in medical sociology, intended for graduate students at the Sociology Department of the University of Leuven (Belgium). After an outline of the origin and development of the program, there is further discussion concerning the role of the medical sociologists, the teaching objectives that can be derived from it, and the learning activities necessary for realizing these objectives. The program was developed around the dimensions theory-research-policy, which are also at the basis of the general sociology training program. Objectives, form, content and evaluation are discussed for each of the training components; indications are also given as to how well they link up with knowledge, skills or attitudes. Recommendations are formulated, pointing out their necessary links with general sociology and their close connections with research.

McEwen, J., Finlayson, A., A medical sociology course in a revised curriculum, *Brit. Journal of Med. Education,* 9 (1975) 4, 236-243.

A discription of the course of medical sociology introduced in Dundee in 1972, and of the factors that have been involved in the development of it. A survey is given of the diversity in course content and the wide variation in the organization of courses and the teaching methods that are currently being employed in medical sociology.

Mechanic, D., The Sociology of Medicine, Viewpoints and perspectives, *Journal of Helath and Human Behavior,* 7 (Winter, 1966), 237-248.

This paper deals with the organizational context of medical practice, help-seeking and illness behavior in a manner which attempts to show their relevance to more extensive sociological issues. The author concludes that if workers in the sociology of medicine are to contribute in a more basic way to the mainstream of sociological thought and to the general issues involving medicine in our society today, some redirection is necessary in the kinds of problems that are chosen to be attacked and in the methodological approaches that are most commonly used.
The sociologist must retain his basic professional perspective, and he must attune himself to the basic sociological considerations relevant to the organization of medicine and the health professions generally, and to the relevance of health care for other institutional sectors.

Pacoe, L.V., et al., Training Medical students in Interpersonal Relationship Skills. *Journal of Med. Education,* 51 (1976) 9, 743-750.

This paper reports a description and experimental evaluation of a training method designed to increase the student's comfort in dealing with emotionally intense material and to increase his skills in the core facilitative qualities.
Comparison of the experimental and control groups reveals a training effect on the student's ability to recognize and communicate empathic understanding and on attitude and personality variables

Sheldrake, P., Reid, M., Student expectations of behavioral science, *British Journal of Med. Education,* 6 (1972) 2, 105-107.

Investigation among students of the Edinburgh Medical School about their expectations and knowledge concerning behavioral sciences, as a part of the medical curriculum.

Sheldrake, P., Behavioral science: medical students' expectations and reactions, *British Journal of Med. Education,* 8 (1974) 1, 31-48.

This paper considers some of the factors which contribute toward students' attitudes. It also reports the results of a research project conducted in the medical schools of Edinburgh and Dundee, where, during the last few years, the behavioral sciences courses have been included in the program. 'Before and after' questionnaires were given to students taking courses in behavioral sciences. The results from the questionnaires show, with the aid of a scale of values, the diversity of expectations that students have of the behavioral sciences, and the limited contact they have had with the subject matter.

Shulman, L.S., Cognitive Learning and the Educational Process, *Journal of Medical Education,* 45 (1970) 11, P. 90-100.

The author defends the position that a most fundamental purpose of medical education is to instruct the student in a general body of cognitive skills and attitudes which are not unique to medicine alone. Curricular or instructional decisions should be made on the basis of an analysis of three elements: the student individual differences (the entering characteristics), the instructional setting, and the application setting. The author discusses the significance of each of these three elements and examines how the findings of the large body of educational and psychological research bears upon many of the general problems in medical higher education.

Sokolowska, M., Two basic types of medical orientation, *Soc. Sci and Med.,* 7 (1973) 10, 807-815.

The fundamental dividing line between doctors is determined by the types of their medical orientation. There are two basic styles of medical orientation: the individualistic orientation which corresponds to the traditional character of medical knowledge, and the mass orientation which shifts the point of interest toward the group, thereby changing the fundamentals of the way of thinking and becoming a qualitatively different medicine.

Van Egeren, L., Fabrega, H., Behavioral science and medical education: a biobehavioral perspective, *Soc. Sc. and Med.,* 10 (1976) 11/12, p. 535-539.

Description of a model for the teaching of behavioral science in medical schools.
In this approach, attention is concentrated on behavioral (psychological, social, cultural) factors linking the individual with physical illness and the medical care system.
These factors are organized by means of an illness behavior model (illness as a behavior as well as a biomedical construct – with a dynamic interaction between these 2 systems of organization).

Volpe, R., Behavioral Science Theory in Medical Education, *Social Science and Medicine,* 9, (1975) 8-9; p. 493-499.

This paper deals with the contribution behavioral science theory may make to medicine and the problems that arise when its relevance is to be shown to students who are mostly practice-oriented.

'Much of the question of relevance surrounding behavioral science theory stems from the false separation of theory and practice... Possible ways of communicating the potential importance of behavioral science theory to the practitioner include clear statements of expected outcome competencies, the presentation of conceptual schemes that enable the integration of experience, team teaching, biobraphical study, and theory explication.'